FAGAN OF HOBOKEN
& THE HORSESHOE

In a gilded, manly age of disorderly industrial
Armageddon and progressive urban reform

NICHOLAS FAGAN DEALY

Printed in the United States of America

—Photograph of Lawrence Fagan on page 4, courtesy Fagan Album—

Publisher's Cataloging-in-Publication Data

Names: Dealy, Nicholas Fagan, 1976-, author.

Title: Fagan of Hoboken & the horseshoe : in a gilded manly age of disorderly industrial Armageddon and progressive urban reform / Nicholas Fagan Dealy.

Description: Includes bibliographical references and index. | Barrington, RI: Arch Kincaid Press, 2025.

Identifiers: LCCN: 2025918665 | ISBN: 979-8-9993934-0-1 (hardcover) | 979-8-9993934-1-8 (paperback) | 979-8-9993934-2-5 (ebook) | 979-8-9993934-3-2 (audio) Subjects: LCSH Fagan, Lawrence, 1851-1921. | New Jersey--Biography. | New Jersey--History. | New Jersey--History--1865- | Hoboken, (N.J.)--History. | Politicians--Biography. | Businesspeople--Biography. | Publishers and publishing--Biography. | BISAC BIOGRAPHY & AUTOBIOGRAPHY / Historical Classification: LCC F133 .F34 D43 2025 | DDC 974.9/092--dc23

To Clau
&
Connie
&
Aunt Meg and Uncle Bob

Lawrence Fagan

CONTENTS

Introduction 7

Part 1: 1851–1887: Migration................................23

Part 2: 1888–1893: Nicknames 36

Part 3: 1893–1899: Over Work.............................55

Part 4: 1899–1901: Under Fire 82

Part 5: 1901–1909: Schemes 109

Part 6: 1909–1921: Circulation 131

Afterword 151

Acknowledgements 160

Bibliography 161

Notes 168

Index 198

INTRODUCTION

"Why did I come downtown? Why, I don't
know; why did you?"

—Lawrence Fagan, as quoted in the Jersey Journal, June 27, 1903

THE HOUSE AT HUDSON AND TENTH STREETS in Hoboken, New Jersey, was tall and square, a stately Italianate-style brownstone with a commanding view and a colorful past. Following its purchase at the end of the nineteenth century by the Mayor of Hoboken, Lawrence Fagan, it was often referred to as the Fagan Mansion. Standing upon the Elysian Fields in Hoboken, the cradle of American baseball, and with views looking out across the Hudson River to Manhattan Island and the New York skyline, the house was, by any name, impressive. Its architecture was "severe but substantial" and included a distinct fourth story, a splendid square-shaped cupola with four pairs of little arch windows encased in the siding. A mast rose from the cupola on the roof and pointed up to the atmosphere. A bay, rising one story high and taking the form of a conservatory, adjoined the south side of the house on Tenth Street. An animal keeper's cabin, a barn, and a brick stable stood on the grounds surrounding the north side of the house.[1]

Built in 1867, the functional urban estate was constructed to the specifications of the original owners, brothers Henry and Charles Reiche of Germany. The Reiche brothers were the foremost animal importers of the day. Their customers included circus and animal show promoters, managers of municipal menagerie exhibits, zoo owners, and a bevy of other pet collectors and enthusiasts. A myriad of animals, the likes of acrobatic elephants, marching guanacos, and intriguing ibex, were kept on the property at Hudson and Tenth. Snakes and other reptiles may have been found there also. The Reiche family was also well known for their commerce in birds, bringing parrots, troupials, cardinals, goldfinches, and numerous other varieties to Hoboken. Not surprisingly, the sale of birdcages was also a part of the business, with models available in bronze, brass, "enameled" wood, as well as more ornately "gold and silver plated."[2]

This photo, probably from the early 1870s, shows the house at Hudson and Tenth Streets standing tall and imposing (in the far left). The clubhouse of the old New York Yacht Club appears behind the two men standing on the Elysian Fields in the foreground. While the man closer to the clubhouse looks to be doing some landscaping work, the other man poses with his bicycle and absorbs the view, which looked out across the Hudson River to Manhattan. (Courtesy Images of America: Hoboken, copyright Patricia Florio Colrick.)

In the head of a young Lawrence Fagan, a view of the affluent merchants' house, alive with activity and shining with promise, could well have planted a seed or two. Fagan, indeed, may have first spotted the property some thirty years before he purchased it, while crossing the Hudson River aboard a steam-powered passenger ferry boat at age seventeen in 1868. Fagan, who had graduated from high school in New York City, moved to Hudson County, New Jersey, in search of employment. He found work in Jersey City, the city bordering Hoboken to the south on the Hudson River. Fagan's career began at Blackmore's ironworks on Railroad Avenue. He was employed there as an assistant to a blacksmith and resided in a nearby area of the city known as "The Horseshoe."[3]

From the Horseshoe to Hoboken and back, in the five decades that followed, Lawrence Fagan's distinct vision and diverse body of work—likely more than any other figure's—shaped the history of Hudson County. "Historians view," writes historian Eric Foner, "the constant search for new perspectives as the lifeblood of historical understanding."[4] This first historical perspective on the energetic and prominent urban leader Lawrence Fagan provides a basis for further analysis of him and his influence on early twentieth-century New Jersey.[5] Fagan, who was born in Ireland in 1851 and brought to America as a small child, rose to own a large ironworks business with factories in Hoboken and in the Horseshoe section of Jersey City. Fagan also served four terms as the Democratic "reform" mayor of Hoboken. As well, Fagan headed the *Observer*.[6]

The *Observer* was perhaps the most influential newspaper in New Jersey at the time of the gubernatorial election of 1910. That year saw the arrival of Woodrow Wilson, then the President of Princeton University, onto the American political scene. As Wilson waged his first campaign for public office of any kind, he came to understand that the road to the governor's mansion in Trenton went through Hudson County's "Elysian Fields of politics,"[7] and therefore through Lawrence Fagan. In addition to the role he had in Wilson's formative political education, Fagan, both as the template of a "reform" mayor and by way of his position at the *Observer*, also shaped the political rise of Frank Hague, who won the job of mayor in Jersey City in 1917. From there, Hague began his long and legendarily forceful run atop American urban politics, reigning as Democratic leader-boss of Hudson County until 1946. (On a side note, the Fagan legacy even played a part in Hoboken native Frank Sinatra's early years; before he was "Chairman of the Board," Sinatra had a job working on the circulation trucks for the *Observer*.)

Lawrence Fagan touched the lives of a diverse many during his long life. By the time of his death in 1921, he had not only amassed influence but also a fortune estimated at $5,000,000.[8]

Fagan of Hoboken & The Horseshoe in a Gilded, Manly Age of Disorderly Industrial Armageddon and Progressive Urban Reform is a book guided by themes in academic historiography and falls into a category somewhere between biography and micro-history. Historian Jill Lepore makes the distinction between these two genres, explaining that they are "founded upon almost...opposite assumption[s]. Biography is largely founded on a belief in the singularity and significance of an individual's life and...contributions to history." Whereas "micro-history is founded upon" a belief that "however singular a person's life may be, the value of examining it lies not in its uniqueness, but in its exemplariness, in how the individual's life serves as an allegory for broader issues affecting the culture as a whole."[9] As biography, chronicling Fagan's previously unrecognized contributions to history fills in many holes and widens colorfully the scholarship given to late-nineteenth and early-twentieth-century urban America. As micro-history, Fagan's chronicles make him into a "human vehicle," whose purpose is to make the overall time period in which he lived more "comprehensible to the reader."[10]

Historians have long grappled with the task of assigning an appropriate moniker to the years that spanned the end of America's Civil War to its involvement in the First World War. A few of the many monikers, names, and labels—gilded, industrial, urban, reform, progressive, in search of order, Armageddon, manly—constitute some of the more popular and prevalently used and serve as inspiration for the wordy subtitle of this book.[11] This book's new perspective and fresh character—its theatre essentially fixed and finite, the action fast but chronological—provides a manageable, logical means to the study of Fagan and the period.

The events to be described, their vast majority happening in or very near Hoboken and the Horseshoe section of Jersey City, are a physical history—a history of places high and low, emblematic or exceptional to the period. One way to understand Fagan as a "human vehicle" for history is to consider him always in motion. In the neighboring cities of Hoboken and Jersey City, Fagan moved up and down physically between the highest and lowest geographical points and in society between the top and bottom echelons. Fagan's longevity—living and working in Hoboken and Jersey City for more than five decades—makes him a remarkably fixed point through which to understand the region's history.

Fagan's Hoboken and Jersey City were ever growing but also shrinking. These were places perpetually blooming with congestion, more people and construction, more and changing industry, more problems and evolving solutions; they were spaces expanding and contracting at once. Fagan's life was lived amidst a crowded mix of old- and new-world energies, where animal muscle met human ingenuity and steam engines required validation in horsepower. In this setting, the going and getting back and forth between Hoboken and Jersey City was not always simple. It often required some degree of concentration, energy, and agility. Jagged, rocky palisades formed much of the border between the two cities where Jersey City was substantially elevated above Hoboken—a long, steep, uneven line of topography. Innovations of varying complexity sought to facilitate travel to and from the cities—mechanical, electric elevator, and passages more stationary in nature (such as ramps and stairs) used by load-bearing man, animal, and machine.

Shown here is a portion of the steep incline between Jersey City and Hoboken (bottom). In these photographs, circa 1910, pedestrians negotiate the one hundred steps that linked Jersey City to Hoboken at Franklin Street. (Courtesy Hoboken Historical Museum Online Collections: hobokenmuseum.org.)

During a spring day in 1897, an example of peril in negotiating the terrain happened on the North Hudson County Railway Company's elevator at Palisade Avenue and Ferry Street in Jersey City. The elevator carried the rail company's horse cargo wagons "up and down the slope of the hill." With its "motive power" supplied by a large engine, the elevator was constructed of two outsized platforms which ascended and descended "simultaneously," one from "the top of the hill...the other from the bottom." The day's mishap began with a startled wagon horse. The force of the frightened horse's bucking was sufficient to snap a safety chain. At the time, a man using the elevator to transport a cargo of eggs from Hoboken experienced the brunt of the mechanism's failure; he was jettisoned from the elevator and fell about fifteen feet down into a ditch. Fortunately, the man sustained no serious injuries. His cargo, however, was a total loss; moreover, he was left drenched from top to bottom, soaked in smashed eggs.[12]

Human ingenuity, horse, and machine power are depicted in this postcard, dated March 28, 1908, which illustrates the difference in elevation on the border of Jersey City (top) and Hoboken. (Courtesy Maggie Blanck: maggieblanck.com.)

Fagan's Hoboken, comprised of approximately one square mile of territory, was small but significant. The city afforded generous views of water and skyline; it had both ample "sea-level access" and "flat...solid land to build on."[13] These impressive natural characteristics helped turn Hoboken, largely undeveloped in the mid-nineteenth century, into valuable real estate by the century's end. It was a city perhaps exceptionally well-suited for people rising in stature. During Fagan's lifetime, the house at Hudson and Tenth Streets, or Fagan Mansion, with its uppermost stories and cupola, probably occupied close to the highest if not the highest altitude in Hoboken.

From that perch, Fagan, whether serving as mayor or just acting like it, was often seen running downtown and to sea-level. He was a figure anxious to diffuse or stir the action down on the streets and on the waterfront. There, constant activity and situations of unexpected turmoil often broke loose, with the Great Hoboken Fire providing a striking example. The fire, which began on June 30, 1900, was the biggest during the period in size, scope, and drama—a grisly disaster that killed hundreds and caused millions in damages. It was there, amid the smoky stench and carnage left in the fire's immediate aftermath, and with the harbor's docks badly damaged, that Fagan once descended. In an instant, he cooled a heated, particularly macabre exchange between rival "morgue keepers" before fists were thrown. The city awash in corpses, they were greedily squabbling over rights to the remains. Fagan's loud, energetic appearance brought an immediate end to their disorderly discussion; he commanded them to "keep still" or "get off the dock."[14]

In contrast to the heights of the Fagan Mansion at Hudson and Tenth Streets in Hoboken, the Horseshoe section in neighboring Jersey City sat low, both in topography and on the socio-economic pecking order. The Horseshoe ran inland from the Hudson River along the Hoboken border and below the looming specter formed by the palisades; much of the area was comprised of very low ground and, in some parts, swamp. It was a place often subject to flooding. Stagnant water was prone to stink and fester in an unsanitary fashion. The air could sometimes be quite foul smelling, reflecting rising pollution and population. When Dutch settlers arrived in the seventeenth century, the area was made up of numerous small islands. As Jersey City grew and the number of railroad tracks to and from New York increased, the ground was filled in, and factories, tenements, saloons, and other commercial buildings were built upon it. During especially warm, inclement weather, rainwater and sewage often mixed, creating foul smells and public health hazards that were frequently neglected by Jersey City authorities.[15]

During the summertime heat in 1904, an example of the Horseshoe area's problems was found in an overrun sewer at Thirteenth and Division Streets. The smell there and potential for the spread of disease had grown. Jersey City authorities, however, had paid little attention to the problem as it worsened. Fagan Iron Works had its factory located just a block away from the growing "pool of nastiness," as the *Observer* described it. "The open ditch allows the tide to back up all the dirt and filth from 1,900 families north of the Erie tracks," dumping it twice-daily onto "the sunken lots" of area meadows. Horseshoe residents, their anger intensified, ultimately galvanized. They gathered for a big raucous neighborhood meeting. Residents demanded city officials "plug up the offending drain" immediately; they also made "threats" against those they blamed for the unacceptable conditions. In the Horseshoe, "they mean business," the *Observer* reported. "Fighting blood [is] up."[16]

Lawrence Fagan was a part of the massive infusion of Irish Catholic immigrants who settled in Jersey City following the Civil War. The emigration surge caused Jersey City's total population and, in particular, its number of Democratic voters to increase rapidly. This demographic shift was troublesome for Republicans, who exercised an inordinate amount of power in New Jersey state government during Reconstruction. They attempted to mitigate the growing political impact of the mostly poor Irish immigrant laborers with a gerrymandering scheme. To lessen the number of representatives that Democratic votes might propel to the New Jersey State House in Trenton, the Republicans tried to reduce Democratic representation on the Aldermanic Council through the Redistricting Act of 1870. This gerrymander created a newly drawn Second Ward political district full of Democratic voters in Jersey City. According to local lore, Dennis McLaughlin, an Irish born Democratic leader-boss in Hudson County, gave the Horseshoe its moniker. The lines of the newly-fashioned ward plotted on a map of Jersey City appeared shaped like a horseshoe, and the name stuck.[17]

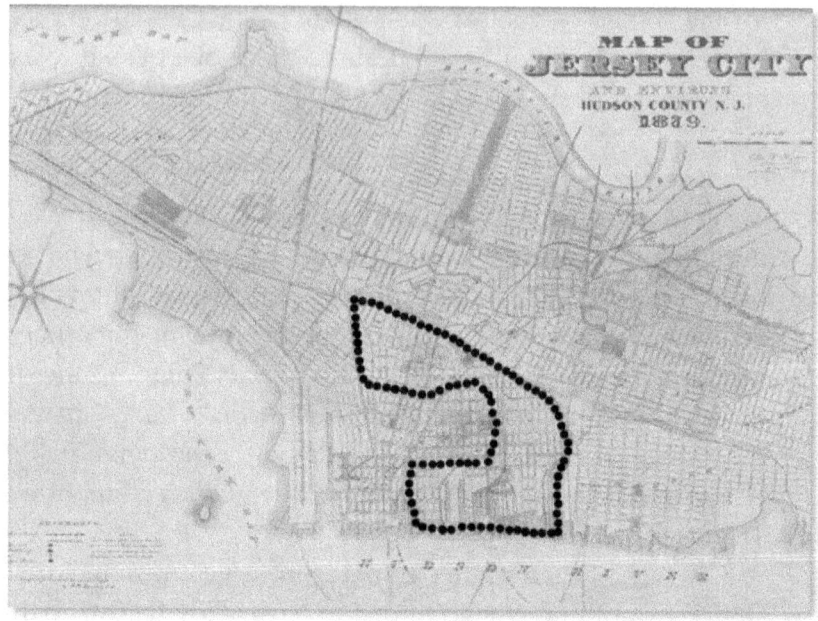

The darkened area outlined on this 1879 map approximates the original Horseshoe section of Jersey City. (Surface image courtesy genealogicalsurveyor.com.)

The gerrymandering by Republicans in the state capital was easily identified by the Irish-Americans in Jersey City's Horseshoe as an act of non-home-rule oppression. At the same time, the moniker the Horseshoe provided an enduring and easily identifiable symbol around which to rally. The image of a lucky slab of iron—strong and adroitly cast, then hammered into a pounding hoof—captured well the imagination of the area's largely hardscrabble, long battered but resilient population. A symbol of collective identity, the Horseshoe came to represent the history, politics, and culture, as well as the work, religion, and social lives of its residents.[18]

For Fagan, a resident living in the Horseshoe in 1870, the Republican gerrymander probably affirmed an allegiance to the Democratic Party and to the principle of independent home rule that otherwise might not have taken form. These tenets he took up to Hoboken. Three decades later, he brought his ironworks factory down to the Horseshoe. Fagan's career was spent both moving bottom up and top down, to and from the highest and lowest geographic positions of Hoboken and Jersey City. He lived in vertical extremes. From the high-set house at Hudson and Tenth Streets in Hoboken to the low-set Fagan Iron Works factory in the Horseshoe, the physical high levels and low levels navigated by Fagan provide something of a blueprint for the idea that he lived very close to the top and very near to the bottom of society in urban America simultaneously. This variation on the "top-down" and "bottom-up" historical approaches—one capable of describing types of movement—emerged in this project as one helpful way to view and interpret Fagan.

Historians often use the terms bottom up and top down to differentiate between two seemingly opposed perspectives, that of the lower versus upper classes. Historians ask, "Whose story is being told?" Is the story being told from the perspective of the people who were trying to survive, working to acquire status and power from the "bottom-up"? Or, is the story being told from the perspective of the people who held wealth and standing and whose actions powerfully impacted many lives from the top down?[19]

Looking at history from a top-down perspective has traditionally been popular in American historical writing. Arthur Link's *Wilson: The Road to the White House* (1947) is an example of top-down history, with the presence of the "bottom of American society" virtually absent. However, at least by the beginning of the 1970s, the top-down perspective began falling out of favor. This was especially true of scholarly writing, where looking at history from a bottom-up perspective became preferred and prevalent. Jennifer Guglielmo's *Living the Revolution: Italian Women's Resistance and Radicalism in New York City* (2010) is an example of "bottom-up" history, with the presence of "the top" of American society virtually absent. Both works provide different perspectives on American and New Jersey political and intellectual history; both were extremely helpful in researching and providing context for this project.[20]

Fagan's absence from these works, perhaps his wider absence altogether from historical writing, might be attributed to there being a certain enigmatic peculiarity to him as a historical figure. Fagan was of Irish-Catholic blood and a first-generation immigrant. Therefore, the fact that he became so wealthy in late-nineteenth century America was highly unusual in the first place. At the time, a lower-middle-to-middle-class Irish-American demographic was only just emerging. This group was comprised mostly of educators, clerks, and salesmen. "Unskilled labor" for men and "domestic services" for women continued to be unequivocally the principal type of work done by the Irish in America.[21]

Even among the very small group of first-generation Irish Americans who rose above the middle-class, it was extremely rare for an ironworks to be the main source of wealth—as it was for Fagan. In *The American Irish* (1963), journalist, author, and future Ambassador to Ireland William V. Shannon noted that, although a small handful of Irish businessmen made "great fortunes" during the Gilded Age's "great industrial expansion," the very vast majority did not. They were neither "notably creative" nor "distinctive in business." Those who did reach any notable level of prosperity "climbed slowly" to affluence. Being "pupils of native businessmen," Irish businessmen acquired "their techniques," "their habits," "their values." Therefore, "there has never been a stereotype of an Irish businessman," added Shannon. "Evolving slowly, over a long period, he did not differ significantly from other businessmen;—his progress was...noiseless."[22]

Fagan's progress, however, was fast and loud. His distinctive industrial success can partially be attributed to his extraordinarily high level of energy, a peculiar force which also propelled him ahead in politics. "[Fagan] has not been asleep lately," as one booster described in 1903. "Everyone knows him," making "things hum...in Hoboken. [Fagan] can make...more progress in two weeks than any other candidate can in two months."[23]

If the ground that Fagan covered in his lifetime more typically took successful Irish-Catholic immigrants at least two generations to cover, the case of Irish-Catholic immigrant Philip Tumulty and his son Joseph provides something of a more measured example of the difference between first-generation and second-generation success in America. After fleeing famine-battered Ireland for America, fighting in the Civil War, and briefly working in an iron foundry, Philip Tumulty opened a small grocery store in Jersey City. His son Joseph Tumulty became a notable Irish success in America, rising to become Woodrow Wilson's White House Chief of Staff, then known as Secretary to the President. Joseph Tumulty maintained that "the foundation stones" for his father's "modest fortune" and his own rise in politics, from leading a small "Democratic faction" in the neighborhood to advising Wilson in the White House, were put down at that "little grocery store."[24] There, with politics often on their minds, many first- and second-generation American-Irish immigrants regularly gathered to confer.[25] "They were a very simple folk," however, they were "independent in their political actions and views," Joseph Tumulty asserted. "They would not submit to tyrannous dictation in this free land of ours, no matter who sought to exert it."[26]

Fagan was probably more complex, but there exists an important shared characteristic between him and the politically engaged Irishmen assembled at Tumulty's store. Fagan was intensely protective of his independence and unfettered in making that message known. Fagan, as Woodrow Wilson was advised in 1910, was "independent," then likened to "that New York policeman who said: 'I bate you, not because I hate you, but to show my aut'ority over you.'"[27]

If wider justification is warranted for an academic or liberal arts study of Fagan, his independent streak might be usefully assessed within the scholarly framework of "manliness." Since at least the mid-1980s, historical writing on America's late-nineteenth and early-twentieth centuries has lent substantial attention to the subject of manliness and/or the "manly" identity.[28] Within this framework, historians have largely focused on concepts of white Protestant middle- and upper-class male anxiety, and made arguments to demonstrate how such anxieties, related nervousness, or fear about the onset of such, have facilitated acts of domestic and international—often racially-motivated—violence and subjugation.[29] Some recent scholarship has also examined the process by which "respectable" middle- and upper-class Protestant reformers, deemed afflicted with a crisis of masculinity, have appropriated manly traits from Irish-Catholic urban bosses. In turn, those bosses, deemed afflicted with a crisis of respectability, have appropriated respectable traits from Protestant reformers.[30]

Fagan, however, across a range of activity, rose so quickly from near bottom to near top in the American pecking order that he seemingly embodied a manly ideal in more than one social station at a time. Moreover, in the period in which Fagan lived, the concept of manliness appears with such prevalence and ambiguity that it might be ascribed credit or blame broadly for almost any societal triumph or tribulation. While manliness may be too broad a lens for interpreting Fagan or his era, a narrower view is possible: in him, manliness appeared both as a social virtue as well as a vice. For example, during his first term as Mayor of Hoboken, Fagan received an award from the Independent Citizens' Association of Hoboken. The award, inscribed with the group's guiding tenet "to secure an honest and economical administration of our public affairs," honored Fagan for having "kept his pledge... to give [Hoboken] such an administration," for his "manly and determined stand...taken in all matters pertaining to the welfare of our city."[31] Nevertheless for Fagan, manliness might also be blamed for bringing social trouble. In 1903, Fagan assaulted a visiting labor union representative, whom he believed had come to extort money from him. Subsequently, Fagan was called before a court of law to answer for the charges.

"I will not be bulldozed," Fagan testified without remorse. "Any man in my place would have done what I did."[32]

Although specific historical figures who stood in the same or similar place as Fagan, as previously discussed, are not so easily found, Fagan's multi-faceted life stands out. Whether standing out as an embodiment or disembodiment of the times in which he lived, Fagan shows us reflections: the story of the famine immigrant, the artisan apprentice, the industrial worker, the iron master, the iron baron, the gambler, the banker, the volunteer firefighter, the ethnic political boss, the erudite business reformer, the education-minded progressive, the pugilist, the self-promoting publisher, and surely numerous more.

Dramatic typecasting, such as the distinction between the venal political "boss" and the virtuous urban "reformer" established in a 1940s generation of historical writing, evolved into a popular but contentious topic in later historical writing. During the late 1960s and throughout the 1970s, previously cut-and-dried distinctions and rigid classifications on ethics, occupation, and social station underwent substantial reinterpretations. Or, as historian David Kennedy described, discourse on the period became a "babble of disagreement."[33] The difference between the "progressive" reformer and the "machine" boss, for example, became foggily unfixed, often indistinguishable or irrelevant, and perhaps made nearly obsolete.[34]

At the beginning of the twenty-first century, historian Glenda Gilmore offered a more universal and authoritative summary judgment on the disputed nomenclature used by historians and the challenge in defining the historical actors of the period. Gilmore warns readers in *Who Were The Progressives?* (2002) that trying to find any singular answer to the question posed by her anthology's title will only bring frustration because they are "studying something on which historians cannot agree."[35] To the contrary, yet simultaneously consistent with Gilmore's assessment, William J. Atto and

Ronald J. Pestritto, albeit from a more political science historian perspective, write "emphatically" in *American Progressivism* (2008) that "progressivism can be understood as a coher-
ent set of principles with a common purpose." Any "differences among progressives" were "over particular means, not
over fundamental ideas."[36]

If labels and names lay down some awkward, painfully
slow, or misleading tracks for understanding Fagan's life
within the wide lines of American historiography, then the
use of new perspectives, both from the bottom up and the top
down, is productive. For over half a century—whether in Hoboken, the Horseshoe, somewhere in between, or wherever in
the northern or southern portion of Hudson County—it was
never long before Fagan was found moving up and down.
Whether identified as a bird of a different or familiar feather,
he brought a phenomenal continuity to a peculiarly energetic
period in American history. Fagan's story began in Ireland
during the Great Famine in the mid-nineteenth century. As an
infant, he was carried across the Atlantic Ocean to America.
After a grooming through lessons learned in New York City
and further knowledge gained by going back to the old world,
then back again to the new one, Fagan landed permanently
on the west bank of the Hudson River. Once there, his independent mark, built in a gilded, manly age of disorderly industrial Armageddon and progressive urban reform, was
made.

MIGRATION

The great questions of the day will not be settled
by speeches and majority decisions...but by
blood and iron.
—Otto Von Bismarck (1862)

LAWRENCE FAGAN'S BIRTH AND EARLY TRAVELS during the mid-nineteenth century were set against the deteriorating circumstances that afflicted Ireland. Food shortages and Great Britain's oppressive colonial rule had long stifled Ireland's growth, piling hardship upon its Catholics and prompting many to emigrate in search of more promising conditions. The situation in Ireland took a grave turn for the worse during the summer of 1845 when the clandestine fungus *Phytophthora infestans* infected the soil and potato crops. The fungus, which most likely made its way to Europe aboard a ship from America, fast brought about catastrophe.[37] One observer in Ireland recalled that, "coming on the harvest time of the year 1845...the crops looked splendid." Then "the hand of death...struck" and "everything...was rotten; [everything] laden with a sickly odor of decay."[38]

Subsequently, Ireland experienced an incredible remission of life. The "Famine Decade" (1845–1855) saw Ireland's peak of human attrition and misery. The population, approximately 8.5 million in 1845, plummeted to around 6 million in 1855. Approximately 1 million Irish died of malnutrition; over a million left for the United States; hundreds of thousands more left for Canada, Scotland, England, and other foreign destinations.[39]

African-American abolitionist Frederick Douglass, who toured Ireland in 1845 and 1846, was taken aback by the condition of the people but recognized the symptoms of suffering. "The shuffling gait," "open, uneducated mouth," "long, gaunt arm," "retreating forehead," "vacant expression," "and their petty quarrels and fights," Douglass observed. "All reminded me of the plantation, and my own cruelly abused people."[40] British writer Thomas Carlyle visited Ireland in 1846 and 1849; he described it as "a human dog kennel."[41]

Probably more kennel-like were the ships that brought Ireland's emigrants across the Atlantic to North America during the Famine Decade. The Irish made their journey, which took between five and six weeks, in wooden cargo vessels designed to move large loads of idle goods, not large numbers of living people. These ships, sometimes referred to as "coffin ships" and later as "famine ships," had severely overcrowded quarters.[42] Confines were dark, damp, poorly ventilated, badly cramped—friendly to the spread of disease and poor health. Disorderly or unlawful behavior on board made for further danger.

Aboard one of these ships, a very young Lawrence Fagan landed in America, probably in 1852 or 1853. While no official record of Fagan's birth or baptism has been found, he was, by all accounts, born in Dublin, Ireland, on January 1, 1851. Details of young Fagan's passage and arrival in the Americas are not clear. There is some reason to believe that he was aboard a ship that landed in Canada or New England and lived with family in Portland, Maine, for a short period. There is also the possibility that he landed in Philadelphia and lived for a spell with family in western Pennsylvania.[43]

If the future ironmaster Fagan did land in Pennsylvania, which shared a border with New Jersey and was a popular destination for Irish immigrants, it would have been appropriate.[44] Representatives from Pennsylvania's iron industry were especially outspoken about their need for more workers at the time.[45] In December of 1849, the *Convention of Pennsylvania Iron Masters* sent a memorandum to Congress—a proclamation that "an ample supply" of iron was "indispensable" to the "progress" and "welfare" of the nation and warning that the present supply was very much insufficient. Immediate and dramatically increased production was needed to avert a crisis. America had to surpass all other nations in her iron, in manufacturing and industrialization, and be the "scene of industry," the Iron Masters told Congress. Such transformation demanded more labor. Millions of workers were needed; they would have to come from "all quarters of the world."[46] The Iron Masters also let it be known that, more so than any other sector of manufacturing, the production of iron relied on "the consequent skill" of its workers. Their training was longer and weightier than that of workers in other industrial sectors, but necessary. Every worker needed to be proficient at his job—his own unique function, or "peculiar duty...in the rolling mill"—where every task was interconnected. "Iron passes through all...hands before it is finished," explained the Iron Masters. "Ignorance" or "awkwardness" of one worker will "destroy" the work done by twenty.[47]

While there is substantial ignorance on the subject of Fagan's early life, census data provides some clues and a small part of the picture. The United States Census of 1860 shows a nine year old Fagan in New York City, residing in a tenement building in the Nineteenth Ward, and in a unit shared with six relatives, all born in Ireland: Job, a twenty-one-year-old laborer; Mary, an eighteen-year-old seamstress; Bernard, a sixteen-year-old laborer; Bridget, age seventeen; Anna, age fourteen, and Elizabeth, age eleven. The Fagan family members and their specific relationship to Lawrence and one another are unclear.[48]

In any case, the Fagan family, living together there, almost certainly had little personal space. New York City's mid-nineteenth-century tenement buildings were characterized by the hot, sardine-can-like packing of their residents. The Fagans' apartment building was very probably an austere five-storied structure. Their apartment unit inside was likely extremely compact, comprising one small and narrow common room for sitting, working, cooking, and eating, and one microscale bedroom.[49] James D. McCabe, a history and travel writer of the period,[50] flavorfully wrote of tenement living in the higher-numbered wards of the city where the Fagan family resided:

> Few rooms are properly ventilated. The sun never shines in at the windows....The whole house is dirty, and is filled with the mingled odors from the cooking stoves and [sinks]. In the summer the natural heat is made tenfold greater by the fires for cooking and washing. Pass these houses on a hot night, and you will see the streets in front of them filled with occupants, and every window choked up with human heads, all panting and praying for relief and fresh air.[51]

Notwithstanding huffing and hardship, city living's close confines may have afforded young Fagan the benefit of more than just his own relatives to serve as in-house adult mentors. The census record shows a man named Martin Crushing, an Irish-born blacksmith, lived with his family only a few doors away from the Fagan family.[52] Perhaps there were occasions which saw Crushing catch young Fagan running errant or standing idle about the premises; these may have been opportunities to offer the boy some direction, perhaps lessons in discipline or of the blacksmith's craft, hard knowledge from old Ireland, or that acquired in the new urban world.

In addition to whatever was learned at home, Fagan was afforded a more traditional education as a student in the free public school system of New York City. At that time, the curriculum for a boy of age nine or ten was generally comprised of "lessons about common objects, or 'object teaching'" intended to "form habits of accurate observation." The curriculum also would have had rudimentary instruction in "reading and spelling easy words," honing these skills on "the blackboard or chart," as well as "morals" and "manners," and "counting" and "simple addition" with help from a "numerical frame."[53]

Perhaps evidence of Fagan's early aptitude for observation, calculation, and etiquette was seen later by the fact that the newspaper he co-founded was named the *Observer*, or in the following letter that Fagan, as Mayor of Hoboken, sent to the city council. "Gentlemen, ...the applications for liquor licenses are getting very large and I would recommend that you pass a resolution limiting the number....Grant no license to any person unless he is a citizen and a resident of this City" for "one year...at least."[54]

One way or another, by the time Fagan was age ten, he was gone from New York and back in Europe. Although the reason for the move is unclear, issues associated with the Civil War seem a likely impetus. The Draft Riots in New York City would have made a far from ideal atmosphere for a ten-year-old boy to remain focused on hitting only the books.[55] Whatever motivated the move, England's census, conducted on April 7, 1861, showed Fagan residing in Liverpool at 67 South Andrew Street. This time the census recorded him with two adults marked as his parents: his mother noted as Bridget, age forty-five; his father as Thomas, age forty-two; as well as siblings: John, age seventeen; Eliza, age fourteen; and Mary, age six. Forty-two-year-old William Fagan, perhaps Thomas's brother, was also recorded as a resident of the household. "Whitesmith" is the recorded occupation of William, Thomas, and John Fagan.[56] A whitesmith's work, which also encompassed the duties of a locksmith, involved filing, grinding, and performing other processes upon the surfaces of iron objects that brought their "brightening." A whitesmith's primary instruments were the turning lathe and file. A blacksmith, in contrast, primarily finished off his objects with an anvil, making objects such as railings, bars, ties, and chains.[57] The census does record a blacksmith residing close to the Fagan family in Liverpool, with a bricklayer, marble mason, and cabinet maker also nearby.[58]

Other members of the Fagan family remained active in Dublin, Ireland, about one day's travel from Liverpool.[59] In around 1855, some Fagans started up a small ironworks at 18 Great Brunswick Street in Dublin. The ironworks, "James Fagan and Sons, 'Housesmiths and Bellhangers,'" did iron work of both the blacksmith and whitesmith variety. James Fagan, probably Lawrence's uncle, advertised his shop's keen facility for producing "ready-made, or made to order" iron work as well as its repair. The shop made iron "gates," "railings," "bedsteads," "kitchen ranges," "smoke jacks," and "grates," with all work done "on the most reasonable terms" and "most improved principle." Services such as picking locks and, of course, hanging bells were also advertised.[60] The use and popularity of iron products in building construction were growing, a trend owing in large part to an increased interest in making structures more "fireproof."[61] The optimism implied by the opening of a Fagan family ironworks in Dublin, however, should not be overblown. There was the backdrop of the Great Famine. Ireland was calamity-rattled and population-depleted as never before. Prospects for an Irishman entering a new trade or opening a new business, whether in Ireland or England, were extremely uncertain.[62]

Whether or not a career in Dublin or Liverpool was contemplated, Fagan's remigration to America was prudent. Already with some urban experience and iron in the family blood, he was ripe to find bigger and better opportunities in post-Civil War America. Fagan returned to the United States and to the classrooms of New York City probably in 1866 or 1867. He would have graduated from high school after spending about a year studying English grammar, American history, geography, astronomy, penmanship, bookkeeping, and possibly French or German.[63] At that time, the public schools of New York City possessed a stellar reputation; it began a quick decline in 1870 after Tammany Hall leader-boss William Marcy Tweed secured control over the entirety of municipal operations, including all public schools.[64] In 1870, the Orange Riots also broke out in New York City.[65]

Like returning to the United States and completing high school before it was too late, Fagan's next move, crossing the Hudson River for New Jersey, proved a wise one. Fagan's opportunity to quickly evolve into a big fish was greater in Jersey City and in Hoboken. The sister cities upon the Hudson were speedily growing and hardy manifestations of America's post-Civil War urban expansion. Between 1860 and 1910, the population of the United States increased from approximately thirty-one million to ninety-two million. The number of cities—those areas occupied by more than fifty-thousand people—went from sixteen to one hundred and nine.[66] In Hoboken the population grew from 9,662 to 70,324; in Jersey City from 29,226 to 267,779; in Hudson County from 62,717 to 537,231; in New Jersey from 672,035 to 2,537,167.[67] The urban expansion was fueled by an astonishing proliferation of immigration acting along with an astounding "acceleration...of industrialization," "commercial expansion," and "technological change."[68]

Modern iron steamships, bigger and faster than their wooden predecessors, brought more and more European immigrants to America. The 3,000-mile trip, which once took between five and six weeks, became achievable in twelve to fourteen days. On board accommodations were also made more comfortable. With quartering no longer so kennel-to-coffin-like, it was possible for those in search of a better life across the Atlantic to have a reasonably "pleasant voyage."[69]

Sea travel's technological advances had, in part, their origins in Hoboken. An engineering pioneer named Colonel

John Stevens purchased the land that became Hoboken at auction for $90,000 in 1784. From his estate there, Stevens unveiled the Julianna, the world's first steam-powered ferryboat, in 1811. Stevens died in 1838, but his sons, Robert L. and Edwin, continued in their father's footsteps. Robert L. Stevens made innovations to the internal mechanics and external design of steam-powered ferryboats, improvements which propelled them to reach speeds far greater than previously thought achievable.[70] At the behest of Edwin Stevens, the Stevens Institute of Technology was founded in Hoboken in 1868; the Institute's doors opened to students in 1870.[71] The establishment of the Stevens Institute furthered a shift in Hoboken's identity, its transformation from an undeveloped picnic "pleasure grounds," a tourist and recreation destination for mostly residents of New York City, to a coastal urban center with its own culture and characteristics.[72]

During the mid nineteenth century, Sunday picnicking in Hoboken with food and drink upon the plush Elysian Fields was a popular pastime for New Yorkers, especially Germans. The congenial, liberal atmosphere was the reason that many Germans chose to put down roots in Hoboken on a more permanent basis.[73] The environment in Hoboken stood in contrast to that of New York City, where there was a marked rise in strident Evangelical Protestant crusading for Sunday temperance and even, during the 1840s and 1850s, for the total prohibition of alcohol.[74]

Given the German culture's custom of both praying and partying together on Sunday, many German-Americans felt that Puritan-minded campaigns were a direct affront to their German identity and heritage.[75] In the wake of the European Revolutions of 1848, many Germans immigrated to America and soon found Hoboken an attractive place to settle. By 1855, the German population in Hoboken reached about 5,000.[76]

In 1862, Germany's Chancellor, Otto Von Bismarck, wielded the famous geo-political forecast, "The great questions of the day will not be settled by speeches and majority decisions...but by blood and iron." Iron steamships, German-built and modern, a large infusion of them, were directed to Hoboken the following year. Shipping corporations, the North German Lloyd and Hamburg-American, made Hoboken the American home port for their lines in 1863. Thus, the link between Germany and Hoboken was made stronger.

Another German business that contributed to Hoboken's growth was the importing of exotic animals. During the second half of the nineteenth century, animal acts became popular and profitable attractions. Promoters of circus-style shows tapped their talents, or maybe sometimes talons, to draw big crowds at venues such as Madison Square Garden. Animals also entertained very large numbers of spectators at free public menageries in municipal areas such as New York's Central Park. The Reiche family, operating on the waterfront in Hoboken and out of the property at Hudson and Tenth Streets, was the national leader in this commerce until the tail end of the nineteenth century. By then, another German, Carl Hagenback, had emerged as the industry leader. Hagenback's animals were also transported across the Atlantic in German steamships docking at Hoboken. The wide array of animals that landed in Hoboken included lions, tigers, bears, boarhounds, swans, cranes, elephants, guanacos, hyenas, leopards, apes, and hippopotamuses.[77]

This bird's-eye view of the house at Hudson and Tenth Streets with its pointed cupola roof was part of a panoramic perspective map published in 1881. The long rectangular structure paralleling Tenth Street likely housed a multitude of interesting, imported wildlife. The smaller structure next to the house facing Hudson Street served as a stable for horses and barn for smaller domesticated animals. (O.H. Bailey & Co. map, courtesy Library of Congress Digital Collections.)

On one afternoon in October of 1886, an unexpected convergence of mammals occurred on the Hoboken waterfront. A commotion was caused when some of the people emigrating from Europe aboard a German steamship found themselves face to face with a particularly large, hoofed passenger. The peoples' fright began when an enormous box of cargo freight, brought by a North German Lloyd steamship, was released down onto the pier in a fast and reckless manner. The box contained a hippopotamus, and it was headed for an area of the dock where an abundance of people, not long disembarked from the steamship, stood. They had to move with extreme dispatch to get out of the way of the box and narrowly avoided being squashed. Then with the "forbidding...headpiece" of the box's "oleaginous" occupant the first thing visible to the startled emigrants, some of the females were reported to have screamed, panicked, and ran. That reaction, while quite understandable, did not go unpunished. The hippopotamus had a handler—a short, corpulent German man who took advantage of the situation. He "seized" and "slapped" some of the frightened women with an "undue familiarity." Later as some semblance of order returned, the handler, left only the opportunity to keep his hands where they belonged, was seen petting the hippopotamus's back. He did so with affection, sharing "endearments" while the hippo's chunky little bristled tail wagged with "childish glee." When the name "Murphy" was included in the kind words called out, the tail wagged "with redoubled vigor." Murphy was a female hippopotamus. Sometimes she was given the name "Fatima" when performing on the animal entertainment circuit. Murphy, or Fatima, was native to the Sudan and only three years old. While still approximately one ton less than her ultimate size, Murphy, or Fatima, was already a proven box-office attraction nevertheless.[78]

The scene, while its comic allure as historical theatre is perhaps distasteful, may offer some keen insight into Fagan's Hoboken and the social dynamics at play. Historian Richard Hofstadter, writing in *The Age of Reform* (1955), explained that those recently arrived in America's cities often had mixed feelings towards their new surroundings. The "new urban world," while "strange, anonymous, impersonal, cruel, often corrupt and vicious," was also rich with "variety and fascination."[79] The emigrants introduced to the City of Hoboken by the hippopotamus and its handler surely had some strong first impressions. Some may have been dazzled and delighted by the animal and its exciting out-of-the-blue entrance, and perhaps also entertained by the scrum that followed. Conversely, or simultaneously, others may have viewed this new city as dangerously unpredictable, prurient, and rude. Some may have been left with the impression that in Hoboken human life, at least theirs, was less valuable than animal life, at least less than Fatima-Murphy's. The women, presumably mostly Irish and Catholic, who had the displeasure of being accosted by the German animal handler probably felt violated and angry. As to Fagan's position in Hoboken and the broader social pecking order, the scene might suggest that his metaphorical sack of tools was, in the language of more contemporary identity politics, only somewhat "invisible."[80] Fagan was an Irish-Catholic immigrant, an identity that was still very much an impediment to status in America in 1886. It was still several years before those commissioning free public menageries, made more aware of the cultural shift in audiences and calls to end "offensive names," stopped the prevailing practice of giving animals Irish names like "Murphy."[81]

Nevertheless, Fagan, by making a life for himself on the west bank of the Hudson in Hoboken, afforded himself some more favorable circumstances. Hoboken, unlike some of America's older, more established cities, lacked an overwhelmingly large and well-entrenched white Protestant population of European, English speaking stock. Excepting for these anglophiles (many of them Stevens family descendants) and the earlier-settled or second-generation Germans, Hoboken's demographics posed fewer socio-structural impediments to Fagan's upward mobility than those he might have faced had he remained in New York City.

Following his apprenticeship at Blackmore's foundry in Jersey City, Fagan began working in Hoboken for an architectural ironworks firm owned and operated by Isaac Mansfield & George Scudder. Mansfield & Scudder was located between Sixth and Seventh Streets on Willow Avenue. After Scudder died in 1872, Mansfield took Fagan on as his partner. The new firm, Mansfield & Fagan, soon moved to a new location in Hoboken at Jefferson Street between Third and Fourth Streets.[82] Mansfield & Fagan set up shop there with room to grow, the firm's operations housed in a sizeable four-story building. By 1887, there were around sixty men working for the firm. The manpower in the factory worked alongside a fifty-horsepower steam engine. Mansfield & Fagan manufactured iron products such as railings, girders, columns,

storefronts, door and window lintels, beams, building castings, coal chute and manhole covers. A promotional description reveals the importance Fagan and partner placed on being at the forefront of new technology changing the iron industry.[83]

> *Mansfield & Fagan—The widely known and progressive firm
> [brings] intimate knowledge of the industry and the require-
> ments of builders and contractors...The mechanical equipment of
> the works embraces all the latest improved machinery, tools, and
> appliances known to the trade, [adopting] every improvement or
> invention that tends to perfect the production...The partners
> have spared no pains or capital...in the production of building
> materials.[84]*

The firm's "progressive" business model was a successful
one. Mansfield & Fagan furnished the iron work for Hoboken's City Hall, which opened in 1883, as well as for Lorillard's tobacco factories and Snake Hill almshouse in Hudson County, and for many other projects in New Jersey and
in New York.[85]

As Fagan grew more successful in the iron industry, he
also became involved in other businesses. Fagan bought a
small stake in the Guttenberg horse racing track, which
opened in Hudson County's North Bergen Township in 1885.
As well, he was one of the co-founders of The Second National Bank of Hoboken, which opened in 1887.[86]

Fagan had come a long way by the late 1880s. Once an infant immigrant, crossing the Atlantic Ocean in the hold of a
wooden cargo ship, his fortunes had grown in urban America, where he was a man of rising influence. The next five
years saw Fagan, with what became his trademark independent energy, setting his sights further and farther, making his
name known to wider circles and larger audiences.

NICKNAMES

Lawrence Fagan is a Democratic member from
Hoboken, where he is employed in an iron
works. He is an Irishman by birth, with a bald
head...but a thinking brain.

—Trenton Evening Times, February 13, 1890

ON MONDAY EVENING, OCTOBER 8, 1888, the "streets were alive" with politics in Jersey City and Hoboken. The fall political season was set to roll, and conventions were being held in Jersey City and Hoboken. The former saw the arrival of a large and enthusiastic group of African-American voters. The African-American men, who numbered approximately three thousand, hailed from New Jersey and New York and were part of a political parade. They had come to raise the banner of the Republican Party, the first time that African-Americans were afforded the opportunity to do so in Jersey City.[87] Jersey City at that time had approximately two thousand African-American residents; Hoboken, approximately seventy-five.[88] While Republicans got together in Jersey City, Fagan's political career began in earnest at the Hudson County Democratic Convention in Hoboken.[89]

Fagan had previously served a minor appointment as a tax assessor; however, his service in a volunteer firefighting company, Hoboken's Old Excelsior Engine #2, probably functioned as his introduction to the logistics of local politics.[90] During the second half of the nineteenth century, service in volunteer firefighting companies often provided young men in America's cities an experience full of excitement and camaraderie, competition and acclamation, and frequently was the catalyst for an interest in political life.[91] Whatever role volunteer firefighting had in prompting Fagan's ambitions for elected office, it seemingly served him well. Fagan emerged from the Hudson County Democratic Convention with the nomination for a seat in the New Jersey State Legislature. The nomination for the office of assemblyman meant that he was in the running to represent Hudson County's Ninth District, comprised of Hoboken's First, Second, and Third Wards, a population of approximately 28,000.[92]

Fagan's nomination was something of a surprise. The nomination was expected to go to a Hoboken police commissioner and saloon owner named Michael Coyle. Coyle, however, for reasons that are unclear, removed his name from the running just moments before the start of the convention and "threw his support" to Fagan.[93]

In the general election, Fagan's opponent was the incumbent, Republican Assemblyman William Letts. Fagan and Letts were the same age and presumably had some degree of familiarity with each other through volunteer firefighting; both were members of Hoboken's Old Excelsior Engine #2.[94] Whatever the sometime firefighters' feelings towards each other, Fagan beat Letts at the polls on November 6, 1888, capturing 61 percent of the 3,482 votes cast.[95]

More firefighting experience might have come in handy in the New Jersey State House only a few years earlier. In late March of 1885, a big fire broke out at the state house building in Trenton. Fortunately, the fire was without casualties, but it caused massive structural damage. The trifecta of the fire, the water the Trenton Fire Department used in putting it out, and a "subsequent action of the elements" amidst weathering early spring conditions left the state house building damaged beyond repair. A new building was promptly constructed, designed by an architect from Jersey City, Lewis Broome. If Mansfield & Fagan sought the contract for the iron work, the firm's bid was passed over. A New York firm, Post & McCord, was awarded the job. Nevertheless, Fagan now had a seat on the floor of the freshly minted government building under its 145-foot-high rotunda and dome.[96]

Fagan's time as an assemblyman would be remembered mostly for fathering "The Hamilton County Bill." The goal of the legislation was to split Hudson County into two separate counties. Fagan argued that the bifurcation was necessary because in Hudson County, the southern portion of the county had too much power over the northern portion. In making his case, Fagan brought attention to the fact that the county's southern portion (that which included Jersey City) had leadership and interests that often conflicted with those of the county's northern portion, which included Hoboken.

If the Hamilton County Bill were passed, Jersey City and Bayonne would become one county and maintain the name Hudson County. The northern portion—comprised of Hoboken, Weehawken, Guttenberg, West Hoboken, Union, West New York, North Bergen, and Secaucus—would become a second county named Hamilton County. Each county would then elect its own representatives to the state senate and assembly.[97]

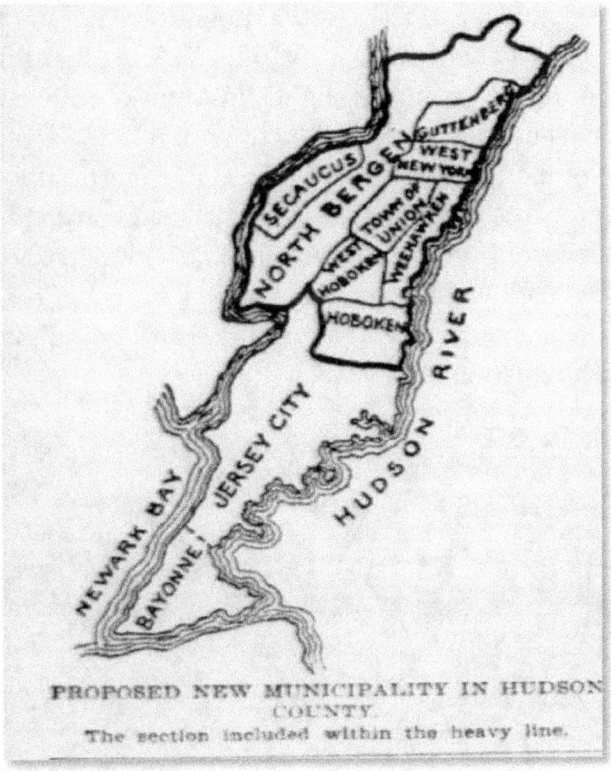

PROPOSED NEW MUNICIPALITY IN HUDSON
COUNTY.
The section included within the heavy line.

This map illustrates how Fagan's Hamilton County Bill might have split Hudson County into two counties. Jersey City and Bayonne would have remained in Hudson County. Hoboken, Weehawken, West Hoboken, North Bergen, Secaucus, Union, West New York, and Guttenberg would have become Hamilton County. The map was published in the January 4, 1901 edition of the New York Daily Tribune in a story examining the argument that continued to be made for bifurcating Hudson County in the manner envisioned by Fagan. (Courtesy Library of Congress Digital Collections.)

The name of Fagan's proposed legislation was a tribute to Alexander Hamilton, whose ties to the west bank of the Hudson River were significant. Hamilton was predeceased by his nineteen-year-old son, who died while dueling on a sandbar accessible only at low tide in Paulus Hook, a hamlet later consolidated into Jersey City. Hamilton, of course, famously died following a duel with Aaron Burr in 1804, the shootout going down on a stretch of beach in Weehawken.[98] Just months before, Hamilton, while practicing law, filed a notable action on behalf of some clients in Paulus Hook. Hamilton's clients were property owners desiring that the boundary between New Jersey and New York waters on the Hudson River be made clear and legal. The case was not resolved promptly; the matter kicked about the courts until 1833. At that time, the water boundary was made slightly less murky with demarcation between New Jersey and New York ruled "fixed...in the middle of the Hudson River."[99] Though superficially simple to comprehend, the ruling lacked in detailed maritime specifics or surveyor precision. Hence, the line between New Jersey and New York waters continued to be a source of confusion and controversy, including in events surrounding the Great Hoboken Fire in 1900.

This map shows the close proximity between Hudson County and New York City. The tight space suggests how determining a clear and absolute water boundary between New Jersey and New York had the potential to be problematic. (1904 Lackawanna Railroad map, courtesy Hoboken Historical Museum Online Collections: hobokenmuseum.org.)

In any case, Fagan's paying homage to Hamilton in the naming of legislation was understandable. Hamilton was a founder in a new nation, its creation the product of the successful fight for independence from British colonial rule. Fagan, seeking to make Hoboken independent of Jersey City, wanted to create a new county. A further affinity for Hamilton was also very probably explained by a shared faith in the future development of the Hudson River's west bank. Hamilton predicted that someday it would give rise to "the greatest city of the world."[100] And, so too did Fagan. Popular historian Walter Lord took note of Fagan making such a Hamilton-like forecast on the eve of the twentieth century. "Wise men gave their prophecies and predictions," Lord wrote. "Mayor Lawrence Fagan of Hoboken saw a 'Greater Jersey City' which would eclipse New York across the Hudson."[101]

Unlike that prediction, as yet, Fagan's Hamilton County Bill actually came close to becoming reality. Versions of Fagan's legislation were agreed to in the House and Senate, but not in a manner sufficiently simultaneous for it to become law. At one point, with a new Hamilton County in New Jersey appearing imminent, a fellow legislator was seen congratulating Fagan—suggesting that when Fagan next returned to Trenton it would be as "the first Senator from Hamilton County." Fagan, however, was heard rebuffing that idea, at least the part about returning to Trenton as a state senator. He explained that he could not afford to do so, that he had not paid sufficient attention to his ironworks while serving as an assemblyman.[102] In any event, the Hamilton County Bill's ultimate failure to pass was, not surprisingly, mostly attributed to its opposition amongst Jersey City representatives. The concept of in any way losing power and influence over the whole of Hudson County found an icy and litigious audience in Assembly Leader William C. Heppenheimer and Speaker Robert S. Hudspeth. The duo, Democrats from Jersey City, had heated exchanges with Fagan on the state house floor, with cold silence and the utmost distance maintained during meals in the dining room of the nearby American Hotel. In the end, Heppenheimer and Hudspeth, by acting in "collusion," at least as Fagan saw it, helped to thwart off Hudson County's divide. In acknowledgment of his Hamilton County Bill's all but certain defeat, "Hamilton County," Fagan remarked, "was in the soup."[103]

Although Fagan's envisaged divergence of Hudson County may have been unsuccessful, there was still reason to be optimistic about his future prospects in politics. Fagan won a second term in the assembly in 1889, capturing 63 percent of the 4,106 votes cast.[104] Fagan's time at Trenton also gave him knowledge and experience. He served on the New Jersey House and Senate Joint State Library Committee, the house committees for Ways and Means, Municipal Corporations, and Unfinished Business. Fagan's decision not to seek a third term in the assembly created speculation that he would be running for Mayor of Hoboken in 1891. Fagan, at least publicly, rebuffed the suggestion that he harbored mayoral intentions. The mayor's office, Fagan remarked, in fact, was one he had "never cared for."[105] Fagan, for the time being anyway, remained true to his word and did not run for mayor in 1891.

Rather than a lack of interest, family and business commitments probably explained the decision to take a short break from politics. Fagan had married a woman named Hannah McHale, often called "Annie," around 1880. McHale was born in 1855; her parents were Irish immigrants who settled in New Jersey. Hannah and Lawrence made their home together in Hoboken at 383 Park Street, their apartment next door to Isaac Mansfield and family.[106] The Fagans had a daughter, Catherine, born in 1881, and a son, John, born approximately fourteen months later. Hannah McHale Fagan died in 1888 or 1889. Her cause of death may have been related to childbirth. Fagan, widowed, soon moved to 413 Washington Street in Hoboken, where presumably he had help caring for the two children.[107]

Fagan soon married again, finding a match in the significantly younger Mary A. Foley, born in 1867 and often called "Mollie." Foley and Fagan exchanged vows on Wednesday afternoon, September 9, 1891. One reporter, pointing to the May–December model of the engagement, noted, "Fagan...'cut' the boys."[108] Foley, however, had shouldered more adult responsibilities than her relative youth might suggest. She was the oldest of seven children and sixteen when her mother died. To help her father, Michael, and the family, she had spent the past several years in charge of her six younger siblings, taking care of them and the Foleys' spacious home on Garden Street in Hoboken. Michael Foley, an Irish immigrant, was a successful contractor. In fact, he was successful enough to afford Mary a role as a "belle" at the New Jersey Governor's Ball in Spring Lake, New Jersey. The big dance was held not too long before the Foley/Fagan courtship began. In contrast to the presumed pageantry at Spring Lake, the occasion of Mary and Lawrence's wedding was exceptionally understated. Only immediate family attended the Catholic service held at Our Lady of Grace Church in Hoboken and the dinner that followed at the Foleys' home. The newlyweds were then off to Canada and the western part of the United States for a honeymoon. Upon return, Mary moved into the house on Washington Street with Lawrence and her new stepchildren, Catherine and John.[109]

Before the start of the new marriage, Fagan would finish an old one by ending his nearly two-decade-long business partnership with Isaac Mansfield. Fagan bought out Mansfield's share in Mansfield & Fagan for $90,000.00. Fagan then formed Fagan Iron Works, incorporated on June 4, 1891.[110] If Fagan sought a business loan to finance the deal, he presumably obtained it on favorable terms from The Second National Bank of Hoboken. Mansfield, on the other hand, now had more money and time for other business interests, including ownership of a saloon called "Mansfield House." The saloon was located in the Township of North Bergen in Hudson County. In 1896, trouble found Mansfield in the endeavor. A judge ruled that Mansfield House was willfully hosting illegal activity; that it was an unlawful "disorderly house." As a consequence, Fagan's former partner eventually served a short sentence behind bars (presumably iron). The judge's opinion was that, because Mansfield was warned on several occasions to heed the appropriate laws regulating saloon operations, i.e., hours of operation, Sunday closings, liquor sales to children, gambling, etc., but chose to ignore those warnings, he had both broken the law and "flaunted...defiance in the face of the courts."[111]

Seemingly better off for the breakup, Fagan began work with some new partners to enter the newspaper business and form the *Observer*.[112] The *Observer* started in Hoboken as a weekly newspaper. The first issue was published on Saturday, February 6, 1892. Fagan may have anticipated running for mayor when he got into the endeavor. Either way, the newspaper created something of an ideological framework for such a campaign. That is, the *Observer* provided insight into how a politically independent mentality might square with an allegiance to the Democratic Party. "The Observer enters the field of journalism not as a rival of anyone but upon the broad ground that we believe necessity has placed before it," the newspaper's inaugural issue declared. "We are in favor of clean openhanded management of the public business of the City, County and State;" "shall support no man for public office who manifestly seeks it for private gain rather than the public good;" "shall on all proper occasions condemn false democracy." The new newspaper maintained it was unabashed in its affirmation of "the principles of the Democratic party." Simultaneously, it made clear its definition of "the word Democratic," that it must be "a synonym for public and private integrity."[113]

For the *Observer*, the integrity lacking in the Hoboken Police Department was a frequent topic of discussion. In one editorial drubbing, there was pointed discussion of policemen in Hoboken "on duty, in full uniform" drinking inside saloons at all hours of the day and night. The irresponsible imbibing was "a notorious fact," according to the *Observer*.[114]

The Hoboken police commissioner and saloon owner Michael Coyle, who years earlier had unexpectedly removed himself as a contender for the Democratic assembly seat nomination, making way for Fagan to secure it, probably now regretted whatever role he may have had in facilitating Fagan's rising influence. Coyle was something of an easy target for the *Observer*. "Michael Coyle's Liquors and Tavern" was located in Hoboken at one corner of Washington and Newark

Streets.[115] Hoboken City Hall, inside which the police department was headquartered, was located at another corner of Washington and Newark Streets. The *Observer* had its own building on Newark Street, located not more than an earshot away from the south side of the city hall. Therefore, any policemen accustomed to something of an easy flow-and-go beat between headquarters and the commissioner's watering hole found themselves with a nosy new neighbor. The *Observer* was now right there, ready to report on officers' drinking or other dallying while on duty. There was further negative attention brought Coyle by the newspaper's attack on municipal policies that did not prohibit public officials from holding more than one office at a time. This multitudinous practice, argued the *Observer*, created conflicts of interest and wastefully enabled public officials to fatten their coffers by drawing multiple salaries. Coyle was called out as a prominent example of the problematic practice. Pointing to Coyle serving simultaneously as a police commissioner, state assemblyman, and as a Hudson County freeholder, the *Observer* dubbed him "One Man Three Offices" Coyle. Further, the paper blasted him for his part in the broad "false democracy" that had taken root in Hoboken.[116] The *Observer*, in further analysis of the political power structure currently in control in Hoboken, condemned Coyle even more magically:

> We are acquainted with the clever tricks of the conjurer who presents a hand full of cards to us and asks us in his most bland style to select one, at the same time forcing a card to the front of the pack, which, naturally, we take as being the one we would select. Having forced this card, the work of the conjurer is complete. Political jugglery does not differ materially from any other....When conventions are packed with [and] by the friends of the nominee, there is little choice left to the voters, who 'rather endure the ills they have, than fly to others that they know not of.'....Coyle and [the likes] are far from being the representatives

of the majority. They are 'forced cards' and a 'Hobson's choice' in every sense.[117]

Comparing the deceptions used by magicians on their marks to the tactics used by unscrupulous politicians upon the electorate, giving the unwitting the illusion of choice, creatively expressed the *Observer's* frustration with the status quo. The analogy not only took aim at Hudson County's Democratic circular-machine, sometimes referred to as "the ring," but also suggested the difficult task of electing Democrats independent of it. Notwithstanding that some moving parts may be inevitably particular to their time and place (early-1890s Hoboken, growing with Jersey City to the south and New York City to the east across the Hudson River) or the often challenged usefulness of names and labels, a very general, but expert, description of the period's prevailing power dynamic in urban politics may be helpful to readers. In *Rainbow's End: Irish Americans and the Dilemmas of Urban Machine Politics, 1840–1985* (1988), political scientist Steven P. Erie writes:

> *The machine emerged as the major urban political institution in the late nineteenth century; the Irish were among its leading architects and practitioners. A form of clientele politics, the party machine organized the electorate in order to control the tangible benefits of public office—patronage, services, contracts, and franchises. The machine employed these resources to maintain power. Bosses purchased voter support with offers of public jobs and services rather than by appeals to traditional loyalties or to class interests.*[118]

As the *Observer* saw it in Hoboken, the reason for the Democratic circular-machine's sustained success was twofold. First, it maintained its "perpetual grip" on power by its secretive dealings, deciding its candidates months, if not years, in advance of elections. The circular-machine's leader-bosses were "able-schemers," as the *Observer* called them. Secondarily, the *Observer* attributed the circular-machine's sustained reign to the unmotivated indifference of the independent voter. For this reason, there was some cause for optimism. If the independent voter could be sprung from "apathy," so too could the circular-machine be sprung from power. The *Observer*, therefore, issued a summons of sorts, calling on earnest and honest "young men" to assume their civic duty — to vote; to run for office for the good of the growing city.[119]

In 1893, Fagan, perhaps inspired by his own call to service in the pages of the *Observer*, reentered politics. He ran for Mayor of Hoboken and was successful in securing the Democratic nomination. "In unity there is strength," Fagan told fellow Democrats on the evening of March 27, 1893, at the city convention. "And, I trust, as your standard bearer, success will be ours, and if it is, and I have no doubt it will be, I shall serve you as an honest, upright man."[120]

A sketch of Lawrence Fagan that appeared in various newspapers identifying him as a candidate for office. (Jersey City News, March 25, 1893, courtesy newspapers.com.)

Fagan was not humble in his belief that he was easily the right man for the job. "I am as confident as the day is long" that "I will be...Mayor," and "elected...by the biggest majority ever given to any Mayoralty candidate in the city," said Fagan, who predicted his win in an interview with the Democratic "reform" newspaper the *New York World*.[121] The *World*, with its New Jersey edition, was an important part of the media landscape in Hudson County.

Although Fagan emphasized the importance of Democratic unity during his speech at the city convention, his interest in bringing the party together was not so apparent in his interview with the *World*, published just hours before the convention. "I will give the people a clean, honest, and economical government," Fagan told the *World*. "If any frauds exist, I'll expose them without fear or favor" and "without any dictation from McLaughlin."[122]

Fagan's finger was pointing at Dennis McLaughlin, the big leader-boss of the Democratic circular-machine in Hudson County at the time. McLaughlin, born in County Cavan, Ireland, and brought to America as a small child, grew up in the area of Jersey City later known as the Horseshoe, the name, as noted earlier, credited to him.[123] McLaughlin owned a cigar shop, from which he also operated a newspaper distribution service. His personality, assessed affable by many, made his smoke shop a popular hangout for the men in charge of the neighborhood's political primaries. Eventually, McLaughlin became their fugleman and rose from there in Hudson County politics.[124] William Edgar Sackett, a Republican attorney from New York City turned New Jersey newspaper editor and political history author of the period, wrote colorfully and critically of McLaughlin and the political scene in Hudson County.[125] "McLaughlin was a shrewd and frank kind of fellow," running "his dingy...little shanty." As "a man of sober habits," he was "attentive to business, good-natured and genial," with "a rough and hearty air well calculated to make him popular among his kind." Sackett's assessment of Hudson County was slightly less kind. Like "no county in the state," Hudson was "overrun...by a rabble of cheap sports and barroom loungers who looked to the spoils of place for their living."[126] Sackett's creative commentary, while best taken with a rough and hearty grain of partisan salt, nevertheless suggests how voters seeking lean and independent governance may have found McLaughlin, his circular-machine's interconnected "sports" and "loungers," less-than desirable.

Connection to McLaughlin proved to be a significant liability for Fagan in achieving his goal of being elected Mayor of Hoboken. While prior dealings between McLaughlin and Fagan in Democratic political circles are not clear, the two men were linked by their shared involvement in the Guttenberg racetrack business. McLaughlin, who owned approximately seventeen percent of the racetrack, was its second-largest shareholder. The largest shareholder was Gottfried Walbaum, who owned approximately 20 percent. Fagan's stake was slightly less than 3 percent.[127] Still, any involvement in horse racing was potentially problematic for a candidate seeking office in New Jersey at the time. Moral reformers were raising increased ructions about gambling and betting on horses. Increasing numbers of lawmakers were taking notice. Attacking the gaming industry, or at least creating distance from it, often became politically expedient.[128]

The Democratic *Hoboken Evening News* was indignant about Fagan's nomination for Mayor of Hoboken. Fagan, according to the *News*, was the Guttenberg bookmakers' "professional bondsman." Democrats were "desperate" to "flaunt...a race track man" for mayor, said the *News*. The publication proceeded to make a further charge. Fagan was not the "reform candidate" his "business friends" had "posed" him to be. "Larry Fagan," in fact, was "the machine candidate," and backed by "Denny McLaughlin."[129]

The *News's* referring to McLaughlin as "Denny" and Fagan as "Larry" was, of course, intended as a slight, inferring boyish immaturity and unsuitability, in particular, for a leadership role in government. The nicknaming was similar to the early pejorative tagging of Theodore Roosevelt, referring to him as "Teddy," which occurred while Roosevelt was serving in the New York State Assembly in the 1880s. In that case, however, "Teddy" probably also implied an entitled, or blue-blooded, foppishness.[130] Whereas for McLaughlin and Fagan, "Denny" and "Larry" were nicknames likely intended to underscore their similar Irish backgrounds. So too, the nicknaming reinforced the *News*'s allegation that Fagan was "the machine candidate;" that choosing "Larry" was the same as choosing "Denny," making it no choice at all; or, in the vernacular of the *Observer*, "a Hobson's choice."

The owners of the *Hoboken Evening News*, William H. Wall and Gustav E. Seide, were both of German backgrounds. Wall was born in Germany; Seide was from Milwaukee. The *News* had supported a German for mayor, a candidate bested by Fagan in the primary.[131] Wall and Seide may have preferred Hoboken have a German leader, but their aversion to Fagan was most likely more motivated by business interests. The *News* had been in business for nearly a quarter century. So too, it began the year 1893 as Hoboken's only daily publication; daily meaning here published every day except Sunday. The *Observer*, while in its relative infancy and published just once a week, had Fagan's backing, financial and political. If the *Observer* transitioned to a daily publication, which certainly was not improbable, it would be a major competitor to the *News*, and presumably much more so if Fagan was elected mayor.[132]

The Mayor of Hoboken until late 1892 was a man named Edward Stanton. Stanton's term ended early when he resigned. He did so after the Hudson County Board of Freeholders appointed him sheriff of Hudson County. The sheriff's position was made vacant unexpectedly after the death of then-Sheriff John McPhillipps. Subsequently, the Hoboken City Council, at the behest of Stanton and McLaughlin, selected an interim mayor, William H. Ellis.[133] This moving around of offices maintained the circular-machine's control of the mayoralty, while also benefiting Stanton more directly. Stanton, by assuming the sheriff's post, did not have to face reelection in the spring, guaranteeing him an additional six months of job security. Voters would cast their ballots for sheriff in fall of 1893.

Whatever the prior maneuvering, Fagan's campaign to be elected Mayor of Hoboken required some extreme distance be put between himself and McLaughlin, probably Stanton too. Fagan likely couldn't do too much about his shared business interest with McLaughlin in Guttenberg. The public relations damage was already done. Fagan, however, could make it absolutely clear that he was an independent Democrat, not in any way beholden to leader-boss McLaughlin or to the circular-machine. Fagan needed to make it loud and clear that, in "political actions and views," he was just as fiercely independent as the old-time Irishmen assembled at Philip Tumulty's grocery store. Fagan's interview with the *New York World* would go a long way toward achieving that goal, covering extraordinary ground. "McLaughlin came to me several months ago and he told me that as I was a candidate for mayor, I would need all the support I could command," Fagan revealed. "[McLaughlin] said he had made arrangements with Seide, Coyle, and Stanton to meet me so we could talk about our differences and arrange an amicable settlement," Fagan added. "I was surprised at McLaughlin's proposition and said to him: 'Those men to meet me at a conference? No, sir,' I replied...'I don't want to meet them, and...I will not meet them,'" said Fagan, whose remarks then turned hard-core. "'I would sooner cut my own throat than have anything to do with those men.' I told McLaughlin that he was a big stuffed pig, and that I wanted nothing to do with him," Fagan added. "I told him to tell Seide, Stanton and Coyle that the more they pounded me the better I liked it."[134]

The interview created a big buzz. A reporter from the *Jersey City News*, a Jersey City Democratic daily publication, immediately headed to Fagan Iron Works in Hoboken to ask Fagan for comment on his incendiary comments. Fagan initially had no comment on the interview, but soon commented, with his comments assuming a non-denial denial approach of sorts. He said that he did not entirely recall mentioning McLaughlin during the interview, but categorically denied calling him "a stuffed pig." Anyway, "the leadership of the party," Fagan commented, "has nothing to do with this fight whatever."[135] McLaughlin, meanwhile, thought Fagan's remarks were outrageous; so outrageous that McLaughlin initially thought the whole interview had been a fake. After McLaughlin was alerted to all signs pointing to a real interview having been conducted, he got burning hot.

On Tuesday, March 28, 1893, shortly before high noon, McLaughlin confronted Fagan. McLaughlin was traveling in his light wagon when he spotted Fagan walking on the sidewalk at Newark and Washington Streets in Hoboken, the location essentially the intersection of city hall, the *Observer* building, and Coyle's Liquors and Tavern. McLaughlin promptly stopped, then bounded out of his carriage. McLaughlin briefly spoke with Michael Coyle, who was standing nearby, then turned his attention towards Fagan and began loudly interrogating him. McLaughlin wanted to know if Fagan had been running around calling him "a stuffed pig." Scores of citizens, many aware of the growing heat between Fagan and McLaughlin and hearing McLaughlin's ructions, rushed to see the two men square off. With the lunch hour scene turned a small spectacle, the quarrel picked up steam. "No sir," Fagan told McLaughlin. "I never called you a stuffed pig." To that, McLaughlin fast retorted, "Why don't you come out like a man and say so in a letter to the newspapers then?" Fagan snapped back, "Because I don't have to...besides, I've nothing to say about it." Infuriated, McLaughlin proceeded to let loose a barrage of simmering verbiage. Meanwhile, the crowd, fascinated, watched and waited; they anticipated fists to be thrown. Fagan, however, kept his hands down and remained quiet during McLaughlin's tirade, allowing the leader-boss to vent. But as soon as McLaughlin's alarmingly ruddy and hot-under-the-collar condition appeared to drop by a degree or two, Fagan reengaged. He defiantly declared his independence from the circular-machine's leader-boss. "You may run Guttenberg," Fagan said, "but you can't run me... I don't believe you can fix things to beat me for Mayor of Hoboken... though, I don't doubt you'll try." At that, McLaughlin had heard enough and got back into his buggy. However, before leaving, he steered in towards Fagan. "I have no further use for you," McLaughlin belted out, an avowal repeated again and again as he rode off and away in his buggy. They were words to which, condescendingly, Fagan howled back, "Well, I guess I can get along—Denny."[136]

On that point, Fagan was correct, for he emerged from the campaign trail and its swinish mudslinging with his arms raised and the keys to Hoboken City Hall in his hands. Fagan was elected Mayor of Hoboken on April 11, 1893, defeating Republican John Tangeman. Fagan captured just under 57 percent of the 6,123 votes cast.[137] The *New York World* described Fagan's victory to be "a death blow" to the circular-machine's long hold upon power, an end to the use and abuse of the people's tax dollars in Hoboken.[138]

However big the win, it was morbidly presumptuous to think that the circular-machine didn't still have a strong foothold in Hoboken. McLaughlin remained county leader-boss; Stanton remained county sheriff. Down but not out, the circular-machine would be breathing down the new mayor's independent neck, jockeying to secure a new means to the power lost in Hoboken. Fagan's victory, nevertheless and with few caveats, can be reasonably assessed as providing a foundational breath of life into a larger "reform" movement, only then taking root in New Jersey.

As to the memorable sidewalk spat with McLaughlin, Fagan offered some clarification after winning the election. He revealed that he was, in fact, misquoted in the interview with the *World*. He also denied lying to McLaughlin's face when confronted. Fagan explained that he never called McLaughlin a "stuffed pig." Rather, Fagan gleefully acknowledged that he had called McLaughlin a "stuffed hog."[139]

By any name, by whatever way, winning the mayoralty was the first of more victories to come for Fagan. During his eventful, but rarely peaceful, long run as Mayor of Hoboken, he would oversee the city during its greatest phase of growth. Fagan's influence would be wielded broadly, impacting the lives of people who were trying to survive, working to acquire status and power from the "bottom up," as well as people who held wealth and standing and whose own decisions influenced many lives from the top down. To lead the city, Fagan would come face to face with an ample supply of combustible situations and fiery personalities. His mettle as mayor, "reform" or otherwise, would be put to the test.

OVER WORK

Mayor Fagan...jumps on the
Hoboken Police with both feet.
—New York Sun, May 2, 1893

ON MONDAY, MAY 1, 1893, Fagan took office as Mayor of Hoboken and began by issuing a searing message to the city
council. After giving praise to firefighters and public-school
educators, Fagan blasted the Hoboken Police Department.
"Official negligence," said Fagan, was to blame for the city
being driven into debt and "criminal classes of other cities"
operating unencumbered in Hoboken. The police department
was "a story of unworthy promotions, unrewarded merit,
...injustice and failure," Fagan said. "Careless" work, "lax"
habits, "loose" discipline, poor management, and shameless
cronyism had become the norm. "We have seen [a] department whose sole duty is the enforcement of the law...be officially unconscious of evil," Fagan asserted. "Only by a thorough reorganization will the injustice of past official acts be
made right."[140]

Fagan's dramatic reform rhetoric was generally well received by the press, but it mustered limited confidence that
his leadership would really bring about a lot of change in

Hoboken. Fagan was talking "like a man," remarked the *Jersey City News*, but the public would have to watch and wait for his actions.[141] The *New York Daily Tribune*, the foremost Republican paper in New York, looked favorably on Fagan's "extreme" arraignment of the police department and aim of overhauling management of the city "from top to bottom." Even so, the *Tribune* added that "reputable" people in Hoboken can only hope that Fagan's first "indignant outburst" will not be proven simply a "clean sweeping by a new broom."[142]

Only time would tell if Fagan could be a successful cleansing agent for reform in Hoboken, but he did promptly put in place some measures aimed at that end. Fagan ordered a recently built police substation on Fourteenth Street shut down, explaining that the maintenance and upkeep costs of operating an additional station were an unnecessary expense. Moreover, the substation, in Fagan's view, was not being utilized for police work; rather, it was being used as a lounge, a popular one for public officials commanding high salaries. Fagan also promoted a police sergeant named John Fanning. Fanning would assume the newly created position of "Chief of Detectives." One of Fanning's first assignments was to investigate a slew of Hoboken shop owners' alleged involvement in the unlawful sales of "policy slips" (tickets for lotteries and numbers games) and "green goods" (counterfeit currency or fraudulent documents). More troubling than any illegal gaming or forgery at the shops were accounts of police involvement, that members of the force were providing protection to the businesses, which explained Fagan's decision to right away put Fanning to work on that front.[143]

To that end, with Fagan's authority obviously making the process of providing police protection more difficult in Hoboken, Chief of Detectives Fanning and his detectives promptly arrested several shop owners for illegal gaming and counterfeiting activities.[144] As several policy slip brokers made plea bargains, an incriminating affidavit emerged. It showed one shop owner's testimony that he had long paid protection money to Detective James Gallagher, a member of the Hoboken police force for over twenty years. Upon receipt of the affidavit, Fagan conducted several interviews before suspending Gallagher from further duty until the police board resolved the charges against him.[145]

Fagan's efforts found support in the Democratic "reform" *New York World* newspaper. The *World*, sold by financier Jay Gould to the once penniless Hungarian immigrant Joseph Pulitzer in 1883, had emerged as the largest newspaper in New York.[146] The editor of the *World's* New Jersey edition was a man named Mathias Cowell Ely. It was Ely who probably conducted, or at least approved for publication, Fagan's memorable "stuffed pig" and/or "hog" interview addressing McLaughlin. Not long before Fagan took office as mayor, the *World* had begun reporting on the illicit sales of green goods and policy slips in Hoboken and Jersey City, later concluding that McLaughlin and Stanton knew of the schemes and received a cut of the protection money paid to officers.[147]

McLaughlin was much worse for wear by autumn 1893. The *World's* investigative reporting and Fagan's efforts to curb police corruption had pinched some of his revenue sources. Voters were also going to be returning to the polls. From within the ranks of the Democratic circular-machine, pressure on McLaughlin to redeem himself was growing. Confidence in him to influence election outcomes, naturally, had greatly diminished since Fagan's win. Getting Stanton elected Hudson County Sheriff would be critical for McLaughlin. In addition to all that, racetrack gaming remained a significant topic in New Jersey culture and politics, important for McLaughlin with his big stake in Guttenberg.

"The gambler is now in the saddle," testified Reverend Dr. John L. Scudder from his Jersey City Tabernacle in October of 1893. "But respectable people [are] determined to pull him off his high horse and put him behind bars." Reverend Scudder then, somewhat begrudgingly but seemingly genuinely, put Fagan on his "respectable people" list. Scudder described

Fagan to his congregation as "a Democrat from his shoes to his scalp" but representing the "better half of his party." He added, "Mayor Fagan...declares Stanton to be 'a creature of the gang,' and on a question of this character, [he] is competent to judge."[148] Scudder's endorsement suggests he recognized Fagan's reform efforts and independence from the Democratic circular-machine in Hoboken, even if some aspects of Fagan, presumably his involvement in Guttenberg, and that he was not a Republican, were less than ideally righteous. Fagan's leadership, for Hudson County anyway, was the far lesser of two evils. Scudder's assessment of conditions in waterfront politics became more bullish the following Sunday. "The tide has turned," he told his faithful. "The ring politicians of Hudson County...are thoroughly frightened. [They] persisted in standing knee deep in the mud, and now the advancing tide has almost reached their nostrils."[149]

Reverend Scudder may have had it right, for it was thought that leader-boss McLaughlin was desperate; that circular-machine plans were in place to pull out all the stops to keep above water on election day. Newspaper reports suggested that Hoboken might be overrun with foul play; that police officers or sheriff's deputies aligned with Stanton might oversee circular-machine men double or triple voting; tampering with or destroying ballots; using intimidation or violence to secure votes or keep voters away from the polls.[150]

Fagan took the scuttlebutt seriously. "The police," he said, in a declaration addressing the potential for trouble, "will be instructed to arrest any person, sheriff's deputy, or whoever" attempts "to intimidate or bulldoze election officers or voters," assist "looked-for repeaters in their nefarious work..., or who, in any way [tries] to interfere with the election."[151]

There were, however, few assurances that all members of the police department would follow the mayor's instructions. When Fagan took office, his criticism of the police force was so public and extreme. Some officers may have been waiting for a chance to stick it to Fagan. As well, Stanton, at least for the time being, was Hudson County Sheriff. Hence, when and how the authority of his office might be wielded to support him in the election really was unknowable. With such issues to consider, Fagan tempered his heavy-handedness by encouraging the virtues of civic and autonomous duty. "The policeman, who fails [to perform] his duty will be summarily dealt with," he said. "But, I expect the force" will "do themselves and Hoboken credit," and ensure "the people an honest election."[152]

On Tuesday, November 7, 1893, no doubt in good part due to Fagan's readiness, the polls in Hoboken were peaceable and votes cast without any visible signs of malfeasance. Voter turnout was smaller than expected, something to which Fagan's appointment of a special anti-fraud detective at every polling place to watch for repeat voters very probably contributed. Under these carefully controlled conditions, the Democratic circular-machine candidates were almost entirely defeated in Hoboken. The trend extended throughout Hudson County. In the most significant result of the day, Stanton lost his bid to remain county sheriff. Stanton was bested by Colonel John J. Toffey, a German Republican.[153]

The *Jersey Journal*, a Republican daily newspaper headquartered in Jersey City, applauded the management of the voting in Hoboken. The paper called the election "a great triumph" for Fagan and reform both. Also eager to describe the unfavorable cards dealt the Democratic circular-machine all about Hudson County, the *Journal* declared its defeat a "heavy, unexpected blow," its unknowable impact leaving its men to "wander...in a dazed, bewildered manner."[154]

Stanton took his loss sorely. He spent what little time he had left of his term as Hudson County Sheriff crafting a silly plot to get revenge. Stanton issued dozens of clumsily drafted indictments before leaving office. Stanton's indictments included charges against Mathias Ely, the *New York World*, and its management, as well as Fagan, the *Observer*, and its management for their part in a "maliciously liable" campaign to defeat him at the polls.[155] Stanton remained on the political scene in Hudson County, but only on the outer rung, his part in Democratic circular-machine operations never approaching the importance it had in 1893.[156]

The election's consequences were just as bad for leader-boss McLaughlin. Stanton, a close ally, lost, losing a very important job for the circular-machine. Virtually all the other candidates McLaughlin backed lost, too. Then, a rival Democratic circular-machine leader-boss named Robert Davis reemerged, ready and eager to capitalize on McLaughlin's weakness.

Robert Davis, who later became Fagan's primary antagonist, had a long career in politics. Born in Carlow, Ireland, in 1848, Davis was a young child when he was brought to Jersey City. There, essentially as soon as the law allowed, he began serving on various district commissions and was selected a member of the Hudson County Democratic Committee in 1875. Davis was elected an alderman in 1885, then elected to a three-year term as Hudson County Sheriff in 1887. Simultaneously, Davis was appointed a police judge by Democratic Governor Leon Abbett, a Jersey City resident. In March of 1892, Davis was further appointed jail warden by the Hudson County Board of Freeholders. The jail warden job came with a five-year contract to board all county prisoners at a rate of 30 cents a day per prisoner, with a residence provided for Davis and his family. The jail warden also billed the county for all the gas and fuel necessary to operate the detention facility and his residence, an arrangement particularly advantageous for Davis; he also worked for a local gas company.[157]

Davis's double or triple dipping was duly noted in the March 19, 1892, issue of the *Observer*, which pointed to him as a circular-machine man who, in particular, benefited greatly from the iniquitous policy allowing multiple-office holding.[158] By that time, Davis was a virtual co-equal to McLaughlin as leader-boss. Davis, however, was punched down a rung by the end of the year after he waged a fiercely unsuccessful campaign to prevent Stanton's appointment as Hudson County Sheriff.[159] The miscalculation forced Davis to assume a lower profile with no part in kingmaking; hence, he had been biding his time, seeing detainees were well-warmed at his detention center, and staying busy with his other jobs.

After the votes were counted and the election done in November of 1893, Davis seized the opportunity to reclaim the spotlight, to be the undisputed leader-boss and stick a fork in McLaughlin. Davis was asked for comment: who had led the Democratic circular-machine to its "disaster" at the polls? "McLaughlin," Davis replied. "The only leader at present" was McLaughlin, Davis clarified. Davis added that he had "not been the boss or leader of the Hudson County Democrats for some time," for "the past two or three elections." The losing candidates "were not," said Davis, "suggested by me." When asked to assess McLaughlin's future in politics, Davis took a fast second to reflect, then replied, "Hard times."[160] Just days after Davis's remarks, the fifty-three-year-old McLaughlin was indeed visited by some hard times health-wise. Pneumonia symptoms knocked McLaughlin flat on his back, leaving him laid up for an extended period at his home on Pavonia Avenue in Jersey City.[161]

The *New York World*, while, of course, not assuming responsibility for making McLaughlin sick, took a good deal of credit and satisfaction in McLaughlin's disposal from power. The *World* also credited Fagan, describing him as "the leader of the revolt" inside the Democratic Party, responsible for "the splendid reform victory."[162] Upon a return to good health, McLaughlin, his political influence on the present scene minimal, opened a new saloon in the Horseshoe.[163]

The political transformation in Hudson County was superficially alluded to in *Forum*, a national magazine, in an article called "The Irish Conquest of Our Cities." The article, written by John Paul Bocock appeared in the April 1894 issue. "The Irish Conquest" was a pointedly nativist, but perhaps also slightly satirical, essay lamenting the positions of political power reached in recent years by Irish-Americans across a broad swathe of urban America. "The Irish-American 'ring' in Jersey City was recently broken—for the time being... at least," wrote Bocock, but "its hold" remains "still strong...on the offices" and "revenues of the citizens."[164] It's evident that Bocock was either uninformed of or, for purposes of not complicating his narrative, intentionally looked past the nuance of Fagan's role in ejecting McLaughlin from power. Bocock, his limited knowledge or interest in detail noted, wrote further, "The race-track bosses, whose shameful control of legislation of the State capital caused a popular uprising last year, are dominated by Irishmen." Now, "even the 'reform' mayor of Hoboken is Mr. 'Larry' Fagan." Bocock's "Irish Conquest" came to conclude that only "a veritable revolution" could now rid America's cities of the dominance held by their "Hibernian oligarchy."[165]

Fagan's reaction to the article is unknown, but two years later, he did participate in an event making his Irishness into something of a public political statement. Fagan was the first speaker and stood in solidarity with John Parnell, brother of Charles Stewart Parnell, who was visiting for a charity event sponsored by the Irish-American Society of Hoboken. The fundraiser, held at St. Mary's School Hall on the evening of Wednesday, April 8, 1896, was in support of "Irish Patriots" held captive "in British Prisons." The event raised $1,000 for the cause.[166]

Ethnic patriotism aside, with McLaughlin out of the picture, Fagan could better concentrate on establishing a favorable legacy for himself as Mayor of Hoboken. Fagan had long viewed the establishment of a free public library as something important for the city. When Hoboken's Second National Bank, co-founded by Fagan, opened its doors for business in 1887, the bank's basement served as a temporary site for the city's public library. Fagan, who then accrued more knowledge on the subject by serving on the House of Assembly's State Library Committee, made finding an improved location for the library a focus once he assumed office as mayor. Initially, Fagan proposed that the top floor of Hoboken City Hall, a space where he asserted public officials were too often found lounging, be made the new location for the library. That proposal, presumably a negotiating tactic, helped to further muster interest and momentum for the Hoboken Free Public Library to secure a suitable permanent location of its own. Eventually, such a location was found at Park Avenue and Fifth Street. Construction began there on April 20, 1896, and was completed just less than a year later. "I hope these keys," said Fagan, as he opened the doors of the new library to the public on April 5, 1897, "may be used to open and never close this library."[167]

While the building of the library occurred during a period of incredible expansion for Hoboken, the project was undertaken at the tail end of a significant recession in the United States. The economic decline, which became apparent in May of 1893, saw over 350 American banks and 8,000 businesses close by the end of the year. The economy then began bouncing back during the second half of 1896.[168] Gauging the recession's impact on Hoboken, assessing something of a cyclical economic downturn in a place experiencing a once in forever generations' growth, would be more than a rudimentary endeavor, and it is not one undertaken seriously in this project. With that stated, there are some statistics and events to consider. In 1890, Hoboken's population was 43,648; by 1900, the population had grown to at least 59,364.[169] From 1855–1889, 5,727 buildings were constructed in Hoboken; whereas, from 1890–1900, 6,570 buildings were constructed in Hoboken.[170] New Jersey's business-friendly climate probably also mitigated recessionary effects for Hoboken and greater Hudson County. New Jersey was a state favored by many companies to headquarter their operations and do business in during the 1890s.[171] A significant portion of John D. Rockefeller's Standard Oil Company was based in New Jersey, with large operations in Jersey City and Weehawken in Hudson County. With sales of illuminating oil and industrial lubricants continuing to be robust during the recession, Standard Oil continued to thrive there during the period of national economic decline.[172] George Werts, the Democratic Governor of New Jersey, boasted grandly of his state's fiscal vitality in 1896. "With no tax for State purposes and practically out of debt, [New Jersey] is unique among her sister States. No such showing can be made by any other state," bragged Werts. "Nor, I apprehend, by any civilized nation anywhere."[173]

Civilized might have been a good way to describe Fagan's competition for mayor in 1895. With the support of several independent clubs, reform and good government groups, Fagan was reelected by a margin of over 1,000 votes, defeating Republican Elbridge V.S. Besson. Besson was anything but a sore loser. "I do not think," he reflected, "that there was ever a cleaner or more gentlemanly contest than that just ended."[174] Two years later with heavier voter turnout, Fagan was again reelected, winning a third term by a margin of over 2,800 votes.[175]

Fagan did not avoid further business entanglements while serving as Mayor of Hoboken. In 1896, Fagan and a group of Hudson County businessmen created The People's Safe Deposit and Trust Company, opening its main office in Jersey City and a branch in the Town of Union. In 1899, the group organized a new bank in Hoboken, The Trust Company of New Jersey, with Fagan serving on the board of directors. The Trust Company of New Jersey was headquartered in the southeast corner of Hoboken near the Jersey City border at Twelve Hudson Place, where it operated out of a three-story 11,340-square-foot building with a stunning central stained-glass rotunda.[176] Fagan also co-founded the Colonial Life Insurance Company of Jersey City, formally chartered on December 31, 1897.[177]

Between 1897–1898, Fagan Iron Works was also busy with an especially big job, the construction of the Jackson Street Bridge. The bridge ran a length in excess of 200 yards over the

Passaic River, connecting the City of Newark at Jackson Street to the Township of Harrison. The use of "curved chord quadruple intersection trusses" by Fagan Iron Works in the fabrication of the bridge made it architecturally advanced for the time. On April 11, 1898, the Jackson Street Bridge opened. The bridge acted as the last local-traffic overpass before the Passaic River emptied into Newark Bay, making it important in serving New Jersey's ever-growing number of motorists during the twentieth century. (Of note, the Jackson Street Bridge closed at 6:00 p.m. during the period of the Newark Riots in 1967, with authorities enacting emergency measures to help restore order.)[178]

This postcard, dated July 5, 1906, shows wagon traffic crossing the Jackson Street Bridge (Courtesy bridgehunter.com.)

In 1898, Fagan, his notoriety and resources growing, moved his family into the large house at Hudson and Tenth Streets in Hoboken, purchasing the property for $45,000.00 from J. Nicholas Crusius. Crusius was a German-born liquor importer with a significant stake in the Guttenberg race track. William Edgar Sackett once unflatteringly described him as "blubber-like."[179] If so or not, Crusius purchased the house

from the Reiche family in the late 1880s and upheld a finger-
ling of the property's tradition as a showplace for fine animals. He garnered some small acclaim for raising several
prize-winning breeds of chicken and hens in the barn on the
property.[180] Increased regulatory scrutiny of New Jersey's
racetrack gaming industry during the mid-1890s, however,
brought about legal and financial challenges for Crusius.[181]
These events may have contributed to his decision to sell the
house.

Another bird's eye, or panoramic perspective, view of the house at Hudson and Tenth Streets (middle left) reveals Hoboken's
incredible growth by the end of the nineteenth century. The image is taken from a map of Hoboken published around 1903.
(Hughes & Bailey Co., courtesy Library of Congress Digital Collections.)

If being an Irish Catholic in America during the late nineteenth century were set aside, Fagan, the businessman and independently Democratic mayor, shared some similarities
with two other colorful, business-background "reform"
mayors of the 1890s, Hazen Pingree and Samuel Jones. Both
were Republicans. Pingree was born in America in 1840 and
grew up on his family's modest farm near Denmark, Maine.
In stepping away from a life there, Pingree became a cobbler,
ultimately an affluent shoe manufacturer, and then Mayor of
Detroit, serving from 1890–1897. In one particularly memorable meeting of members of the Detroit School Board, Pingree
startled everyone with his announcement, "There are quite a

number of members going to jail tonight."[182] Pingree, while born in America, was an urban emigrant. And, like Fagan, Pingree became a successful businessman and then pursued public office. Business accomplishment, bringing financial security, executive experience, and confidence, no doubt in part explained the fearlessness both Pingree and Fagan brought to the political arena. Samuel "Golden Rule" Jones, Mayor of Toledo from 1897–1904, was also a successful businessman before he brought his colorful persona to politics. Jones was born in Wales in 1846 and was brought to America at age three. Jones began as a laborer in the oil fields and eventually started a small oil company. Before long, Jones sold his business to Rockefeller's Standard Oil. With profits from the sale, Jones established a successful oil-well pump manufacturing company in Toledo.[183] After being elected Mayor of Toledo, Jones, as his "Golden Rule" moniker suggests, helped implement many programs to help the poor, especially children; this included support for building public playgrounds. Jones, like Fagan, had crossed the Atlantic as a small child, then turned the opportunities afforded him in America into great affluence. As mayors, both Jones and Fagan seemed, at least generally, to understand the wisdom of acting out of enlightened self-interest to procure the public good while keeping up with the demands of their cities' rapidly growing populations.[184]

Hoboken had certainly emerged as a much bigger city than it was when Fagan may have first considered making a run for mayor. According to federal census data, the population of Hoboken, recorded at 43,648 in 1890, increased to 59,364 in 1900. Mayor Fagan and Dr. Samuel H. Helfer, President of the Hoboken Health Board, however, disagreed with that number when it was recorded. According to their calculations, the population of Hoboken was 70,000–72,000 in 1900.[185] Whatever the exact tally, Hoboken had grown a lot. In terms of growth, people per pavement foot, Hoboken, comprised of approximately one square mile, may have expanded faster than any other place during the 1890s.

Hoboken's expansion included its active Jewish Community.[186] On Wednesday evening, August 9, 1899, Fagan presided over the cornerstone ceremony for the building of a new Orthodox Jewish Synagogue on Grand Street between Newark and First Streets. There, those in attendance not only heard Fagan declare, "Hoboken...proud of her Hebrew residents," but also saw him work, losing sight almost of the ceremonial nature of his role. Fagan, literally and skillfully, laid down the cornerstone for the new synagogue, working in fastidious fashion. "Over the work of plastering up the cornerstone," as one reporter described, "[Fagan] lingered...for several minutes." Attendees were surprised. Their mayor, they remarked, "handled the trowel like a professional bricklayer."[187]

Entertaining, but also instructive, the scene points to Fagan's identity as a figure constructing the new urban world, doing so from the top down and bottom up simultaneously. Speaking for the people of an entire city, Fagan led from above. As well, he led hands-on—in the mortar, bent over, and doing the job. New immigrant groups of the late nineteenth century shared variations of the aphorism: "I traveled to America because I heard that the streets were paved in gold. When I arrived, I quickly learned a few things about America: the streets were not paved in gold; the streets were not paved at all; and, I was expected to pave them." Fagan's physical labor, his ironworks, including the iron manhole covers in the roads, made him part of the literal paving of a new urban world. The top side of the covers, marked Mansfield & Fagan until 1891, thereafter as Fagan Iron Works, physically bore Fagan's name. As an immigrant, Fagan came to America and literally left his mark on the pavement of its streets.

Mansfield & Fagan Cover (Courtesy Walter Grutchfield: waltergrutchfield.net).

Fagan Iron Works Cover (Courtesy Erica Fagan).

Getting the streets properly paved was important to the growth and modernization of Hoboken. Fagan and twenty-five other Hoboken citizens formed The Good Roads Association in a meeting held at the Quartet Club in Hoboken on Thursday evening, January 28, 1897. The new organization was especially interested in the roads needed to provide safe and direct access between the lower plane of Hoboken and the higher plane of Jersey City. Fagan, perhaps with the Jackson Street Bridge build and Fagan Iron Works in mind, shared his support for some Hudson County assemblymen introducing legislation to build a viaduct from the Jersey City Heights down to Hoboken. Alexander P. Hexamer, a Hoboken native and one of Fagan's partners in The Trust Company of New Jersey, was elected chairman of The Good Roads Association. Hexamer noted that the physical challenges posed to vehicles trying to get to and from Hoboken had caused many residents to move out of the city, with some relocating to Orange, New Jersey, and Brooklyn, New York. "There is no city with such poor roads," said the apparently well-traveled Hexamer. "They are a disgrace to Hoboken," he lamented. "There is not a single road to take us to the Hudson Boulevard."[188]

Hexamer's German immigrant parents were some of the many Germans who lived in New York City before electing to settle permanently in Hoboken.[189] By the mid-1890s, Germans had lost their majority status in Hoboken, having become equaled in numbers by the Irish. The ethnic composition of Hoboken had become 40 percent German, 40 percent Irish, 15 percent Anglo-Protestant, and 5 percent Italian. For many Germans, the initial appeal of Hoboken was that it was a great place to celebrate "Continental Sunday." The custom of observing the Sabbath with revelry, energy, and enthusiasm was almost universal for German immigrants, whether Roman Catholic, Lutheran, German Reformed (Calvinist), Jewish, or Freethinking (anti-religion intellectuals). On Sundays, men, women, and children enjoyed music, dancing, and sometimes athletic spectacles such as gun-shooting or gymnastics contests. Food and drink, which generally included Limburger sandwiches, pretzels, frankfurters, sauerkraut, and beer, were indispensable to the festivities.[190] On Continental Sundays and other occasions, Hoboken's more affluent Germans entertained in their homes; others might be found at the Deutscher Klub (German Club) at Hudson and Sixth Streets. Meanwhile, some of Hoboken's more affluent Anglo-Protestants interested in drinking on Sunday might be found at the Columbia Club at Bloomfield and Eleventh Streets. For most Hoboken residents, Sunday was their only day off from work. Sunday, therefore, was generally the best day for people interested in drinking and socializing in saloons to do so. Between 1885–1895, the number of saloons and/or liquor stores rose from 134 to 240 in Hoboken. German ownership of these establishments was approximately 95 percent in 1885, declining to approximately 80 percent in 1895. Catholic priests often had ominous warnings about the dangers of self-indulgence during sermons for their mostly Irish and Italian listeners. The priests were, however, generally not particularly strident about calling for Sunday temperance. They knew it was the only day of the week that the majority of their parishioners had off from work, often rigorous physical labor.[191]

Saloons, in Hoboken and across America, became increasingly popular destinations during the late-nineteenth and early-twentieth centuries. The saloon provided a convivial club-like atmosphere for people of modest means to drink, eat, and socialize. A saloon, moreover, might serve a myriad of additional functions. Some of the wide array of offerings one might find in a saloon included: temporary lodging; mail and message delivery; banking services; treatment for minor illness, injury, or infection; antidotes for animal bites or impotence. Prostitution was often an attraction to be had in seedier saloons where trade tricks typically transpired in back rooms and stalls, outside in backyard sheds, or in nearby alleys. Gambling, while not omnipresent in every saloon, was regularly part of the scene. Saloon patrons might be found betting on horses, playing cards, tossing dice, shooting craps, buying lotto policy slips, making impromptu wagers, or participating in other forms of gaming. Saloons, in addition, quite often served something of a more useful civic function, providing meeting space to political organizations, labor unions, benevolent associations, and fraternal orders.[192] In 1896, the Republican New York Daily Tribune editorialized on the idea that the saloon was "the poor man's club." The Tribune concluded the

idea was largely accurate, then noted, "The saloon...is a political power in New Jersey."[193]

As Mayor of Hoboken, Fagan's interest in saloons appeared mostly limited to rooting out their connection to police
corruption. In Hudson County, saloons and/or liquor stores,
as well as most forms of commerce, were, in fact, officially
supposed to be closed on Sundays in observance of the Sabbath. These laws, however, had for decades been all but ignored in Hudson County. This was especially true in Hoboken, where Continental Sunday celebration was part of its
German cultural identity. Fagan, but for the very occasional
instance when the city's lack of enforcement of Sunday closing laws brought about a tangible legal threat, such as from a
grand jury, was for the status quo and generally disinterested
in high-minded or antiquated declarations on saloon regula-
tion.[194] Unfortunately for Fagan, he would be forced to spend
more time and energy on the issue when a new law across the
Hudson caused a dramatic spike in the number of New Yorkers heading to Hoboken to celebrate on Sundays.

On April 1, 1896, the "Raines Law," a strict New York state
statute governing the sale of alcohol on Sundays, went into
effect. Sponsored by Senator John W. Raines, a tall, stern,
blue-eyed son of a Methodist minister, the Raines Law called
for stringent enforcement of a ban on liquor sales in saloons,
clubs, and restaurants from midnight on Saturday evening
until five o'clock on Monday morning, with severe penalties
promised to be imposed on violators. The Raines Law had the
support of New York City's Republican Mayor William
Strong. Strong's election in the fall of 1894 helped oust from
power, at least temporarily, the Tammany Hall Democratic
circular-machine, then guided by leader-boss Richard "Dick"
Croker. Democrats were far more likely to utilize saloons as
centers of political organization than their Republican counterparts. Hence, support for the Raines Law was driven by
both temperance and partisan-minded forces. Mayor Strong's
police commissioner was Theodore Roosevelt. Roosevelt was

resolute. The Raines Law would be vigorously enforced by his officers.[195]

With the new statute to consider, it was anticipated that New York City's devoted drinkers would be hesitant to test the waters at their neighborhood saloons on Sunday, April 5, 1896. Rather, it was thought that they would ferry across the Hudson River and do their drinking in Hoboken. Saloon proprietors in Hoboken welcomed the prospect of serving an additional market. Hopeful for a strong bump in business, Hoboken's saloon owners prepared by adding bartenders on duty. Their preparations were proven wise. The first Raines Law Sunday generated more business for Hoboken saloons on a Sunday than had been seen in a very many months. With saloons fully open, drinks gotten easily, and the scene effervescent, the waves of New Yorkers who traveled to quench their thirst in Hoboken were reportedly highly satisfied with their experience. By contrast, the very vast majority of saloons in New York City remained closed that Sunday. The Raines Law there, its enforcement and/or the threat of its consequences, proved effective.[196]

A week later, on Sunday, April 12, 1896, New Yorkers arrived in Hudson County in far greater numbers. Eager to imbibe and enjoy a hassle-free Sunday, the tourists brought not only their thirst but also unwelcome attention to Hudson County's liberal alcohol culture. As one group prepared to board an early morning ferry for Hoboken, a reporter asked whether or not they had heard the rumors that Hoboken planned to keep its saloons closed in accordance with the official Sunday closing law. They all laughed heartily, with one member of the party retorting wryly, "Hoboken without beer? [Might] as well talk of Coney Island without merry-go-rounds."[197] One exceptional newspaper account of that Sunday afternoon in Hoboken described the saloons clearly open and doing strong business on Fourth Street, where there were no police officers anywhere to be seen—except one. That police officer was posted outside of a saloon that was open and operating far more brazenly than the rest. Flowing in and out through its swing-hinge doors, the number of customers was robust, making the big crowd drinking at the bar clear for anyone outside on the street to see, notwithstanding the thick clouds of tobacco smoke being generated. At one point, a young man emerged from the saloon, greeted the officer, and gave him a cigar. With that, the policeman "nodded understandingly."[198]

The Reverend Dr. John L. Scudder was far less understanding about everything that happened that Sunday. That evening at his Jersey City Tabernacle, he spoke to his followers, bearing witness to the large volume of New York City alcohol enthusiasts landing in Hudson County that day. "Disorderly characters," Scudder testified, "thirty thousand drinkers," their "normal abode...lower New York, ...swarmed across the Hudson and held high carnival on Jersey soil....The Sabbath was made a day of revelry," our "waterfront...a Sunday saloon." Scudder then called on authorities to take "prompt and vigorous action" in response to the "deluge of drunkenness and debauchery."[199] In a subsequent sermon, the formidable religious rhetorician declared himself, his "Christian friends and fellow citizens" in holy "battle" against the "liquor dealers." They were defenders of "sobriety, purity," and "righteousness," virtues now under assault by the "filthy tides of wickedness" thirsty to serve "Bacchus and Venus...a monopoly on the Sabbath."[200]

Scudder was not the only Christian leader eager to mobilize against the alcohol-friendly culture in Hudson County. On Thursday morning, April 23, 1896, over one hundred women met at the First Methodist Episcopal Church in Hoboken for the semi-annual convention of the Women's Christian Temperance Union of Hudson County. "Our cause," said Mrs. John. O. Bush, President of the Hoboken chapter of the W.C.T.U., in delivery of the convention's opening address, "has inspired many noble women to make it their lifework, and all over the land we hear glorious reports of the results of their labors. I welcome you to Hoboken because we need your counsel, encouragement, help and inspiration. My experience in this city is that in temperance, morals, and religion it is behind our sister cities."[201]

With the tides perhaps turning, at least temporarily, in favor of the moral reformers in Hudson County, a grand jury convened in Jersey City and warned public officials that indictments would be served if the Sunday closing laws were not enforced.[202] Fagan, wishing to avoid indictment and understanding the heightened seriousness presently about the topic, made plans to get a better handle on the situation. With hopes to mask the surge in drinking revelry, a "confidential circular letter" was created. The secret memo was officially attributed to no authority but very probably came from Fagan's office. Julius Schlatter, the secretary of the Hoboken Saloon-Keepers Protective Association, distributed the document, instructions for Sunday, April 26, 1896. Saloon keepers were to keep their shades pulled down and front doors closed. They were to conduct business as "quietly as possible." Owners of establishments failing to maintain the protocol were warned: they were "liable to be arrested" and "stand the consequences."[203] With some semblance of order and discretion reigning in Hoboken on that last Sunday in April, Fagan's attention to detail had seemingly paid off. "Even Hoboken liquor-sellers," the *New York Daily Tribune* patronizingly reported, found themselves "compelled to do a side-door business."[204]

Fagan made preparations to continue that trend. He summoned all Hoboken police officers in for special duty the following Sunday.[205] Fagan appeared intent on bringing discretion and order to the Sunday law-breaking done in his city. His efforts would be aided by a change in the conditions in New York City. Saloon keepers there, many of whom were now having their establishments designated as hotels, had figured out enough loopholes in the Raines Law to take the teeth out of the statute. Hence, New York saloons quickly got back the clientele they had lost to Hoboken on Sundays.[206]

Since Fagan's attitude towards enforcing Sunday saloon legalities was pragmatic, not ideological, it fluctuated in its seriousness of purpose, a lack of consistency sometimes leading to conflict with the Hoboken City Council. Such was the case with Fagan and Councilman Anthony Capelli from the Third Ward. Capelli possessed significant influence amongst the city's rapidly growing Italian community. He served as the chairman of the Licensing Committee for Hoboken saloons and owned a saloon at Fourth and Adams Streets. Capelli and Fagan were once considered to be close allies. However, at some point during the spring or summer of 1896, the men had a falling out. They stopped talking and no longer acknowledged each other when passing by at Hoboken City Hall.[207]

Precisely what soured the relationship cannot be known for certain, but it's reasonable to speculate that some of the unwanted publicity brought to Hoboken in April 1896 could have been a source of tension between the two. Capelli's saloon was located on the same street as—and may, in fact, have been—the establishment described in the embarrassing newspaper account of an open-door saloon operating brazenly under the guard of a cigar-smoking policeman.

Whatever the source of the ill-will, a frigid silence between Mayor Fagan and Councilman Capelli had been going on for over a year when the city council convened on Wednesday, June 30, 1897. Capelli was at that time informed of Fagan's decision to veto the renewal of his saloon license. The news came as a shock. Capelli protested vociferously. He declared his saloon "a model," pointing out that not once had he been "compelled to call" the police there to "quell any disturbances." Many council members were also taken aback by Fagan's decision; his stance was judged "peculiar." The week before, in a motion considered a formality of ordinary business, and with no objections offered to it, the council had voted in favor of renewing Capelli's license. Fagan, however, saw the matter quite differently. Fagan declared Councilman Capelli "not-fit to keep a house of public entertainment [or] saloon" and "not-fit to be a Councilman."[208]

Any action taken by Fagan against saloon operators was likely to have been judged insufficient by the Hoboken Branch of the Women's Christian Temperance Union. On Monday, July 5, 1897, just days after Fagan's dramatic denunciation of Capelli, Fagan presided over a meeting of the Hoboken Police Board at city hall. It was not long before the president of the Hoboken W.C.T.U., Mrs. John O. Bush, showed up unexpectedly. Mrs. Bush was accompanied by two other members of the organization, a Miss Arnold and a Miss Decker. The women promptly interrupted the meeting. "We have come, Mr. Mayor," greeted Mrs. Bush, "to tell you that [there are] stores open on Sunday." And, had the women come to city hall to inform Fagan "that the water in the [Hudson] River was wet, ...the information would not have been more of a surprise," wrote a cheeky reporter on the scene from the *New York Sun*. First with "round eyes," then with "appealing eyes," Fagan gazed at the police commissioners who "sat stiff" and "said nothing." They remained "silent," the *Sun* reporter added, "like stony-faced automata with broken main springs."[209]

It's of interest to note that some of the colorful style used by the *New York Sun* reporter to describe the scene at Hoboken City Hall was, with little doubt, a reflection of the journalism philosophy of Charles Anderson Dana, the *Sun's* iconic owner. English Professor George Douglas, author of *The Golden Age of the Newspaper* (1999), credits Dana, "more than anyone else in journalistic history," for "the art of the newspaper story," making writers "the eye, the ear," as well as "the emotions of the reader." Every story in the *Sun* had to be accurate, have all the facts, and get them straight. However, as Douglas explains, "A bland, straightforward catalog of facts about a trial, or a street encounter, or a society ball," that kind

reporting "was exactly what Dana did not want." A reporter
must call on "imagination, wit, instinct," and "education....to
create an ambience, a world perhaps, for every story."[210]

Meanwhile, the ambient uneasy silence in the room at Hoboken City Hall brought by Mrs. Bush's revelation of open
Sunday commerce in the city was ultimately broken by Fagan,
his idea for more clarity on the subject his best at the time.
"What kind of stores?" Fagan asked Mrs. Bush cautiously.
"All kinds," replied Bush, Miss Decker, and Miss Arnold in
chorus. Bush then elaborated, "Grocery stores...milk stores,
butcher shops, and liquor stores—Liquor stores, Mayor Fagan: Saloons!" To which, in a respectful fashion, Fagan replied: "Oh." Bush continued: "It is a shame that they should
be open. [It's] a burning shame—Isn't it, ladies?!" To which
her cohorts, on cue, soberly asseverated: "It is." With hopes
of bringing the matter to a polite resolution, "Madame," said
Fagan to Bush, "If you will put your complaint in [written]
form, [the] Board will gladly—"[211]

"That's what it always is," said Bush, cutting Fagan off.
"Always telling us to write and write: and where do our written complaints go?" she inquired, then exclaimed with disgust and damnation. "Into the fireplace!" Fagan then looked
down at the waste basket silently and sheepishly, for, as the
reporter from the *Sun* noted astutely, there was "no fireplace
in the room." Bush continued her lecture, "So...Sunday in Hoboken [stays] desecrated" with "drunken men upon the
streets..., ball playing upon the cricket grounds...and Sabbath
breaking on all sides!" And, "I see remonstrance," Bush hol-
lered just before she marched her colleagues out of the room,
"is useless!"[212]

"Whew!" exclaimed Fagan, as soon as the door had closed
securely behind the women. One of the police commissioners
then blurted, "Move we adjourn at once;—they might come
back." And immediately, without the mayor and the commissioners even waiting to vote on the motion, the meeting "dis-
solved."[213]

Grievances the likes of Mrs. Bush's may have sometimes been hard for Fagan to take seriously when he saw parts of the city made like papers for a burning fireplace. Mrs. Bush's memorable call on city hall occurred not that long after a sad and ruinous factory fire hit Hoboken. The fire of Thursday, May 20, 1897, began around 8:00 pm inside a large six-story factory building between Washington and Hudson Streets at Twelfth and Thirteenth Streets. The cause of the fire could not be conclusively determined. There was strong speculation that a cigar or cigarette discarded carelessly inside a bathroom on the first floor of the factory was to blame. In any case, flames first crackled through a section of the building's interior woodwork, then spread furiously out onto the first floor. The first floor was occupied by a manufacturer of toilet articles and a supplier of electrical apparatuses, with cache of chemicals and other flammable materials also stored in various areas there. The fire spread quickly. Flames burst up the airshaft to the rest of the building, occupied primarily by a Macy's factory and a wallpaper company.

Hoboken firefighters were overwhelmed from the get-go. By the time their first piece of firefighting equipment was in position, the conflagration was raging, volatile burning on every floor of the factory. More gear and manpower were soon on the scene to help combat the blaze. Firefighters from Weehawken, Union, West Hoboken, and Jersey City arrived to help. Fagan telephoned the high-service station of the Hackensack Water Company and requested an increase in water pressure but was informed that the maximum force had already been reached. With a distance of little more than ten yards separating the burning factory from a row of fourteen tenements on Washington Street, the situation was perilous. This slim buffer between urban industry and city living was breached at around 9:00 p.m. Very loud noises were heard at that time. Drums of fire-sensitive chemicals housed on the factory's first floor began exploding. The pressure-cooked combustibles spit out a salvo of fluid-fueled flame and sparks, some of which rained down onto the tenements. Hence, just as the factory's walls began crumbling, new flames were burning hot inside thirteen of the fourteen adjacent tenements. There would be no saving them. The dwellings, although constructed with solid exterior walls built of brick, had cut-rate interior construction—finished on the cheap with particularly light, flimsy woodwork.

The most dangerous point of the fire occurred around 10:30 p.m. when shifting winds began carrying slivers of burning debris to the waterfront. Some landed on the dry docks at Seventeenth Street on the Weehawken border, causing another fire. A tarpaulin-covered oil barge and six canal boats there quickly began burning. Hoboken, fortunately, had some small amount of good luck that evening. Several Pennsylvania tugs were on the Hudson River and in close proximity to Hoboken. The tugboats, equipped with pumps and other specialized firefighting equipment, responded to help. The fire slowed; the situation was soon under control. The tugboats prevented the fire from spreading to any waterfront buildings and even from causing major damage to the dry docks.[214]

Outcomes that evening were less favorable back at the fire-ravaged tenement buildings. A great deal of anxiety and hardship was found there, with 140 families made homeless. Hoboken public servants had their hands full, as the *Trenton Evening Times* reported.

> *The police had great difficulty in keeping the frenzied tenants from rushing back into the flames for valuables left behind. ...For blocks around [the fire], the people were almost panic stricken....Mayor Fagan of Hoboken reached the scene early and started the work of supplying the destitute with shelter and clothing and at a late hour the many families were made as comfortable as families can who have lost everything in the world.[215]*

In addition to big problems brought by fire, innumerable small annoyances brought by saloons continued to be a theme of Fagan's time as Mayor of Hoboken. In 1898, Fagan sent a memo to the Hoboken City Council expressing concern about the city's alcohol-fueled social scene's impact on families in the community after dark. A "species of crime...traceable to saloons" often "abounds...during the evenings," Fagan explained. "When under the influence of drink" and "musical sound,...seafaring men are usually noisy," making "mostly...not a very acceptable neighborhood to live in."[216]

A year later, indictments, a large number of them, aimed to curb "Sabbath breaking" in saloons were delivered to public officials in Hudson County, including Fagan.[217] The indictments specific to Fagan and Hoboken, in fact, involved musical sound. These indictments charged a select group of saloons in Hoboken with having music abounding from them on Sundays when saloons were supposed to be closed. Fortunately for Fagan and other Hoboken officials, a favorable interpretation of the law was found. A judge ruled: the establishments in question should not be classified as saloons; they should be classified as musical theaters; and musical theaters could lawfully remain open on Sundays. Thus, the indictments were dropped.[218]

UNDER FIRE

A reader of words of wind-demons might
have [seen] a dialogue pass to and fro
exhorter and...hearers. 'You are damned,'
said the preacher. And the reader of sounds
might have seen the reply...'Soup?'
—Stephen Crane, Maggie, a Girl of the Streets (1893)

IN THE SPRING OF 1899, FAGAN SOUGHT REELECTION to a fourth term as Mayor of Hoboken in the face of criticism that he had been in office for too long and was in lust with power. The Republican *New York Daily Tribune*, which commented frequently on Fagan's activities, lampooned him. "One finds a lot of unappreciative citizens...in Hoboken," the *Tribune* remarked. It's "cruel." Those "who say they have had enough of Mr. Fagan" are either "unmindful of the great sacrifices [he] has made for them" or "forget how nobly he has championed their interests."[219]

Republicans had high hopes for Fagan's challenger for mayor, William S. Stuhr. Stuhr, a former New Jersey state senator, was running in the general election as an independent Democrat with the backing of Republicans. As the election approached, the Odd Fellows Hall in Hoboken hosted an energetic meeting in opposition to Fagan. Stuhr took Fagan to task there, raising a variety of issues including: rising property tax rates; the price paid by the city for a water contract; and the low prices the city charged companies for franchises. Stuhr also alleged Fagan was using the police force for his own political purposes. Hoboken was "not a monarchy," said Stuhr. Public officials were "servants," not "masters," of the city.[220] Notwithstanding the hard charging, Stuhr fell short of victory. Fagan was reelected on April 11, 1899, winning a fourth term by a margin of over one thousand votes.[221]

The result was particularly disappointing to a man named Edward Russ, the Hoboken Public Instruction Commissioner. Russ had served on the body that governed public education in the city for ten years but resigned just days after Fagan was reelected. Russ attributed the decision to Fagan's flawed, imperious leadership.[222] Russ's disdain for Fagan was primarily the result of an episode from the prior fall, a strong disagreement about the treatment of a Hoboken school principal named Eugene Kiernan.[223]

The conflict not only well illustrated differing attitudes towards the appropriate use of power in city government, but also probably towards the abuse of alcohol. Kiernan, a graduate of the Stevens Institute, was the principal of Hoboken Public School No. 5. Mysteriously, Kiernan was gone—"absent without leave"—in October of 1898. Very shortly after his disappearance, the Hoboken Commission of Public Instruction, the body headed by Russ, received a message regarding Kiernan. The letter explained, rather ambiguously and only kind of, sort of officially, that Principal Kiernan "had left town" on a sabbatical of sorts "for his health." Russ, wholly dissatisfied with that explanation, promptly began his own investigation. He conducted a search of Kiernan's desk and discovered two whiskey bottles; a third was found in the schoolroom closet. After Russ presented his findings to the school board president, Kiernan, although already missing, was officially suspended. However, when Kiernan reappeared five weeks later, he was not brought before the board to face charges. Rather, Kiernan was simply told to resume immediately his former duties. The decision came from Fagan, who also ordered Kiernan receive full pay for the time of his absence. Fagan's specific thinking in backing Kiernan so strongly was not clear, but his use of mayoral power severely antagonized Russ. After Russ submitted his resignation, he discussed the Kiernan incident publicly. Russ said that he had protested Kiernan's reinstatement vociferously, but Fagan told him: he did not care about his feelings on the matter; the decision had already been made, and he already had all the support needed from the other members of the commission. According to Russ, Fagan said, "I have the votes and Kiernan will go back." Feeling his authority unjustly usurped by Fagan's, Russ was simply too angry and fed up to continue his duties. "It was once an honor to be a School Commissioner," Russ told the *Tribune*. "Now [It's] an insult to a man's intelligence."[224]

The *Tribune* welcomed the story of Russ's resignation, using it as an opportunity to take a dig at Fagan. "A true friend to our public schools," with a "lively interest in everything pertaining to their management," Russ will be "sorely missed," the *Tribune* declared. Fagan's "interfering" in the schools, by contrast, brought only "a demoralizing effect."[225]

Whatever the effect, Fagan wasted little time in catching his critics off guard by offering an olive branch to his former opponent, William Stuhr. Fagan offered him the Hoboken Public Instruction Commissioner position vacated by Russ. Stuhr, unlike Russ, did not feel his intelligence insulted by the offer and accepted the job.[226]

Fagan's belief in Principal Kiernan, however, was proven a miscalculation. The following year, Kiernan was forced to resign after he showed up intoxicated at a meeting of the Teachers' County Institute.[227]

In June of 1899, Fagan's personnel decisions faced further scrutiny after he dismissed a man named A.K. Banta from his role as the Superintendent of the Police Telegraph System. The telegraph superintendent was a fairly minor part-time municipal position with a small salary. Mr. Banta, however, was also president of the North River Light, Heat, and Power Company. At the time of his dismissal, Banta's company was bidding for a contract to supply electric light service to Hoboken against the city's current provider, the North Hudson Heat, Light, and Power Company. In light of the timing of Banta's termination, Fagan detractors took the opportunity to allege that Banta was being punished for his company seeking to encroach on the status quo. Fagan did not make clear the reason for Banta's release; it may have been one of many simple budget-cutting measures. Nevertheless, the sardonic *Tribune* alleged that Fagan's "friendly" relationship with the city's current provider explained the move and delighted in bringing further attention to the story in a sarcastic editorial. "The offending president of the new electric light company had to be taught a lesson." That is, in Hoboken, "burning money" can be "only for the benefit of Mayor Fagan," his "friends and their allied enterprises," said the *Tribune*. So Fagan, "his bosom swelling with honest pride, ...shouldered his axe" and "cut off his head....What a noble, large-minded, public spirited Mayor Hoboken has! [He's] a marvel of the official seal."[228]

The newsworthy axing coincided with a change in Hoboken's banking policy, which created another, but more easily visible, appearance of impropriety. That issue rose after Fagan signed a resolution making the Second National Bank of Hoboken and the newly organized Trust Company of New Jersey the depositories for all the city's funds. The First National Bank of Hoboken, which had been the city's sole depository for three decades, was not allocated any of the city's business in the new resolution. The Hoboken City Council proposed the change. However, with the mayor's signature, new questions were raised about whether official public influence was being used to further personal business interests.

Fagan held an interest in Second National and the Trust Company, but not in First National.[229]

While Fagan faced criticism for his business entanglements and political decisions in Hudson County, William Jennings Bryan was shaping the Democratic Party's ideological tenets on the national stage. Bryan, a charismatic rhetorician, brought to public life and the Democratic Party a unique and dynamic ethos, something of an enthusiastic brayed tilling of evangelical Protestantism and agrarian populism. Bryan's supporters, as American journalist and novelist Willa Cather described them, were "controlled not by a commercial syndicate or by a political trust, but by one man's personality."[230] Bryan, born in 1860 in Salem, Illinois, was raised a Presbyterian and attended Chicago's Union School of Law, later Northwestern University. He practiced law and headed Nebraska's largest daily newspaper, the Democratic *Omaha World-Herald*. Bryan's rhetoric, in good part, drew from the concept of class warfare. He delighted in discussing a growing clash between struggling small farmers and powerful big bankers, overstrained laborers and fat industrial capitalists. An idea Bryan favored was adopting an economic policy of "bimetallism." Simply put, he thought that implementing some combination of a gold and silver standard to increase the money supply would be a fairer and more democratic way for America to produce more wealth for more people. The recession of the 1890s helped boost Bryan to national prominence; he effectively and dramatically communicated the hardship and frustration of less prosperous citizens, particularly those in more rural parts of America.[231]

On July 8, 1896, Bryan gave what became known as his "Cross of Gold" speech at the Democratic Convention in Chicago. There, he made his preference for the experience and values of rural, middle-America over those of urban and "Atlantic Coast" rather clear. "Burn down your cities, and leave our farms, and your cities will spring up again as if by magic," Bryan told the convention. "But destroy our farms and the grass will grow in the streets of every city in the country."[232] It's unknown if Fagan ever expressed a view on that line there. However, with duties managing the material destruction and human anguish caused by fires in the City of Hoboken, Fagan may have found Bryan's words "burn down your cities," even as analogous rhetoric, imprudent. Moreover, Fagan, as a sharp-witted urbanite, may have found other parts of the famous speech a bit hokey. In one instance, Bryan pointed west, while exclaiming, "The pioneers away out there...made the desert blossom as the rose." He then asserted those "hardy pioneers" were now all but forgotten. However, with Bryan in charge, they would be forgotten no more. The Democratic Party now spoke for them, spoke for those "who endured "the dangers of the wilderness" in order to "rear their children near to Nature's heart," said Bryan, to "mingle their voices with the voices of the birds."[233]

Enough voices in the Democratic Party, anyway, liked what they heard. Bryan got the party's nomination for president. In the autumn of 1896, Bryan chronicled his presidential campaign up the Atlantic Coast, traveling by rail. In Pennsylvania, Bryan described encounters with railroad and manufacturing workers at stops that included Philadelphia, Phillipsburg, and Washington. Bryan wrote, "I found that many of the employees were working only a portion of the time—not finding employment for the whole time." The observation then prompted him to suppose that, "under the gold standard," the "laboring men worked half time" whereas "the farmers...worked double time;" they had to "in order to keep up with taxes and interest." After Pennsylvania, the coastal campaign train headed to New Jersey, where stops included Orange, Newark, Hoboken, and Morristown. For Bryan, the Morristown stop was distinct. He expressed hesitation about the "fashionable" appearance of the crowd there. His speech, therefore, would, at least by his own estimation, be "brief." Bryan's speech, however, at least probably for some of the people from Morristown who had come to support him, was likely a bit long on sanctimony. "Ladies and Gentlemen...in a city like this, where there are so many evidences of plenty of money, I do not know whether you understand or feel the need of more money," Bryan told them. "But, I want you to...remember [that] until wealth is produced it cannot be divided." And "all the wealth [in] this country is first derived from those who toil....You cannot destroy the prosperity of those who produce the wealth without undermining the foundation upon which all society rests," Bryan explained. "A financial system" favoring "itself only to the wealthy is a curse to any land."[234]

For the Pennsylvania and New Jersey portion of this East Coast campaign, Bryan was joined by State Senator William D. Daly of Hudson County, a longtime friend of Fagan's. Daly was a delegate to the national convention in Chicago, having led the charge to muster support for Bryan amongst influential Democrats in New Jersey.[235] Sometimes called "Big Bill," Daly was corpulent in build but full of get-up-and-go. He had an expansive, outgoing personality that endeared him to most. A reporter from New York once described Daly as having "as large a fund of good nature to his credit as any public man in New Jersey."[236]

Daly and Bryan bore some similarities. Both were attorneys, Presbyterians, and brought to politics a genuine interest in uplifting the "struggling masses." Daly, however, was shaped by more humble, urban beginnings. Born on June 4, 1851, in Jersey City, Daly matured early into a sturdily built adolescent. At age fourteen, his parents took him out of school, securing him work in the iron yard. They believed their son was best-suited for intense and physically rigorous work. By his late teens, Daly was a journeyman iron molder, employed at Blackmore's where he worked alongside Fagan. Fagan and Daly, while seeming to develop differing minds on strident union labor activity as their careers progressed, remained long allies in New Jersey politics.[237] After leaving the iron trade to study law in 1870, Daly completed apprenticeships at two Jersey City law firms and was admitted to the bar in 1874. Notably, Daly represented Erie Railroad freight handlers arrested in the Great Railroad Strike of 1877, securing their acquittals. As well, he represented leaders of the Cigar Makers Union facing conspiracy charges in Jersey City in 1887, also securing their acquittals. Daly entered politics in 1890, winning the Ninth District assembly seat previously held by Fagan. In 1898, Daly, after serving several terms in the state assembly and senate, was elected to the U.S. House of Representatives.[238]

Bryan, undeterred by his loss to Republican William McKinley in the 1896 presidential election, was rumored to soon declare himself again a candidate for the Democratic nomination when he joined Congressman Daly for an evening of political activities on Wednesday, January 24, 1900. Bryan was scheduled to speak at St. Peter's Hall in Jersey City.[239] Prior to the speech, the Robert Davis Association clubhouse hosted a festive banquet in honor of Bryan. Dinner guests there were treated to a main course of "stuffed squab a la Bryan." After dinner, Bryan, Daly, and Davis shared a motorcar, which, led by a drum corps, brought them the short distance to St. Peter's College. An enthusiastic audience of over one thousand was there, filling the event hall to "suffocation." Outside, there were several hundred equally enthusiastic, but non-ticketed spectators, whom police officers needed to restrain from rushing inside.[240]

Reports conflict as to whether or not Fagan attended the banquet dinner or Bryan's two-hour-long speech, but it is more likely that he did not.[241] Fagan's distaste for leader-boss Davis had grown. So, to see Fagan dining with Davis, in particular at the leader-boss's clubhouse in Jersey City, at night, in January, seemed a long shot. If not there to experience Bryan live at St. Peter's Hall, Fagan presumably read a summary of the speech in the newspapers and very probably took exception with some of it. Fagan probably shook his head at the way Bryan called on figures from America's past to shape the political narrative of the present. Bryan, in an effort to claim the political principles of Abraham Lincoln for the Democratic Party of 1900, quoted excerpts from a letter Lincoln sent to a group of fellow Republicans in 1859. Republicans stand "for both...the liberty [of] man" and "man's right [to] the dollar," Lincoln wrote. "But in case of conflict," the G.O.P. stands for "the man before the dollar."[242] Lincoln's statement was the "first Republican platform," testified Bryan. This "appealed to all the people" and "to the principles of Washington and Jefferson." Then, in a forceful revelation, Bryan continued, "If you go to a Republican meeting today you will hear what a great man Alexander Hamilton was," for "under Republican administration [today] money is...more precious than human blood."[243] As "Father of the Hamilton County Bill," Fagan probably took issue with Bryan's disparaging, simplistic allusion to Hamilton. Evidence also suggests that the Fagan family preferred the maxim of President Lincoln that advised: "Let not him who is houseless pull down the house of another, but let him work diligently and build one for himself, thus by example assuring that his own shall be safe from violence when built." This "Lincoln on Wealth" adage, clipped from a newspaper, appears as the only quotation from a historical political figure in scrapbooks kept by Mary Fagan—the mantra, moreover, affixed there next to a photo of the house at Hudson and Tenth Streets in Hoboken.[244]

Shortly after Bryan's Hudson County visit, Fagan announced that he was not going to seek reelection for a fifth term as Mayor of Hoboken.[245] The need to provide for additional children may have influenced the decision. By 1900, Mary and Lawrence's family had grown. They had a daughter, Madeline, born in 1895; a second daughter, Marion, born in 1898; and a son, Arthur Lawrence, born in 1899. The couple's firstborn, had it been a boy, would likely have been named Lawrence. Mary's first pregnancy, however, ended with the birth of stillborn twins.[246] Meanwhile, Catherine and

John, Lawrence's children with deceased wife Hannah, were now in their late teens.

There is no evidence to suggest that Bryan in the background and his populist bluster as the Democratic Party's national leader had any influence on Fagan's decision not to run for mayor. Fagan probably felt some political fatigue, but the source was not Bryan's speeches. Rather, Fagan may have grown tired of spending the time and energy required to fend off leader-boss Davis's rising influence over Hoboken's affairs. An example and source of friction between Fagan and Davis arose after Fagan refused to sign a long-term contract extension with the North Hudson Heat, Light, and Power Company to supply Hoboken with electric street lights and service. Davis had brokered the deal between the Hoboken City Council and North Hudson Heat, Light, and Power. North Hudson Heat, Light, and Power was the same company critics had accused Fagan of having a "markedly friendly" relationship with after A.K. Banta was let go as police telegraph superintendent. With Fagan refusing to sign off on the Davis-arranged deal, Fagan's relationship with North Hudson, Light, and Power was proven not as markedly friendly as some once thought. Davis was infuriated. For Fagan, while he may have deflated the charge that he had favoritism for North Hudson, Light, and Power, so too there may have been some conflict of interest in his decision not to grant the long-term contract. Just after Bryan's visit, Daly too had made an announcement. Daly would be starting a utility company of his own, the Municipal Light, Heat, and Power Company. Daly's utility would seek lucrative contracts, including providing electricity to Hoboken.[247] One of Daly's partners in the venture was a man named John Bruning. Bruning was the secretary and treasurer of Fagan Iron Works. The connection, however, seemed to fall under the radar of Fagan's critics at the time.

Another source of heat between Fagan and Davis came in the form of Anthony Capelli. Capelli, who years earlier Fagan called "not-fit" for public service or for saloon-keeping, had reemerged on the political scene. Capelli, however, now had a powerful backer in Davis. Davis wanted Fagan to appoint Capelli to a newly vacant position on the Hoboken Board of Police Commissioners. Fagan, not surprisingly, refused.[248] A good deal of the power granted the mayor in Hoboken was his control over appointing the city's police commissioners. For Fagan, the cost of pushing back against Davis was the loss of support of two police commissioners, Adolph Lankering and Martin Daab. Following Fagan's refusal to appoint Capelli, Daab and Lankering staged a public mutiny. The pair not only attended but proceeded to whoop it up with Davis at his clubhouse at the annual Winter Ball of the Robert Davis Association in Jersey City. The theatrics were viewed as an especially flagrant public affront to Fagan. Lankering and Daab made clear who their leader was; it was no longer Fagan, the Mayor of Hoboken; their leader was Davis, the Hudson County leader-boss.[249]

With Fagan's announcement not to run for reelection also came his public acknowledgment that he and Davis were "not on the best of terms." Fagan, however, denied reports of having come to a "loggerheads" with Davis when questioned.[250] If Fagan downplayed his displeasure with Davis, he probably did so for two reasons. First, he probably sought to limit the amount of credit Davis might take for his decision. Second, he was showing deference to Democratic Party allies who had urged him not to irrevocably blow up the relationship with Davis, in particular because it was a presidential election year. Republicans very much enjoyed visible signs of dysfunction amongst Democrats in New Jersey's lone Democratic county. Republicans had taken to referring to Fagan as the "Davis Stop Gap," a moniker that only served to increase the heat between the two.[251] Nevertheless, and all obstacles being equal, Fagan, by not seeking reelection, afforded himself more freedom to express his independent views of leader-boss Davis and the Democratic circular-machine in Hudson

County; that is, at a future time and date, if he chose to. Before that, however, Fagan would see his city face a far greater and fiery antagonist.

The Great Hoboken Fire began late afternoon on Saturday, June 30, 1900. The fire's exact cause was never determined, but when the first flames were spotted at approximately 3:55 p.m., conditions were clear, dry, and very windy. Flames began rising from bales of cotton piled on the docks of the North German Lloyd company's Pier No. 3. A remarkably rapid ignition of the wooden pier followed. The pace of the combustion was mostly due to the presence of a potent accelerant, several hundred casks of whiskey awaiting shipment on the docks. Before long, wind high-hopped the booze-fueled flames onto the steamship the *Saale* and Pier No. 2. Fire soon fully engulfed the ship and pier both. Within minutes, the conflagration spread to the adjacent pier and to two more steamships, the *Bremen* and then the *Main*.[252]

The late edition of the New York World describes the start of The Great Hoboken Fire on Saturday, June 3, 1900. (Courtesy Library of Congress Digital Collections.)

Along with its usual load of cargo, material, and passengers, the *Bremen* had recently returned to port carrying one item of particular interest and suspicion—the remains of writer Stephen Crane. Crane, the author of *The Red Badge of Courage*, was a native of Newark, New Jersey. He had died weeks earlier in Germany at age twenty-eight. The *Bremen* had transported Crane's body back to the United States for burial. Because many superstitious seamen believed that carrying a corpse across the sea was a harbinger of bad luck, the *Bremen*'s fiery obliteration on the Hudson gave them no reason to doubt their superstitions.[253]

The fate for those unlucky enough to have been trapped below the fire-riddled decks of the ships was horrific. They endured excruciating physical suffering preceded by searing psychological torment. The portholes of the North German Lloyd steamships, probably designed to prevent people from falling overboard, measured only eleven inches wide, making them too small for an average-sized man or woman to squeeze through, no matter how hard they tried. This element made for a grisly tragedy. The people trapped below had "to submit to the torture of being burned to death without hope of escape."[254]

This illustration from Reginald L. Foster's "The Great Hoboken Fire," published in the September 1900 issue of Munsey's magazine, depicts the desperate scene in the harbor. Foster wrote, "Had some master mind planned this tragedy for theatrical effect, he could have found no better setting." (Courtesy Google Books.)

Many others, successfully finding a way to hurl themselves into the Hudson River, also had their hopes of escape dashed cruelly. The captains and crews of many rescue tugboats were seen doing deeds of great malice. Although commissioned for the search and rescue of all people, some tug boat captains and crews saw fit to rescue only those who had money or valuables in hand, literally, to pay for their lives. Those without fare faced severe mistreatment, were immediately given the cold shoulder, or first taunted and then ignored. Many in the river, injured or not able swimmers, were simply left to flail and splash until they were overcome with exhaustion and drowned. Some rescue vessels appeared to ignore people in the water entirely, interested exclusively in helping themselves to a myriad of floating goods liquidated from the German steamships or Hoboken piers.[255]

Not everyone was convinced of the cold-hearted criminality or that it had, in fact, occurred at all. With "so many rescues by tugboat men who might have been seeking salvage instead of saving life," wrote one nativist, uncharacteristically unimaginative reporter from the *New York Sun*, "stories of inhumanity... may be looked upon as the result of excitement, overheated imagination," or a "lack of knowledge of English on the part of the men who make the charges."[256] Not imagined at all, the corpses, whether brought to shore by dutiful rescue workers or carried in by the tide, were numerous. In another shameful turn of events, however, recovered bodies laid out above the shoreline were not left but a moment's peace before their pilfering began. Greedy onlookers groped remains in search of valuables. The body looting made the process of identifying the dead, especially those disfigured by burns, more difficult for authorities and family members.

The Great Hoboken Fire was an Armageddon. The fire was probably the worst of the time period.[257] Approximately three hundred people were killed. Approximately $10,000,000 in material damages were caused. There were also approximately 100,000 spectators who watched the spectacle unfold from the east and west banks of the Hudson River. J. Pierpont Morgan's yacht, the *Corsair*, was one of several hundred vessels seen cruising on the river, allowing passengers a better view of all the dramatic sights.[258]

This photograph of the Great Hoboken Fire was taken looking down at the smoking harbor from the Jersey City Heights on June 30, 1900. (Courtesy Hoboken Historical Museum Online Collections: hobokenmuseum.org.)

Where some saw the disaster as a chance to take in entertaining diversion or steal a fast buck, others saw a more long-term economic opportunity. The president of the New York Dock Board, J. Sergeant Cram, of the Tammany Hall Democratic circular-machine, found a chance to lure waterfront business away from Hoboken and bring it to New York City. On Monday, July 2, 1900, Cram spoke to reporters after a meeting of the dock board adjourned, stating that he had gone to Hoboken earlier that day and conducted a thorough investigation. Cram's conclusion was that Hoboken's piers were "too narrow," and the distance between them "very much too narrow." After then describing the piers as all "rotten" and "nothing but tinder boxes...in the first place," Cram added, "That's the reason the fire spread so quickly and with such disastrous effect." It's unclear whether or not there was any merit to the issues Cram raised about the condition of the piers in Hoboken. In any case, Cram then spread blame to the crew and operators of the steamships. "One thing I desire to emphasize strongly—there's not a bit of excuse in this world for the terrible loss of life that took place on the ships. I found on examination of the three burned vessels that not a single lifeboat had been cut away from the davits. The unfortunate people in those vessels could all have escaped roasting and drowning if there had been proper discipline."[259] On that point, Cram, to a large degree, was probably incorrect. The problem for passengers roasted and drowned inside the ships was the small size of the portholes, insufficient to allow for escape, making access to lifeboats irrelevant. Lifeboats, however, could have helped passengers who had escaped the steamships but drowned in the harbor. Cram was correct there. That stated, had all the rescue tugboats acted more honorably in their duties, access to additional lifeboats would have been less strategic. Moving forward, Cram boasted of the supremacy of the New York City piers, turning the press conference into something more of a promotional appearance for the city's docking facilities. New York's piers were "much wider and much further apart," said Cram, more "modern" too. The New York dock head then reminded reporters that the steamship lines from England, France, and America all docked in New York City. The North German Lloyd corporation should follow suit, Cram advised. The company should stop docking in Hoboken, even if it saves "some slight expense." With the "protection" of the "the best" police and fire departments "in the world," docking in New York City, pitched Cram, was "a great deal."[260]

As New York called out Hoboken, branding its waterfront infrastructure second-rate, Fagan shot back shrewdly. Fagan seized on the rescue tugboat controversy, while calling on the long foggily-fixed water border between New York and New Jersey on the Hudson River to shift the narrative slightly more in Hoboken's favor. Fagan's calculation, in this case, was uncharacteristically amiable to surrendering authority. He spoke with reporters on Wednesday, July 4, 1900. "I have received many complaints" about "the brutal actions of certain tugboat captains....My chief [of police]" was "ordered—to collect what evidence he could...In my opinion," Fagan added, "the dealing with these men rests entirely with the New York authorities." It's "their jurisdiction" which "extends to high water-mark, Hoboken....All the acts so far reported seem to have been committed within New York waters." Thus, it's "not us," concluded Fagan, but "the New York authorities [who] should attempt the investigation."[261] It was not long before the New York City District Attorney's Office seemed in agreement with Fagan's interpretation and assumed responsibility for the investigation and likely prosecution of the relevant rescue tugboat captains and crew.[262]

New York City also exercised its authority to celebrate on the Fourth of July. Calls were made for New York to suspend its usual fireworks festivities out of respect for the family and friends of the several hundred people just burned or drowned to death across the Hudson. Some also suggested that the piers in New York might be equally at risk for disaster as those incinerated in Hoboken.[263] Others thought the catastrophe in Hoboken should be heeded seriously as a cautionary tale. That "terrible holocaust" across the Hudson, wrote one New Yorker, "was like the finger of the Destroying Angel pointing its warning to this great metropolis, which seems to lie at the mercy of the fire fiend on each recurring anniversary of our National Birthday."[264] This view, however, fell on deaf ears at the mayor's office in New York City, then occupied by Robert Van Wyck of the Tammany Hall Democratic circular-machine. The celebration in New York continued as planned, unabashedly voluminous. With a "tremendous...firing of pistols," "cannon crackers," and "pyrotechnics," the "annual jubilee," according to the *New York Times*, "surpassed in noise any...celebration of recent years."[265]The next day, Thursday, July 5, 1900, Fagan led a somber funeral procession through the City of Hoboken, which coincided with a mass cremation of eighty-two victims. Executives at the North German Lloyd company reached out to Fagan and expressed gratitude for his "able efforts" and "orderly manner" in leading Hoboken through the "appalling disaster."[266]

Shown here is the July 5, 1900, funeral procession led by Mayor Fagan for victims of the Great Hoboken Fire. The photo shows the somber procession moving south on Washington Street near Fourth Street. (Courtesy Hoboken Historical Museum Online Collections: hobokenmuseum.org.)

The mass cremation, however, was judged something of a failure, at least by one measure. It was hoped that the bodies' incineration would bring an end to a foul smell that had lingered over the city for the past few days. But it did not. Subsequently, Fagan met with health officials who expressed fears that bodies trapped below the burnt-out piers were dangerously decomposing. The scene, a potential incubator for disease, was determined to be an imminent threat. Fagan, therefore, ordered the wharves destroyed by dynamite. News of the blasting generated a good deal of public interest. A big crowd of onlookers turned out to watch the blasting on the morning of Sunday, July 8, 1900. The first detonation proved disappointing for public officials and spectators alike. It seemed to little impact the targeted wreckage, bringing only a minor concussive tremor and the sight of a column of water that rose only to a height of less than forty feet. The second detonation, however, was far more theatrically impressive and strategically successful. It generated an impressive major concussion, bringing a mighty surge of ebony black water propelled upwards to a height easily in excess of one hundred feet. More importantly, the blast cleared the wrecked portion of the dock and pier, dislodging any clandestine matter from underneath it. Mostly, the explosion liberated a submerged grain barge. The decaying barge, smoked and soaked with soggy grain, smelled, but not too badly. Whatever had been below the burnt piers was not harboring human remains. It could be eliminated as the source of the stink problem. Unfortunately, the rancid flesh-like stench remained about the city. So too did fears that, somewhere in Hoboken, there were un-attended human remains aging badly, creating a situation that might be very hazardous to the health of the city. Fortu-nately, perhaps with attention removed from the burnt piers, the real culprit was soon determined. The smell was coming from animal hides stored in the lower level of the Campbell's Soup factory. The factory by the waterfront was badly dam-aged by the fire. Its basement, where many soup ingredients were stored, was covered in wreckage and debris. As soon as a safe path was cleared to access to the lower level of the building, the smell problem was quickly remedied.[267]

While Fagan's duties as mayor, especially during the fire, must have been psychologically and somewhat physically draining, he did have the luxury of taking some days away from the city during the heat of the summer. When informed of the fire, Fagan immediately returned to Hoboken from the seaside resort of Asbury Park, New Jersey. He had been spending the weekend there with Mary and the children. Shortly after ordering the piers blasted by dynamite, Fagan went back to Asbury Park to rejoin the family. (Further evidence of the family's rising fortune would be found a few years later with the purchase of a vacation home in Deal, New Jersey; then, in 1918, with the building of a larger vacation home in Deal on Ocean Avenue.)[268]

The Fagan family's vacation home on the Jersey Shore in Deal, New Jersey, built in 1918, is shown here. (Courtesy Fagan Album.)

Congressman Daly, who lived in Hoboken with his wife and son, was out of town during the fire. Daly had left New Jersey for Kansas City, Missouri. His political career reached its acme there on Friday, July 6, 1900, when he was prominently featured and delivered a speech to the Democratic National Convention. "New Jersey," Daly declared, "wants...into the Democratic column....When I left my home...I was instructed to sacrifice everything in order that the Democratic Party might win [New Jersey] in the coming election."[269] Shortly after Daly returned to Hoboken later that month, he overexerted himself while rushing to catch a train. Hours later, he died at age forty-nine.[270] Daly, who held ambitions to run for governor, seemed to be a pacifying force between diverse personalities, the likes of Fagan, William Jennings Bryan, and Robert Davis. "Big Bill" Daly's untimely death was a loss for the Democratic Party in New Jersey.

With Daly no longer around to greet him, Bryan returned to Hudson County as the Democratic Party's presidential candidate on Thursday evening, October 25, 1900. Bryan's train arrived at approximately 8:15 p.m. at Marion Station near the Jersey City Heights. A big and boisterous crowd, estimated at fifteen thousand, assembled to see him there. Flocks of supporters from Hudson County joined Democratic contingents from Monmouth, Essex, Bergen, and Passaic counties. All were eager to greet the spectacle brought by Bryan. Davis, joined by a local brewer named Peter Hauck, was the first to receive the candidate. Then, escorted by a troop of police officers protecting him from being trampled or having his trademark black alpaca suit torn from his body, Bryan made his way to an ornamented wagon that had been made into a platform for him to speak.[271] "I am glad to see so many—So much enthusiasm." Here's "the proper spirit—Jersey City tonight," the crowd-pleasing Bryan blurted humbly. "The people are awake and are interested in the campaign and the important issues."[272]

Bryan then spoke disapprovingly of the United States military operations in the Philippines and of Republican President McKinley. Bryan charged that freedom was presently being "menaced" by the Republican Party; the GOP stood for "political despotism" overseas and "industrial despotism" at home. If elected, Bryan assured his audience that trusts in America would be eliminated. He would "make their formation impossible." For "wherever our flag flies," Bryan exclaimed, trying to make sure that he was heard by everyone in the big crowd assembled outdoors near the train station, "we want industrial independence." On that point, Bryan, naturally, did not mean ending American dependence on foreign industry. Rather, he meant ending dependence on America's own "industries controlled by a few, who, to enrich themselves and increase their profits, pay starvation wages," as Bryan, anyway, described the dynamic to his audience in industry-heavy Jersey City. As the speech continued, Bryan expressed "hate" for monarchies and their kings, monopolies and their monopoly kings.[273]

Following the populist open-air oratory, Bryan's spectacle continued with a patriotic political processional. A bugler riding a donkey, along with members of the Robert Davis Association and other Democratic clubs, followed Bryan, now inside a carriage. The carriage, drawn by four black horses with red, white, and blue plumage titivating their harnesses, would bring Bryan to four more speech stops in Jersey City.[274]

Bryan's final stop that night was Hoboken. There was a reservation for him at Meyer's Hotel at the corner of Hudson and Third Streets. It was well after midnight by the time he arrived. Bryan, nevertheless, continued to campaign, addressing a small private gathering at the hotel. A vocal performance by a German-American singing society followed. Two songs, sung in German, were performed for Bryan, capping off his very busy evening. The ambitious schedule was set to continue in the morning, with his first engagement scheduled to begin at 8:30 a.m.[275]

By 8:00 a.m. on Friday, October 26, 1900, approximately seven thousand people swarmed upon lower Hudson Street outside Hoboken's Lyric Theater. The buzzing crowd made the road between Third and Fourth Streets impassable to traffic. The Lyric Theater's official seating capacity was 2,000. The venue was packed. Its doors were jammed; throngs of enthusiasts, hungering for Bryan, piled outside the entrance.[276]

At approximately 9:00 a.m. Fagan, assuming duties presumably intended for the late Congressman Daly, took the stage and introduced Bryan. Understandably but uncharacteristically, Bryan appeared very tired. His voice sounded guttural as he began speaking. The dynamic political showman, however, soon reenergized before the large and lively assemblage of supporters. Bryan told them, "I am glad to have [the] opportunity to defend our cause here."[277] His speech then frequently called on Biblical inspiration to haul President McKinley and the Republican Party over the coals, analogizing that Ahab was to Naboth's vineyard as the United States was to the Philippine Islands. Further, he shared a mocking rendition of how an imperialistic Republican leader might preach. "We are very sorry we got [the] Philippine Islands," Bryan chortled with faux piety. "We did not intend to keep [them]. It is our duty," nevertheless. "God commands it...and it will pay."[278] Finally, Bryan further blasted Republicans for cultivating "industrial despots," declaring "the angels now in charge came not from above, but from below."[279]

When the twenty-five-minute speech was finished, the crowd showed their admiration, showering Bryan with cheers. The plaudits continued as Bryan exited the Lyric Theater, with policemen putting him into a motorcar headed for the Delaware, Lackawanna and Western Railroad station. A sizeable and jubilant group of people ran down the street in pursuit of the car. Many followed it to the train station, where they jockeyed hard for the opportunity to shake Bryan's hand or, at least, to catch a better glimpse of him before he left Hoboken. As Bryan's train pulled out of the station, some ran after it too.[280]

Despite his fandom, the presidential election a week and a half later again revealed Bryan lacking the horsepower to win the White House. McKinley was easily reelected. The large and loving receptions Bryan enjoyed in Jersey City and Hoboken, however, were not misleading. Bryan won in Hudson County. McKinley won in every other county in New Jersey.[281]

While Bryan had been the reason for the packed house at the Lyric Theater in Hoboken, the audience there that morning also witnessed an unexpected act of local political camaraderie. Fagan and Davis shook hands on stage. The handshake, done probably out of respect for the late Congressman Daly, created a small stir. When they shook hands "without exhibiting the point or the handle of anything up their sleeves," wrote the *New York Daily Tribune*, using its often cheeky style, "the surprise of the audience was great." Now "every Democrat is asking every other Democrat" when will they "cut and slash each other? Postponement of this interesting entertainment, everybody is being assured, is only temporary....Robert and Lawrence are still in the ring."[282]

The good faith suggested by the handshake between the Democratic Mayor of Hoboken and the Democratic leader-boss of Hudson County, indeed, was less than permanent. The following year, Fagan expressed his disgust for Davis publicly. Moreover, Fagan endorsed a Republican as his successor. The mayoral election, its timeline made more streamlined for Hoboken voters, was set for fall of 1901. Leader-boss Davis's candidate Adolph Lankering was set to face Republican Frederick William Verdon. Lankering, as earlier noted, was the police commissioner who, with Martin Daab, made a public show of cutting ties with Fagan and aligning with Davis in early 1900.[283] Fagan's support of the Republican candidate, of course, can be explained by his enmity for Davis and Lankering. Verdon's background, however, may have also resonated somewhat with Fagan. Verdon, notwithstanding his French-sounding last name, was an Irish immigrant. Verdon was born in Dublin in 1869 and, like Fagan, educated in the New York City public schools.[284]

One way or another, Fagan shared his thinking in a dramatic interview published in the *Tribune*, which now more warmly welcomed reporting the soon-to-be-retired mayor's side of the story, in particular after he endorsed a Republican for mayor. When asked to give his reasons for opposing the mayoral candidate from his own party, Fagan replied, "Yes, I will give my reasons. I am opposed to [a] crafty politician, seeking office for the purpose of handing up Hoboken to a political boss in Jersey City whose collar he wears....I am opposed to sacrificing, selling or giving away your birthright and your manhood as a citizen to any political boss," Fagan added. "[I am] opposed to seeing this city governed by a Jersey City Boss....I don't want [Hoboken] ruled by 'Bob' Davis at the other end of a long distance telephone....The people of Hoboken can govern themselves!"[285] Fagan then praised Verdon, calling him "a fighter—honest and fearless." And "any man who is not a fighter is no good as a public official," Fagan explained. "The machine will own him in a month." Fagan next pointed out that, in addition to standing for "no bending of the knee to a boss," Verdon stood for "a business administration" and "more schools." Fagan was confident in Verdon's chances at the polls. "He will be elected," said Fagan. "The revolt against Jersey City bossism is in the very air."[286]

The interview proceeded with Fagan expressing displeasure with the greater influence Davis had gained over the Hoboken City Council. Most members of the council, according to Fagan, now managed the city's affairs with "extravagance" and "recklessness." They were "owned...and controlled absolutely by 'Bob' Davis;" "mere puppets in his hands."[287]

Notably, over the summer, a boiling point was reached between Fagan and the city council, with funding for the Hoboken Free Public Library the source of the heat. Fagan was in support of a measure that allocated sufficient funds to pay the library staff as salaried employees of the city. The city council voted in opposition. As a consequence, Fagan, enraged, refused to sign the payroll checks to the council members. Thus, they too were enraged. During the acrimonious impasse, Fagan paid the staff of the library entirely out of his own pocket, their checks delivered paid at the higher rate afforded salaried employees.[288]

Fagan also seemingly acknowledged some of his short-comings as mayor in the *Tribune* interview, expressing regret that the city was failing to meet the educational demands of its surging population. "I am opposed to the crime by which thousands of children in Hoboken are deprived of decent school accommodations, and by which so many of them are huddled in miserable annexes hardly fit for animals to live in," said Fagan. "There are better doghouses in Hoboken, than some of these annexes." [289] Fagan's strong feelings on this matter were probably rooted in knowing that his public-school education in New York City proved an essential build-ing block for his own good fortune in America, his rise from close to the bottom to close to the top. Fagan, now empowered and wealthy, even had the living quarters of the family dog to call upon in point of personal reference. Fagan had a Great Dane, which presumably spent a good deal of time in the same barn where Nicholas Crusius once raised prize-winning chickens at the property at Hudson and Tenth Streets in Ho-boken. [290]

Animal analogies aside, Fagan further took the occasion to comment on a rumor that had hounded him since his an-nouncement not to seek reelection more than twenty months ago. That is, his decision not to run for a fifth term was based on knowledge that he had no chance of getting the nomina-tion of his own Democratic Party. "No sir," Fagan rebuked when asked about it by the *Tribune*. "That story is not true....The fact is that I have been urged a hundred times within the last three months to take another nomination, but I declined....I want to see Hoboken well governed," but "I have had enough. My time now belongs to my business." [291]

As Fagan turned towards business, the keys to city hall were turned over to leader-boss Davis's Democratic circular-machine and Adolph Lankering, who defeated Verdon to be elected Mayor of Hoboken. [292] Leaving office on that note must have been a bitter pill to swallow for Fagan. On the brighter side, he would have the time to be a more hands-on business

owner. Fagan Iron Works, in fact, was in expansion mode between 1901–1902. Fagan's firm maintained its Hoboken facility for smaller projects but moved its headquarters south to
the Horseshoe section of Jersey City. A much larger plant was
built there at Coles and Fourteenth Streets.[293] With some lucrative new contracts secured and Hudson County develop-
ing fast, all signs suggested that Fagan Iron Works was fueled
to grow to new heights.[294]

SCHEMES

The word paralysis had always sounded strange...in
my ears; [it] filled me with fear...yet I longed to be
nearer to it and to look upon its deadly work.
—James Joyce, The Dubliners (1905)

THE EXPANSION OF FAGAN IRON WORKS occurred at a time of
heightened disgruntlement and desperate measures in America. Although William Jennings Bryan was unsuccessful at
capturing the presidency, his fiery rhetoric captured the outrage felt by many Americans at the turn of the century. Scores
of women and men felt that the government and economy
were unjust, with America in business for the betterment of
only a few. To them, the endemic construction of industrial
plants was not a sign of American progress but a symptom of
systematic labor exploitation. In their eyes, the factories of the
new world were not providing opportunity, full-time employment, and upward American mobility. Rather, they were
modern dungeons where workers endured punishing hours
in inhuman conditions.

Maria Barbieri, an Italian immigrant who lived in Hoboken and worked in a silk factory, was near the very bottom of
the pecking order in terms of American status. It was a plight
that made her feel less than human. She had grown careworn

and embittered, and had become a committed anarchist. In 1905, Barbieri described the silk factories' wretchedness and implored workers to revolt against their mechanical treatment. "Locked in the immense industrial prisons," here "we lose our... right to live—our strength, our health, and youth....We have become human machines....Rebel against these abuses," Barbieri exhorted. "[Rebel] against the greed of the bourgeoisie....Shake with rage before the pompous and contemptuous lady" who "from our humble labor...wears a silk skirt."[295]

To battle the injustice, America's most enraged and radical critics were full of more than just tough talk. On September 6, 1901, President William McKinley was shot to death by an American-born anarchist named Leon Czolgosz. Czolgosz, a disenfranchised one-time steel worker, had become a devotee of violent anarchist teachings. Historian Beverly Gage writes of the extreme breed of violence that was contextually paramount to late-nineteenth and early-twentieth-century American culture in *The Day Wall Street Exploded: A Story of America In Its First Age of Terror* (2009). "These years saw the rise of [militant] socialists, anarchists, and other revolutionaries dedicated not to the reform of capitalism but to its abolition....Newspapers were filled with [violent] reports" detailing "attacks against the symbols of American government and business: bombs mailed to mayors and governors, assassination attempts on presidents and capitalists, dynamite found beneath railroad tracks or outside the factory door." Gage points to the union movement's gathering steam bringing with it a marked rise in violence between workers and employers. It was "a 'civil war,'" as many saw it, "between capital and labor."[296]

The relationship between labor and capital clashing violently and the flourishing newspaper industry often appeared symbiotic. Anarchists wanted to make a point with their terrorist acts. Newspaper publishers required a steady stream of "disruptions of the norm" for captivating content.[297] If publishers proffered editorial condemnation for the "wretched doctrines" and "desperate character" of "the incendiary anarchist," as an early edition of the *Observer* did, so too they profited from the disruptive and compelling content. Delivering details of violent anarchist attacks, in all their "peculiar savagery," was part of the business.[298]

Savage, disruptive, and increasingly popular, anarchist dogmas were attracting growing numbers of followers, especially in New Jersey. Anarchists affiliated with the Italian Socialist Federation, in fact, started their own newspaper in Hoboken, founding *Il Proletario* in 1902.[299] Two years earlier, the assassination of Italy's King Umberto I had really put New Jersey on the map, making it known as the American home to one of the violent anarchy movement's biggest stars. King Umberto's assassin was a man named Gaetano Bresci, an Italian immigrant who was active in Hoboken and Paterson, New Jersey, anarchist circles. A silk weaver by trade, Bresci was profoundly impacted by a violent episode that occurred in Milan, Italy, in 1898—a bloody, highly publicized clash that saw over one hundred striking workers killed by Italian military forces. After the incident, Bresci's perspective hardened. He embraced principles of violent anarchy and badly wanted retribution.[300] In late May 1900, Bresci left his home in West Hoboken (the municipality bordering the cities of Hoboken and Weehawken) and traveled by steamship to Europe, where he got the retribution he sought. Bresci assassinated King Umberto in Monza, Italy, on July 29, 1900. Authorities promptly arrested Bresci, who reportedly remained cold-blooded and calm but not repentant while being interrogated. He avowed himself to be a committed "Revolutionary Anarchist," and said that, if released from custody, he was ready "to resume operations."[301]

News of the entire saga came as a shock to Bresci's wife. She was home in West Hoboken with their eight-month-old daughter when her husband was arrested. Sophie Bresci, born Sophie Kneiland in Boston to Irish immigrants, was also a silk weaver. When questioned by authorities, she claimed to know nothing of anarchists or assassinations. She believed her husband went to Europe to collect a small inheritance left to him by his mother.[302] "I did not know that he was an Anarchist" and "do not believe it now," she stated. "His intention was to come back here and buy a house in West Hoboken for me and the baby."[303] An unidentified co-conspirator of Gaetano Bresci from Paterson was a source who gave credence to her story, at least the part of her being unaware of her husband's anarchist activism or role in the assassination plot. The "American" Mrs. Bresci was without ties to "any of our circles," he said. "I do not believe that she had the slightest idea [why] her husband went to Europe." Informing her of the plot, he added, "would be foolish....Women often spoil the most carefully laid plans by talking." That misogynistic tone turned more egalitarian in spirit when the question of raising a relief fund for Mrs. Bresci was mentioned. "She does not need it," he said. "Like her husband, she is a skilled factory hand, ...able to do for herself."[304]

In the wake of the assassination, Peter Esteve, editor of the Patterson-based *La Question Social*, the largest anarchist newspaper in America, issued a public statement that elucidated his movement's objectives. "We are working for 'socialista anarchico,'" Esteve explained. "That is the abolition of all authority. [No] private property...No kings, no presidents;" "No authority." According to Esteve, anarchists sought "everything all equal." In a factory, for example, "no boss," and nobody else, would be in charge. "All the profits," therefore, could be "divided equally" among the workers.[305]

Fagan's name easily could have appeared atop an anarchist hit list in Hudson County. Fagan was well-known, both for having been Mayor of Hoboken for four terms and for Fagan Iron Works. Fagan, if Beverly Gage's terms applied to him, was one of "the symbols of American government and business" likely to be targeted for "violent attack." If an obvious target, Fagan was harder to see as an easy mark. About a quarter century after Fagan's death, one newspaper reporter recalled, "Larry Fagan—a rugged ironmaster" was "the Mayor of Hoboken...at the turn of the century." Not one for "office informality, [he] settled strikes in his foundry with a crowbar."[306] Crowbar in hand or not, Fagan was presumably pleased by anti-anarchist legislation passed by Congress in early 1903. In summation, a new federal law required aliens seeking naturalization to swear that they were not opposed to organized government—all or any government in particular—or to the government of the United States. Aspiring Americans were also required to swear their opposition to "the unlawful assaulting or killing" of government officials or of "generally" anybody else. The new law went into effect, Monday, June 1, 1903. All applicants for final naturalization papers that day were reported to have signed the oath "without protest."[307]

This caricature, published circa 1910 in the Observer, or perhaps the Jersey Journal or Hudson Dispatch shows Lawrence Fagan outside of Fagan Iron Works. The pugilistic satire in the pages of the Observer in his pocket suggests his willingness to use physicality to protect his business. (Courtesy Hoboken Historical Museum Online Collections: hobokenmuseum.org.)

On that very same day, Fagan Iron Works in the Horseshoe was the setting for both protest and unlawful assault. The incident began with the arrival of an itinerant brand of trade union representative, known as a "walking delegate." Builders and contractors' attitudes towards these representatives had been worsening steadily in Hoboken and Jersey City. Walking delegates were increasingly seen as loosely-affiliated extortionists, shake-down men who fomented strikes solely for purposes of pocketing an illegal profit, not for the betterment of the laboring men as a whole. A walking delegate, for instance, might arrive on a builder's doorstep on the eve of a new job for which terms with the union had already been reached. He would, nevertheless, demand an additional payment, seemingly something of an arbitrary tribute to ensure that the men would not somehow decide they should go on strike in the morning. Sometimes making the payment really "was the only way," as one senior labor official reportedly advised a Hoboken contractor, "that business could be carried on quietly and without annoyance."[308] The walking delegate who called on Fagan Iron Works, Daniel Stiles, was a national agent for the Local No. 43, the Union of Architectural, Bridge, and Structural Iron Workers of America. Upon entering the business office at Fagan Iron Works, Stiles found himself face to face with Fagan and John Bruning, the secretary and treasurer of the firm and one of the late Bill Daly's partners in the Municipal Light, Heat, and Power Company. Stiles immediately solicited for a payment, a sum of perhaps $200 or $300, the amount deemed somehow necessary to maintain "peace" at the plant. Stiles' solicitation, however, initiated something far different. While Fagan was initially unfamiliar with the walking delegate, Bruning knew Stiles well. Bruning promptly scolded Stiles; he declared him the source of the "troubles at the plant."[309] Bruning accused Stiles of agitating the men to get up a strike and cast him as an irritant firebrand. Stiles was "[not] a trade unionist," said Bruning. Stiles was "an anarchist."[310] Bruning's indictment got his boss's blood running hot. It was not long before Fagan physically threw Stiles right out the office door. After that, Stiles removed his spectacles. The two men went out on the iron yard where they stiffened for a fight. It did not last long. The walking delegate wanted a payment. Instead, the rugged ironmaster gave him a pummeling.

The story did not end there. Later that summer, the two again faced off, this time settling their differences in a court of law. The case was heard on Tuesday morning, August 18, 1903, in Jersey City's First District Court. Stiles was the plaintiff, seeking $300.00 in damages from Fagan. Stiles alleged that, on June 1, 1903, Fagan assaulted him at Fagan Iron Works and that, as a result of injuries sustained there, he was left "laid up," unable to work for two weeks. Fagan did not deny the allegations. Rather, he freely admitted to the assault. Fagan testified, "I ordered him away from the place, and hit him....Had I been excessively angry at the time, the punishment would have been more severe. I will not be bulldozed. I had to protect my interests against such men as Stiles....Any man in my place would have done what I did."[311]

Fagan's act of aggression was not without consequences. The judge ruled in favor of Stiles, awarding the walking delegate $47.00 in damages ($5.00 for medical costs, and $42.00 for missed wages). Notwithstanding the judgment, Fagan was probably better off for the entire episode. Given his wherewithal, paying fifty bucks for the chance to squash a would-be bulldozer was probably well worth it—a small price to pay. In addition to whatever stress Fagan relieved by administering the punishment, the publicity he received was not necessarily unfavorable. As an owner-operator of an industrial business, Fagan sent a discouraging message to other potential visitors the likes of Stiles. As well, to political friends or foes, Fagan surely appeared defiantly principled, ready to strike back strongly should he decide to make a return to the arena of Hudson County politics.[312] Looked at together, Fagan's independent actions and views out on the iron yard and in the courtroom can be understood as manifest "manliness" both from the bottom up and top down. Feeling his foundry breached, Fagan weighed the evidence, then showed his identity as a force of nature to be reckoned with. And later, when summoned to explain himself in court, Fagan expressed himself didactically. He neither denied his actions nor cited some temporary loss of emotional control when explaining his behavior. Rather, he appealed to a law higher than the courts; simultaneously, he laid down his checkbook, allowing him to move on in defiant deference to established urban law and order. By this time, Fagan's stature, talent, and resources were, at least in Hudson County, sufficient to allow him some degree of freedom for recklessness in his public conduct. To be sure, similar freedom was not afforded to all men at the time.

Charles Reed was an African-American who worked and resided in Jersey City, where African Americans comprised approximately 2 percent of the city's population in 1903.[313] Employed in security, Reed worked for the American Veneer Company at 449 Pacific Avenue. Reed had risen in the ranks as a watchman and established an excellent reputation. He had just been appointed an elite quasi-official police security officer. Reed, as the *New York World* described him, was "the first negro watchman of private property upon whom special police power had been conferred in the past twenty years."[314]

That power notwithstanding, an episode of conflict and consequences demonstrated the limitations of Reed's stature. On Sunday morning, May 31, 1903, Reed was walking home from church when he spotted some trespassers shooting craps "on the premises" of American Veneer's factory. Being Sunday, the factory was closed. Nevertheless, the special police watchman, although not on the clock, was eager to protect the factory. Reed showed his shield; ordered the game over, the trespassers away from the place. The Sunday gamers, however, did not comply. They ignored Reed's order; they also "guyed" him mockingly. With his command flouted,

Reed went home. And there, in hindsight, he should have stayed. But, he did not. Reed changed into full uniform and returned to the factory, where again he confronted the trespassers. But this time, Reed drew his weapon, pointing it at the trespassing craps players. The move quickly cleared the scene. Unfortunately for Reed, it also proved to be a monumental miscalculation. Only hours later, Reed was arrested, chastised for "exceeding his authority" and stripped of his shield.[315]

The following day, the same which saw Fagan administer punishment to Stiles at Fagan Iron Works in the Horseshoe, Reed was summoned to Jersey City's Second Criminal Court. There, Reed faced punishment of his own. Reed, according to the prosecution, was, at the time of his appointment as a special police watchman, "told carefully" by Chief Murphy of the Jersey City Police Department that his powers did not extend beyond the walls of the factory, the physical building or literal structure of the American Veneer Company's plant. Reed testified to the contrary. He explained that it was his understanding that his authority had no such limits. The defense was unsuccessful. The unfortunate incident had unfortunate consequences for Reed. He was fined $10.00 by the court; his police powers were not restored, and presumably American Veneer terminated him.[316]

Fagan, meanwhile, when not at Fagan Iron Works or in court in Jersey City during the summer of 1903, was in Hoboken and plotting a return to the political arena. Fagan was backing a new independent political organization called the "Iroquois Club." The Iroquois Club, its incorporation papers stated, was established "to promote and promulgate the principles of a free and honest government, clean politics and home rule."[317]

The club, to outward appearances anyway, was formed fast. With a brisk efficiency, officers were elected; articles of incorporation were filed with the Hudson County Clerk and the New Jersey Secretary of State; a lease on a clubhouse was negotiated; new furnishings purchased. According to the *Jersey Journal*, the time between "the first rumors...whispered" of the club were heard and the time of the club being up and running, holding meetings, and "doing business" was little over a week.[318]

The new Iroquois Club had a very well-outfitted clubhouse from which to collaborate. The clubhouse, located at 902 Bloomfield Street in Hoboken, was considered one of Hudson County's best. The clubhouse was previously leased to the Knights of Columbus organization; however, the group could no longer afford the rent.[319] The Bloomfield Street clubhouse was swanky, for sure. The space came equipped with a gymnasium and a swimming pool, bowling alleys and billiard tables, a library, and "all the luxuries of a modern club."[320]

Trappings aside, setting up a clubhouse made some sense for Fagan, especially if he was to reenter politics and run for mayor as an independent candidate in the fall. He had long watched the clubhouse of the Robert Davis Association in Jersey City serve as a strategic venue for the Democratic circular-machine. Fagan had, in fact, previously discussed the concept of creating a new independent political organization in Hoboken. The year prior, on the evening of Thursday, February 13, 1902, he hosted a political event at his house at Hudson and Tenth Streets. At this "preliminary conference" of Hoboken's leading anti-Davis Democrats, Fagan and company assessed the potential for "a new branch" of the Democratic Party in Hudson County.[321]

In contrast to that gathering, the peculiar facet of the Iroquois Club's formation was the secrecy Fagan maintained about his involvement. It was all but ubiquitous that Fagan was behind the Iroquois Club. It was mostly assumed that the club would serve as a launching pad for Fagan, or possibly for another Iroquois Club independent candidate, to run for Mayor of Hoboken in the fall. Fagan, nevertheless, maintained a secretive façade and air of contradiction towards the new club, as well as any suggestion of waging a political comeback. In odd fashion, Fagan's name was absent from the Iroquois Club's incorporation papers and clubhouse lease; nowhere to be found on the club's official list of members or officers.[322] Fagan, meanwhile, was openly seen at the clubhouse during meetings, but was uncharacteristically taciturn in making tangible any ties to the club known or plans to run for mayor. On Monday, June 8, 1903, Fagan was spotted leaving the Iroquois Club clubhouse, but not forthcoming in responding to questions posed by reporters. "I am interested in the new independent club. But beyond that, I cannot say anything."[323]

While Fagan's tight-lipped stance was consistent with the inexplicable furtiveness about his part in the Iroquois Club, someone else's might have been attributed to the weather. It was a rainy day. The month of June had, in fact, brought with it unusually cold and rainy conditions. Dr. William H. Guilfoyle of the New York City Health Department even acknowledged the psychological impact of the weather. It "depresses people, to be sure," diagnosed Dr. Guilfoyle.[324]

By Friday, June 26, however, conditions, weather-wise and politically, began to warm up. The day saw clearing skies and rising temperatures, with a high of seventy-one degrees Fahrenheit.[325] By that evening, Fagan's interest in the limelight was also normalizing. Fagan, however, was not found outside the Iroquois Club; rather, he was found outside The Lamp Post. The Lamp Post was a saloon located across the street from city hall. It had become the recognized meeting place for Democratic circular-machine men in Hoboken. The Lamp Post functioned as something of a Michael Coyle's Liquors and Tavern for the next generation or satellite branch of the Robert Davis Association clubhouse in Jersey City. Either way, there were circular-machine men in abundance, enjoying "their regular evening meal of politics" at The Lamp Post when Fagan showed up just before 9:00 p.m., with a small cadre of officially recognized Iroquois Club members behind him.[326] Word of Fagan's call on "the enemy's camp" spread fast, making hullabaloo and attracting a big crowd. Fagan fielded reporters' questions and responded differently than he had weeks earlier outside the Iroquois Club. Fagan, albeit in an enigmatic and mischievous fashion, was now ready to provide entertaining copy and what might, at least, be symbolic hints about future plans. Reporters asked: What was he doing downtown? Why was he at The Lamp Post? "Why did I come downtown? Why, I don't know; why did you?" Fagan replied. His rhetorical response generated only puzzled silence from reporters and the crowd gathered there. Whether or not that was the reaction intended, Fagan soon broke the crickets and continued, "I thought I'd come downtown and see how the electric lights are burning. I heard there were new lights on 'The Lamp Post' and I thought I would come down and see how I looked under them. They are very fine lights...I think they may be useful in my business," said Fagan. "I suppose I came down to see what might be new in this section of the city. I'm taking quite an interest in public affairs nowadays and they say," he postured in rhyme, "there is lots doing down this way. Have I heard anything new? Why, heavens no! I wanted to," Fagan rousted cheekily, "but I haven't done anything but answer questions since I got here."[327]

Fagan's call on The Lamp Post was seemingly successful enough as a publicity stunt. It brought a refreshed jolt of attention for him, and the Iroquois Club too. "Fagan does some strange things in Hoboken," recounted the *Jersey Journal*. "No act," nevertheless, as his "visit to...the machine shrine," could come "with more surprise." To be "showing up...at 'The Lamp Post,'" there "big as life and twice as natural, ...adds only more to the audacity that he started when he started the Iroquois Club."[328]

Audacious or otherwise, Fagan must have liked the way he looked under The Lamp Post's lights. With July bringing a surge in temperatures reaching upwards of ninety degrees, so too it brought Fagan back to The Lamp Post.[329] Five days after the initial stunt, Fagan, seemingly no worse for the heat, re-appeared at the circular-machine men's saloon hub in Hoboken. Again, he attracted a large crowd. This time, however, he was far more candid and direct in his performance. Fagan finally acknowledged that he was behind the Iroquois Club. "The Iroquois Club was organized to put independent politics on a working basis in this county, [in] particular—Hoboken...The time is just ripe for such a move," Fagan told reporters. "People are tired of the reckless way that things are going....Good Democrats who have had no voice in party matters are interested in this movement...and I have reason to believe the Iroquois Club will accomplish all it was organized to do."[330]

That summer evening in Hoboken, Fagan was a human vehicle for spectacle. With a big group of hearers following, Fagan began walking away from The Lamp Post but continued talking, moving up and down the city streets of Hoboken. "Some people have an idea that the Iroquois Club already has things [down] pat." Well, "that...is not right," explained Fagan, showing a bead of humility, presumably many perspiration beads too. "It won't be easy for us," but "people will know there is a fight going on." As to whether or not the Iroquois Club was formed also to launch his candidacy for mayor, Fagan was unwilling to be pinned down. After someone in the crowd suggested that it might be "a trifle hot" for him to be out and doing political work, "Hot?" Fagan replied. "Why this isn't a marker to what it will be next fall, provided the other fellows are able to create enough opposition to cause some friction."[331]

All the attention given Fagan during the summer of 1903 seemed to satisfy his craving for the spotlight. Fagan did not run for mayor in the fall. As to the Iroquois Club, it turned out to be a short-lived gimmick.[332]

Fagan's next interesting move came in late October of 1904, with plans to embark on a six-month vacation to Europe with his wife, Mary. The trip was more than likely Fagan's first out of the country since his honeymoon in 1891. It was almost certainly his first trip back to Europe since his remigration after the Civil War. The Fagans would travel on the *Kaiser Wilhelm der Grosse* of the North German Lloyd company line. A reporter from the *Observer* was there at the waterfront to cover the story of Fagan taking the longest vacation of his life. With Mary soon to join him in the boarding area, Fagan was interviewed in the company of his friend and neighbor, John Keresey. Keresey was an importer of rare rugs who lived in Hoboken at Hudson and Ninth Streets. Keresey was headed out of town on business and would be taking the same steamship as the Fagans, who were good customers.[333]

For Fagan, the thought of being so far away from his business and for such a lengthy period may have been the source of some anxiousness; if so, Keresey lightened the mood. Keresey was a droll and witty character. When the *Observer* reporter asked Fagan about the purpose of his trip, he explained that he was simply taking a vacation. The voyage was "entirely for pleasure." Keresey, however, seemed less than satisfied with his friend's straight-forward remarks. He interjected and began trying to get a rise out of Fagan. "What's that story about you going to see 'Dick' Croker about annexing New York to Hoboken?" inquired Keresey. "For heaven's sake," Fagan retorted, "can't you let a fellow go to Europe without mixing him up in politics? Why the fact of the matter is, we wouldn't annex New York to Hoboken if they paid us a dollar a square foot for the privilege." Plus "the average New Yorker," Fagan added, amusedly, "can't appreciate...the superiority of Hoboken over New York...I don't mind doing my share of missionary work," but to "try...to convert millions of New Yorkers when we only have sixty thousand [in Hoboken] to do it?" And "all of us are not exactly fit for missionary work at that—Eh, John?"[334]

Leaving the reprisal unchallenged, Keresey steered the bantering buffoonery towards topics in international relations. "We may go over to Germany and interview the Kaiser about sending us over a few thousand more Germans," Keresey chirped. "[The Germans] are good people, and, if we are to keep all our Irish friends busy by putting them on the police force, we've got to get enough Germans to make it necessary." Keresey's comic posturing continued with speculation that his friend's trip had something to do with the Russo-Japanese War. To this, Fagan chimed back inquisitively, "What's that? [Am I] going to join the Russian Army?" Fagan then paused, before hooting, "Not on your life [Keresey]. There's one war...to keep still [of]; I'm going...to keep out of it entirely."[335]

Receptive anyway to the idea of avoiding confrontation while on vacation, the Fagans headed to Europe, where plans included a visit to Dublin, Ireland. Fagan reunited with relatives there, introduced Mary, and visited the old iron shop. James Fagan & Sons: Housesmiths and Bellhangers was still in business, producing works at the same location in Dublin where it had opened a half-century earlier. This Fagan family reunion may have brought with it at least some awkward tension. This dynamic can be inferred by a letter from John Fagan, Lawrence's cousin, which came accompanied with a parting gift, a shamrock-shaped iron box. The small iron box and letter, dated March 14, 1905, presumably were not seen by Mary and Lawrence until they returned home to Hoboken later that May.

Dear Cousin Lawrence, I trust you [had] a nice passage across....All here are so sorry your stay was so short but hope soon to have the pleasure of seeing you and some of your family again...Ask your good wife to accept from me this specimen of my works. You can assure her there [is] no mistake about it being Irish Manufactured made and finished in 18 GT Brunswick Street Dublin. I know you can do big things in America and works out there perhaps as good as this but I do not think better. Place it where you can often see it and it will remind you that

there are Fagans [both] in the New World as well in old Ireland
that can do iron works in all class still after 500 years.[336]

John Fagan's emphasis on the "old Ireland" iron work—
that his was a "specimen" that could certainly rival the "big
things" his cousin made in America, suggests he bore at least
a little resentment. This may have reflected a broader cultural
theme in Ireland, a jealousy amongst some Irish families for
their more prosperous emigrant family members abroad.
John Fagan, whether or not a bit amusedly sarcastic in comparing the small iron box to the likes of big iron structural
trusses produced by Fagan Iron Works, likely did not have a
full understanding of the cost of doing business in America—
there was a price paid for making big works in his cousin's
new urban world.

Approximately fourteen hours before the Fagans were
scheduled to dock in Hoboken, returning from their six-
months-long vacation in Europe, there was a large and de-
structive fire at Fagan Iron Works at Coles and Fourteenth
Streets in the Horseshoe section of Jersey City. Iron workers
there had finished work for the day at 5:30 p.m. on Tuesday,
May 2, 1905. Many were still little more than a block away
when the first flames were seen rising about ten minutes later.
The fire intensified rapidly.[337]

Fagan's own newspaper, the *Observer*, described the scene
in vivid, energetic fashion. "As the sun went down...the
flames were seen to shoot heavenward...100 feet above roof-
tops....The heavens were lighted by the flames;" next "a
shower of sparks." Then "as if oil fed them...the flames
spread" and "the spectacle," assessed the *Observer*, "was
beautiful."[338]

Public interest in the fire spread almost as fast as its flames,
with a big crowd soon on the scene to watch. Many spectators
were really wound up and in want of entertainment. They appeared in no hurry to see the factory's incineration brought to
an end. Some, in fact, even acted to impede the firemen. It was

only with the arrival of additional firefighters called from "all points" that the obstructive spectators were finally brought back in line.

The *Kaiser Wilhelm der Grosse*, with Mary and Lawrence aboard, docked at Hoboken at about eight o'clock the next morning. The steamship, which departed from Southampton, England seven days earlier, carried 1,000 passengers across the Atlantic. The Fagans, along with approximately 270 other passengers, made the trip in first-class cabins.[339] Children Catherine and John, as well as John Bruning, were there to meet them on the waterfront. Mary and Lawrence had heard news of the fire the night before by way of a Marconi wireless telegraph.[340]

Built little more than three years prior, the Fagan Iron Works factory in the Horseshoe was almost entirely in ruin. The loss was estimated between $100,000 and $200,000. John Bruning told reporters that the insurance on the facility was minimal, an amount far short of $100,000. Nevertheless, Bruning was eager to appear optimistic. He stated that new building construction would soon be underway. Fagan Iron Works would "be on the same footing" as before the fire, said Bruning, "just as soon as human ingenuity could bring that about." Facilities and machinery could be rebuilt and replaced. The same was not true for a cache of original castings, drawings, patterns, and other valuable articles which were destroyed. Fagan had been accumulating these artifacts since he began work at Blackmore's nearly four decades before. When asked for comment, Fagan replied philosophically. "Worse news," he said, "might have been awaiting me."[341]

In taking a big-picture view, Fagan may have understood how small the loss was in comparison to others that he had seen; perhaps all the lives lost during the Great Hoboken Fire came to mind. As well, Fagan, just back from Ireland, may have returned with a greater appreciation for his opportunities in America; his greater opportunities to build or, in this case, rebuild big things.

Married life may also have encouraged in Fagan a more mature, live-and-let-live ethos. Mary Fagan was a founding member of the Women's Club of Hoboken. The organization, formed in 1904, aimed to do positive works in the community and especially to prevent cruelty to children. "See Big Things Big, and small things small" was the Women's Club motto.[342] For the Fagan family, maintaining a sense of humor and healthy perspective on life's ups and downs appeared important. In a letter to her sister, Mary wrote of a fun-filled, but tiring, weekend in March of 1906. It was one which saw Mary and Lawrence together babysitting an assortment of visiting nieces and nephews. "[I'm] owed...one new pair [of] shoes," Mary stated jokingly. Her shoes were "completely worn out" after all the time spent "chasing Lawrence and several other members of the family up and down the floor and throughout the house" while "they...madly endeavor[ed] to escape me."[343]

This photo, circa late 1930s, shows Mary Fagan holding a grandchild. (Courtesy Fagan Album.)

Family fun time aside, the troubles facing Fagan Iron Works did not end when Mary and Lawrence returned from Europe. The rest of 1905 brought with it several more, albeit much smaller, fires to the ironworks. In 1906, such fires "of mysterious origin" continued. These incidents antagonized the process of the facility's rebuild and repair. Strikes and other labor troubles were also a constant—always a threat to the business of doing business.[344]

For the iron industry, in particular, the second half of the nineteenth century brought with it a great recalibration to the relationship between working people and their work, between labor and capital. Much had changed since the 1849 Convention of Iron Masters. The proclamations detailing the lengthy training and weighty competency required of iron workers were no longer applicable. In *Dynamite: The Story of Class Violence in America* (1934), labor activist Louis Adamic explained the ironworker's shrunken stature by the dawn of the twentieth century. By then, the "trade required little skill....Almost any husky young man with good nerves" could fast and easily know "all its tricks." Ironworkers first came to be "considered inferior" by employers, then "by fellow mechanics belonging to other trades."[345]

As to the mysterious fires hitting Fagan Iron Works, some light was shed on the subject inside a New York City courtroom in late March of 1906. An iron worker named Charles Moran provided some very informative testimony as part of a plea bargain agreement struck there. Moran was charged with several crimes, including arson and other acts of destruction at several factories in New York and New Jersey. Moran's testimony included an account of his attempt earlier that January to burn down Fagan Iron Works in Jersey City. Moran stated that he had just finished dumping kerosene all over one side of the factory when a watchman spotted him, chasing him off before he could properly spark the accelerant. According to Moran, the Employees' Protective Association paid him $80.00 to start the fire, promising him more if "the trick," as he called it, was performed "successfully." Moran expressed remorse for his involvement in the "schemes," but also deflected blame onto those who had contracted him. He told the court that those who put him up to it were cunning and had taken advantage of him and other "soft uns." Moran lamented that he and his cohorts were not paid enough for the risks they took. Moreover, the labor officials had abandoned them once arrested. "Why, they made us feel that we were heroes," Moran testified. "As a matter of fact...we were damn fools."[346] Whether Moran, in fact, was mostly the dim-witted dupe, or merely cast himself as such to lessen his punishment, is unsure.

In October of 1907, Fagan and his son John, now in his mid-twenties, might also be judged as acting foolishly, at least sufficiently so to also find themselves inside a New York City court of law and in some trouble. The problem landing them there began when John Fagan, either independently or at his father's direction, tried to take the law into his own hands. Fagan Iron Works sought to settle a disagreement over the rightful ownership of approximately a half-dozen iron beams (or columns). The principal antagonist of that endeavor became a man named Harry Levin, Vice President of the Dawson Realty Company. Dawson Realty was putting up apartments in New York City at 155th Street and Wales Avenue, building the flats with iron beams purchased from the Municipal Iron Works of New York. Municipal Iron Works had purchased the beams from Fagan Iron Works, where the beams were cast. Fagan Iron Works asserted it delivered Municipal Iron Works the beams, but Municipal Iron never paid its bill. Therefore, presumably after exhausting a diplomatic means of recovering the balance due, John Fagan, accompanied by men and trucks, set off to put right the matter on Saturday morning, October 19, 1907. John Fagan and crew went to New York City and to Levin's construction site on Wales Avenue. Once there, they attempted to repossess the beams, approximately four tons of iron. At Levin's behest, John Fagan was arrested. He was taken to the police station; so too was the evidence, the iron beams at the root of the conflict. John was bailed out promptly. Later that day, Lawrence and John Fagan appeared in court together. Fortunately for the Fagans, criminal and grand larceny charges were quickly dismissed. The court magistrate ruled that the matter belonged in the civil courts. Free to leave, the Fagans went back to the police station. They presumed they could leave New York City with the iron beams in hand. The commanding lieutenant at the station, however, refused to release the iron. Hence, back to the courthouse the Fagans went. They petitioned for a judicial order for the immediate return of their property. This time, before a different court magistrate, a less favorable decision was dealt them. The magistrate ruled that the Fagans were, of course, free to go, but the iron beams needed to remain "in custody." The beams would be held by the property clerk of the New York City Police Department and stay there until the two iron works firms and the property developer could resolve their issues in civil proceedings.[347]

In May of 1909, Fagan Iron Works was delivered another disappointing ruling from the courts, this time in New Jersey. The unfavorable decision followed Fagan Iron Works' purchase of the bankrupt Passaic Steel Company of Paterson. Passaic Steel, once valued at nearly $1.25 million, had shut down two years earlier. Passaic Steel's principal bondholders ultimately put the company up for auction, with Fagan Iron Works purchasing it for $190,000.00. Immediately after the sale, however, additional bondholders came forward and objected. They argued that that they were not given sufficient time to find the business another buyer at a higher price, nor to restructure its debt and resume operations under new management. A United States circuit court judge in Trenton agreed. The sale of Passaic Steel to Fagan Iron Works was ruled null and void.[348]

Although that deal fell through, Fagan remained rambunctious and eager to take on the future. With son John maturing into something of a suitable heir apparent to run Fagan Iron Works, he would again be setting his sights on politics. This time serious, Fagan wanted his old job back. Desire to again be Mayor of Hoboken would put Fagan's well-seasoned political metabolism to the test.

CIRCULATION

The Jerseys seem to have struck a winning gait
since new blood was infused in the team.
—Robert Davis, as quoted in the Observer, June 8, 1910

ON JANUARY 1, 1909, Fagan turned fifty-eight years old. The average American's life expectancy was then forty-nine years.[349] Nevertheless, Fagan showed no signs of slowing down. He was, in fact, energized to reclaim his old job and supremely confident that he had all the right tools and track record to once again be Mayor of Hoboken. "I know what kind of administration Hoboken needs," said Fagan, while boasting about his political vitality in June of 1909. "The people of Hoboken know [it]. I possess sufficient energy and force to bring the City what the citizens desire."[350]

Fagan sought the Democratic nomination amongst a crowded field of candidates. Four other men also wanted the job: Hoboken's two-term incumbent mayor, George H. Steil; Hudson County Clerk and Robert Davis-backed Maurice J. Stack; police commissioner Jacob E.W. Kuper; and chairman of the city council, Martin J. Whelan. The Democratic primary was particularly contentious. It was one "hot mayoralty fight," assessed the *Trenton Evening Times*, the "bitterest...in many years" with "war to the finish" for Fagan and Davis.[351]

By early September, however, it appeared that diplomatic efforts had cooled the hostilities within the party. Patrick Griffin, a Fagan supporter and the Democratic city chairman in Hoboken, struck a political peace treaty with Davis. The terms were simple. When the primary was over, no matter the victor, differences would be set aside. Hoboken Democrats would present a united front in the general election. All would put their full support behind the Democratic Party's candidate for Mayor of Hoboken.[352]

After Fagan won the nomination, the other Democratic candidates and their respective factions maintained the terms of the agreement; that is, until the very day of the general election. Davis, who appeared genuine in supporting Fagan since he won the primary, had something up his sleeve. It was perhaps the joker card from the deck of the old conjurer. On election day, the Democratic leader-boss directed his circular-machine men to put their full muscle and all their wherewithal behind Fagan's Republican opponent, George Gonzalez. Griffin and Fagan were completely blindsided. No plans for last-minute mutiny were in place. There were no special anti-fraud detectives posted at every polling site to guard against repeat voters or ballot-box stuffers. No extra precautions were in place. It was assumed that Fagan would be elected by a wide margin. He was not. Gonzalez won, defeating Fagan by a majority of approximately 400 votes.[353] Gonzalez was the first Republican elected Mayor of Hoboken in twenty-six years. Fagan had seen himself "cut," reported the *New York Sun*, "slashed...with a free hand" by his own party, with news of his defeat generating great "joy" at the clubhouse of the Robert Davis Association in Jersey City.[354]

While Fagan was infuriated by his mayoral loss, he could take some solace in the success of the *Observer*. By 1910, the *Observer* was the largest daily newspaper in Hudson County and largest "Democratic" newspaper in New Jersey.[355] Some of the *Observer's* success had long ago come at the expense of the *Hoboken Evening News*, out of business before the century's end. The animosity, however, between the former owner of the *News*, Gustav Seide, and Fagan, was also a thing of the past. Seide now worked at the *Observer*. Seide and Fagan were the newspaper's two principal shareholders and business was booming. "Circulation Guaranteed Over 34,000 Daily—Biggest in the county: 12,000 more than all other papers published in Jersey City," boasted the *Observer's* masthead in May of 1910.[356] Another appraisal for the year as a whole ranked the *Observer* as Hudson County's largest newspaper, but with an estimated daily circulation of 32,090 newspapers; the Republican *Jersey Journal* followed with an estimated daily circulation of 24,031 newspapers; the Union-based *Hudson Dispatch* came in third with an estimated daily circulation of 9,000 newspapers.[357]

Not destined for a fifth term as Mayor of Hoboken, Fagan used the extra time on his hands to assume a more active and editorial role at the *Observer*, an advantageous position for him to settle some old scores. Fagan could now steer the *Observer's* "muckraking," that is, his newspaper's dramatic expository investigative reporting. The term muckraking, often credited to Theodore Roosevelt, became most widely applied to the work of Lincoln Steffens. Steffens, the son of a seamstress from Hoboken, came to prominence with the 1904 publication of the *Shame of the Cities* series. His artful writing generally depicted the events of the day in stark terms, black and white, right and wrong. "If there is such a thing as treason by a state," Steffens once declared, "New Jersey is a traitor state."[358] So too the muckraker moniker might be cautiously applied to Mathias Ely. Ely, as earlier discussed, was the editor of the New Jersey edition of the *New York World* in 1893 and reported on Hudson County gambling and green goods shops protected by police under McLaughlin and Stanton. Now, Ely was editor of the *Observer*.

With the erudite and experienced Ely behind the editor's desk and Fagan now a fixture in the building, the *Observer* set its sights on a newly formed newspaper, the *Hoboken Inquirer*.

The *Observer* charged the owner of the *Inquirer*, Phillip Daab, with being an unscrupulous profiteer. Phillip Daab was the younger brother of Martin Daab, the police commissioner who paired with Adolph Lankering in 1900, the men flouting Fagan's authority as mayor and embracing Davis's as leader-boss. Phillip Daab owned the semi-professional Hoboken Baseball Club and had previously served a term in the state assembly.[359] He now headed the Hoboken School Board and had just started the *Inquirer*. Daab's *Inquirer* was off to a great start. The newspaper was awarded a profitable contract from the city to publish the minutes of the school board's meetings. The *Observer* expressed its displeasure with Daab and the *Inquirer's* convenient deal, objecting to it on the grounds that it was inked under false pretenses. The size of the *Inquirer's* circulation, so said the *Observer*, was grossly exaggerated to obtain the contract. The *Observer*, in providing a description of circulation and its sanctity, explained that the value of a newspaper's advertising depended upon "the number of readers each announcement reaches" and "into how many homes each publication goes." Advertisers "pay for space in accordance with that circulation." Public officials spending "public money" for that space "pay only the legal price fixed by law." It's "their duty...to get for that price the largest circulation obtainable," the *Observer* added. "Any public officer who uses public funds to pay for advertising in obscure or ill-circulated publications, placing them therein for political or mercenary reasons, is as much an embezzler of the public funds as if he took the money out of the treasury for himself."[360] Fagan and the *Observer* filed a lawsuit against Daab and the *Inquirer*. The suit alleged that Daab and the *Inquirer* perpetrated fraud against the City of Hoboken, knowingly providing false data about their business in order to secure the publishing contract with the city. A court ruled in favor of Fagan and the *Observer*. The publishing contract Daab and the *Inquirer* had with the city was ordered null and void in June of 1910.[361]

The *Observer's* next target was much more prominent: Woodrow Wilson. Wilson, then the president of Princeton University, had begun a campaign for governor in July of 1910. Wilson, a Princeton graduate who earned a PhD at Johns Hopkins University, was considered a distinguished scholar of political theory. However, excepting for some university entanglements, Wilson was a total novice in politics. He embarked on his gubernatorial campaign with almost no knowledge of New Jersey state politics. Moreover, he had not recently, if ever, voted in New Jersey.[362] The *Observer* objected to Wilson's candidacy not because he was inexperienced as a politician but because of his connection to Davis. Davis, along with James Smith Jr. of Essex County and Newark's James R. Nugent, were the three big leader-bosses of the three big Democratic circular-machines in New Jersey. Davis, Smith, and Nugent aligned early to back Wilson. The *Observer* attacked Wilson, calling him "a catspaw," hand-picked "to serve" the leader-bosses; Wilson was a "taken" man.[363] "Induced" to run for governor by the leader-bosses, Wilson, the *Observer* editorialized, embodied "the very elements...progressives are fighting."[364]

One way or another, Wilson's career path had changed dramatically. He exited "the shades of the University," wrote Joseph Tumulty. "The Princeton Professor" was now "to enter the Elysian Fields of politics."[365] Wilson may have begun the campaign as a greenhorn politician but he was soon smartened up. In addition to new "friends" like leader-boss Davis, Wilson, to some extent anyway, already had his own political network, a more socially elite set of contacts, upon which to bring him up to speed. A man named Archibald Stevens Alexander, a member of Hoboken's first family, was one of them. After attending St. Paul's School in Concord, New Hampshire, Stevens Alexander went to Princeton University, where he was a student of Wilson's. He then studied law at New York University, became a partner at the Hoboken law firm, Besson, Alexander & Stevens, and served briefly in the state assembly. Stevens Alexander was also on the board of directors of the Hoboken Trust Company.[366] Hoboken Trust was a competitor to the Trust Company of New Jersey with which Fagan was affiliated. Advising Wilson in a letter dated July 22, 1910, Stevens Alexander wrote, "We have a rather peculiar local condition here in Hoboken which explains the *Observer*'s attitude toward you...Mr. Lawrence Fagan controls the policy of the *Observer*." Stevens Alexander proceeded to educate his former professor on the 1909 mayoral election in Hoboken and some of the history between Fagan and Davis. Stevens Alexander shared with Wilson that it was Davis's endorsement that brought him the denunciation of the *Observer*. "Fagan very naturally attributes his loss to the disloyalty of the Davis wing of the Party," Stevens Alexander explained. He wants "a chance to get even." To that end, the *Observer* was disparaging Wilson and supporting Otto Wittpenn, the Mayor of Jersey City, for the Democratic gubernatorial nomination. Davis found Wittpenn "most distasteful," as the two recently had a major falling out. Stevens Alexander, however, was optimistic about Wilson's long-term prospects with Fagan's publication. He believed the newspaper would support his former professor in the general election. At the *Observer*, Stevens Alexander advised Wilson, "They think nothing of making the most acrobatic changes politically."[367]

A more simple, less lithe, albeit admittedly second-hand, picture of Fagan was given to Wilson by Henry Eckert Alexander (of no determined relation to Stevens Alexander). Eckert Alexander was a longtime Ohio resident before he sold the *Columbus Dispatch* and moved to New Jersey. He now owned and served as editor of the Democratic *Trenton True American* newspaper.[368] In a letter dated July 23, 1910, Eckert Alexander informed Wilson: "As to the Hoboken Observer man, I know nothing directly. I am told that [Fagan] is as independent as that New York policeman who said: 'I bate you, not because I hate you, but to show my aut'ority over you.'"[369] In a subsequent correspondence to Wilson, Eckert Alexander shared more of what he had learned about Fagan and Mathias Ely too. Fagan's "hostile" feelings for Davis account for why "the poor editor takes it out on you," he explained. "It is pretty hard for a gentleman to act as 'the goat' but there you are! I understand the owner is to be taken in hand."[370]

The tone taken by Ekert Alexander in his correspondences suggests he held himself and Wilson, perhaps also the *Observer*'s "poor editor" Ely, men of words, in higher regard than he did Fagan. Calling on a cultural stereotype of an Irish policeman, blunt, brutish or simple-minded in desire and of unpolished brogue, to understand Fagan, may also infer Eckert Alexander to be more comfortable amongst native born counterparts. The phrase "to be taken in hand" may suggest the best approach towards Fagan was not to take him too seriously, that perhaps whatever brand of Irish power was his was to be taken with a grain of salt.

However one chose to take it, Fagan's newspaper continued to claw at Wilson's candidacy. In August 1910, the *Observer* called out Wilson for remaining so vague about many of his political relationships and positions on issues. After Wilson asserted that he had only agreed to run for governor after a "decided majority of thoughtful Democrats" urged him to do so repeatedly, the *Observer* objected and speculated sardonically—who were these "thoughtful Democrats?" Wilson's vacuity, the *Observer* surmised, clearly indicated that he was "against...most," if not "all," of the Democratic Party's "progressive ideas."[371] As summer gave way to fall, the *Observer*'s unfavorable coverage continued. "Wilson did not discuss a living state issue," asserted the *Observer*, reporting on one of Wilson's campaign stops. His audience was delivered merely "a revamped edition" of his "speech on miscellaneous corporations," his same speech given "for five years...with variations." Wilson's rhetoric, as the *Observer* saw it, was both stale and non-progressive, with the candidate wanting only "that the ins...be put out" and "outs be put in control of the State machinery."[372]

Notwithstanding the heat from the *Observer*, Wilson's decision to embark on his campaign buoyed by the circular-machine leader-bosses was not proven a miscalculation. He won the state-wide primary and became the Democratic Party's nominee for governor.

Simply winning the nomination, however, was not enough to bring about a one-eighty at the *Observer*. The *Observer's* reach, moreover, stretched beyond Hudson County. Its unflattering view of Wilson was being echoed by the Republican but independent *Trenton Evening Times*. James Kerney, editor and part owner of the *Evening Times*, had a working relationship with Mathias Ely. The *Observer's* campaign reports and analysis were often referred to by the *Evening Times*.[373] With the negative coverage brokered about by the *Observer* and *Evening Times* sufficient to ensure defeat in the general election, Wilson realized a change in strategy was required. Wilson would need to vilify, and declare himself severed from, the circular-machine leader-bosses who had nurtured his candidacy from its launch.[374]

The plan for Wilson to do so was not sprung until the last week in October, 1910. Wilson's plan would have him renunciate the Democratic leader-bosses in a newspaper interview of sorts. Wilson would answer, in writing, a series of tough questions, his answers provided to all the newspapers. The questions would be posed by a journalist named George Lawrence Record. Record, something of a persistently aggressive reform progressive, was a graduate of Bates College in Lewiston, Maine, a school with a reputation for producing some of country's finest debaters.[375] Record's influential writing made him known as the "intellectual architect" of the "new idea" variation of reform governance in New Jersey.[376]

Record's three most important questions for Wilson pertained to Wilson's alleged ties to the Democratic circular-machine leader-boss system in New Jersey. First, Wilson was asked to acknowledge the circular-machine's existence; second, to identify Davis, Smith and Nugent as its leader-bosses;

third, to repudiate the system and its captains. Wilson, wisely, did all three.[377] Wilson, furthermore, obliged Record in "denouncing and fighting any one and every one" involved in any "such outrages against the government and public morality." Further still, Wilson declared that, should "even in the slightest degree," he "cooperate in any such system" or any "transaction" influenced by it, he would be "forever disgraced."[378]

The *Observer* judged Wilson's responses "frank and explicit," more than sufficient. The *Observer* endorsed Wilson. Fagan's newspaper praised Wilson for his "alert and open mind," a mind eager and able "to learn quickly."[379] The *Observer*'s stance, as Hoboken's Archibald Stevens Alexander predicted, had recalibrated. Another of Wilson's more important contacts, Richard Lindabury of Bernardsville, New Jersey, was eager to share the good news. Lindabury, a prominent corporate attorney, had successfully defended the Singer Sewing Machine Company and the American Tobacco Company, amongst others, in tax fraud and anti-monopoly litigation brought by the state of New Jersey.[380] "The attitude of the *Observer*," once "a little shaky," has turned "enthusiastic," rejoiced Lindabury, in letter to Wilson dated October 27, 1910. "There is no longer any occasion for anxiety....Everything just now looks so bright and promising." Lindabury then gave Wilson some of his additional thoughts on the *Observer*, describing it as a thoroughly "Democratic" publication, but "always...independent" and "for progressive principles." The *Observer*'s endorsement would, according to Lindabury, bring Wilson virtually all the votes cast by Hudson County's independent and progressive voters.[381] With the governorship all but certain, Wilson reached out to the *Observer*. He thanked the publication for its meaningful support. Ely responded on behalf of the *Observer*. He congratulated Wilson and thanked him for reaching out.[382]

The Observer's front page reports Wilson's gubernatorial victory on November 9, 1910. (Courtesy news-papers.com.)

Leader-boss Robert Davis died not long after Wilson was elected governor. Davis's health had declined during the course of the 1910 political season. Davis was at home in Jersey City when he died of stomach cancer on January 9, 1911.[383]

New Jersey Governor Woodrow Wilson, meanwhile, proved not long for politics in his home state. On March 4, 1913, Wilson was inaugurated President of the United States.

Joseph Tumulty, risen from his father's Jersey City grocery store to serve at the White House as Secretary to the President, reached out to Fagan. Addressing him as "Mayor," Tumulty thanked Fagan for having "rendered such excellent service to the cause in which we all are so deeply interested."[384]

If Robert Davis's death left Fagan temporarily without an antagonist with which to tangle, it was not long before trouble again threatened Fagan's interests. On Friday, February 17, 1911, the advertising manager for the *Observer*, Abraham L. Kohnfelder, was attacked and badly beaten. Kohnfelder had been unable to come to terms with James O'Neill and son James Jr., the owners of a newspaper circulation business, on a renewal of their distribution contract. The O'Neills' company delivered the *Observer* to some parts of New York City. After Kohnfelder hired a new group for the job, the O'Neills were enraged and completely lost it. James and James Jr. O'Neill, accompanied by several of their employees, ambushed Kohnfelder. They delivered him a brutal beating. Kohnfelder was left with a crimson mask and knocked unconscious, his skull severely fractured. James and James Jr. O'Neill were arrested, charged with "conspiracy to incite a riot." Fagan arranged medical care for Kohnfelder, delivering him to a head trauma specialist in New York City.[385]

The violent incident may have played a role in the *Observer*'s decision to make a tough Irish boxer named Frank Garrick a mainstay in the circulation department. Garrick often played baseball in Hoboken with a man named Marty Sinatra. The two became close friends. Garrick became the godfather and namesake of Marty's son, Frank, born in Hoboken in 1915. In the 1930s, Garrick secured his teenage godson Frank Sinatra his first job, working on the circulation trucks at the *Observer*.[386] By then, the *Observer* was under the management of Fagan's son, Arthur L. Fagan, as well as members of the Seide family.

Arthur L. Fagan, born in Hoboken in 1899, attended The Lawrenceville School in Lawrenceville, New Jersey, then Princeton University, graduating in 1921. During his freshman year at Princeton, he tried to enlist in the army but was twice excused from service. A minor deficiency of his eyes prevented him from passing the military medical exam. Arthur's father, however, secured his son treatment from an ocular specialist in New York City, then made a special petition on his behalf to Washington, DC. Arthur, granted approval for enlistment, reported for artillery training in Kentucky at Camp Zachary Taylor.[387]

While Fagan's son went south to get battle-ready, Wilson and Congress's declaration of war on Germany had, in fact, made the waterfront in Hoboken the forefront for the war effort. On April 6, 1917, the headline of the *Observer* read:

AMERICA IS AT WAR.

The sub-headline of the *Observer* read:

SEIZURE OF GERMAN SHIPS TAKES PLACE WITHOUT DIFFICULTY.

The comings and goings of the Hamburg-American and North German Lloyd companies' steamship lines, vessels which for over half a century docked at Hoboken, had become a serious issue, a matter of national security. The steamships were made property of the United States government; their crews were arrested and sent to Ellis Island for reclassification. If already somewhat uneasily aware of the war's implications for Hoboken's sovereignty, the *Observer*, long on the ground of the waterfront, was also enamored by the thrilling, almost patriotic, role it had in covering such historically significant, dramatic action. As "Hoboken became the center of the war operations...the weather was miserable in the extreme," the *Observer* reported. This made "it...impossible to gauge what might take place at any moment;" thus, "the newspapermen, and others whose duty compelled them to remain out were drenched through and through."[388]

As the *Observer's* interest in trumpeting its journalistic duties continued in the weeks that followed, so too did its uneasiness with the course of the news, a foreboding that the start of the war had brought the beginning of the end for home rule in Hoboken. "The fact that a portion of the City of Hoboken is at present an armed camp [remains] the main topic of discussion," the *Observer* reported on April 21, 1917. "The reservation on the River...is under the strictest of military supervision....No one, not excepting [city] officials," has been "allowed to enter." The *Observer's* coverage continued, however, only to reveal boastfully that, by "special permission of the Military Authorities," a "Hudson Observer Man" had, in fact, toured the "war zone." The *Observer* emphasized that he was the "only newspaper man to whom this privilege was given;" the "only newspaper man allowed on the docks."[389] The identity of that "Observer Man", and whether or not it was, in fact, Fagan, is unknown.

In any case, Hoboken residents, whether they liked it or not, could only watch as the awesome force of the United States Army repurposed the city. The waterfront hub of international shipping and travel was remade into a mammoth military base, a launch point for soldiers shipping out to the European theatre. The declaration of war, meanwhile, brought about a swift rewriting of the social order in Hoboken. Significant numbers of residents, German-born or of German descent, were arrested, sent to Ellis Island for questioning and potentially prolonged containment. Several hundred Hoboken businesses and properties classified as German-owned or operated were outright seized by the federal government. Two hundred German dockworkers were fired. In other instances, measures restricting civilian and saloon proprietor proximity to military-occupied areas hurt Hoboken's broader economy as a whole.[390] "Khaki-clad regulars [captured] the first German City in America," testified United States Army Captain King W. Snell. "The Army...overran the town." There was "just one motto—'Do It.'"[391]

By comparison, certainly to the doings in Hoboken, springtime in 1917 brought with it something destined to be a more regular experience for citizens of Jersey City, Frank Hague's election as mayor. Hague, born in 1875 to Irish immigrant parents, grew up in the Horseshoe. His early political education took place there inside of a saloon. Hague neither smoked nor drank but thirstily took in the abundant political talk. Although in lesser family-friendly confines, his introduction to politics was not dissimilar to Joseph Tumulty's at his father's grocery store. Hague held several public offices before he was elected Mayor of Jersey City; his first came in 1897 when he was elected a constable.[392]

In 1898, Constable Hague made a call on Hoboken City Hall, which showed him establishing his reputation as a real go-getter. Hague's visit was official, the result of the City of Hoboken failing to make an approximately $600 payment to the estate of a Jersey City contractor. The matter went back nearly two decades when the contractor's company did some street work in Hoboken on Monroe Street around 1880. For unknown reasons, Hoboken did not pay for the work done, or at least not for all of it. It's also possible the contractor failed to send an invoice for the work done. One way or another, the contractor died many years later. Several years after that, a family member hired a new attorney to investigate if any outstanding funds might still be due his estate. In June of 1898, a Jersey City court awarded the estate the sum of $571.63 from the City of Hoboken. When the city council in Hoboken was notified of the judgment, the council referred the matter to the finance committee. After a week went by and no check had been received, the estate lawyer obtained a writ of levy against the City of Hoboken from a circuit court. The lawyer took the court order document to the sheriff's office in Jersey City, from where Constable Hague was promptly dispatched. Hague went to Hoboken City Hall and seized furniture as collateral on the outstanding debt, capturing furnishings from offices, including those of the mayor and city clerk.[393] An absence of news pertaining to a physical struggle or loud argument during the seizure suggests either that then-Mayor Fagan was out of the office at the time or that he did not object to the merits of the collateral's surrender.

In any case, Hague's career in Jersey City politics moved forward. He won a seat on the street and water board, was elected chief janitor (a position which bore brawny powers for making personnel decisions), and was appointed commissioner of public safety. Hague led a coalition of public commissioners elected by Jersey City voters when they went to the polls in May of 1917. The commissioners then elected Hague as Mayor of Jersey City. A year or two in advance of assuming the mayoralty, Hague's identity in politics underwent a rather dramatic transformation. Hague changed from stalwart Democratic circular-machine man to appearing something more like a reform politician. Repackaged, Hague found support in the *Observer*, without which the mayor's office almost certainly would have been beyond his reach in 1917. Fortunately for Hague, the *Observer* saw his politicking with a nostalgic fondness. Notwithstanding "all the mudslinging...indulged in" by the opposition, Hague's win, according to the *Observer*, demonstrated "actions speak louder than words" and "brought to the minds of old-timers the good old days in the political game."[394] Hague's approach in 1917, which included making reform politics combative and theatrical, was reminiscent of Fagan in 1893. Hague turned boldly, and newly, outspoken about the need to reform abuses and corruption in the police department. "Reclaiming the police department [for] the people," assessed the *Observer*, marks "the greatest...achievement" of "Hague's manly fight" and "voters...like a fighter for a good cause."[395]

Before long, Mayor Hague's record as a reformer, however, was called into question. An altercation with some Princeton University students led not only to an inquiry of Hague in Jersey City but to a far-reaching investigation into governance across Hudson County. On election day in the fall of 1920, a group of Princeton students, with no evidence to suggest that Arthur L. Fagan was among them, went to polling places in Jersey City. The students were members of the Honest Ballot Association, a campus group championing good government. The students went to Jersey City intending to serve as watchdogs of sorts at the polls. They were eager to stop, or to at least formally document, any repeat voting, ballot box tampering, or anything else crooked, in their assessment, going on. With their arrival, so too appeared Mayor Hague. Hague reportedly greeted them warmly. He told the Princeton men that they were welcome to observe the voting as closely as they wished, but if somehow they found themselves knocked unconscious, that would be their own "hard luck."[396] Later that day, members of the Honest Ballot Association returned to campus in Princeton, New Jersey. The students appeared roughed up and beaten. Outrage ensued. Everything, however, had gone according to plan; that is, the plan hatched by aides to Republican members of the state house who had encouraged the students to embark on the dangerous mission in the first place. An investigation into the students' manhandling gave way to a wider investigation of public officials in Jersey City, then to an even wider probe across all of Hudson County and the formation of the Republican-led MacKay Legislative Committee. The committee's investigators were keen to leave no stone unturned in their efforts to uncover wrongdoings in the Democratic-controlled municipalities of Hudson County.

Amongst the papery abundance of materials MacKay investigators flagged for further analysis, there were records of an odd Hoboken real estate transaction involving Fagan. Documents from early 1920 revealed that the City of Hoboken purchased the house at Hudson and Tenth Streets from Lawrence Fagan for $100,000.00. The contract stipulated that the property would be converted into a school building at a future date. A seller's remorse clause was also in the contract. Records showed that Fagan exercised that walk-back option, purchasing the property back from the city only one week later and for the same price $100,000.00. Given the parties involved in doing the deal and in its expedient undoing, it's not surprising that MacKay investigators sought some additional information; it certainly appeared a strange exchange. The $100,000.00 figure was, in fact, significantly higher than the property's most recent tax assessment. This raised suspicions of impropriety.[397] A fair market private appraisal of the property, however, might have reconciled the disparity. If so, perhaps new questions might also have been raised.

One way or another, Fagan had not made his thinking known on the matter and was issued a subpoena to appear before the MacKay Legislative Committee during its preliminary hearings. The hearings were held in March and April of 1921 at city hall in Jersey City. There outside, very late in the afternoon on Friday, April 29, Fagan, who had long waited to be called to testify, was heard blustering before a friendly group. "I was willing and anxious to testify before the committee....If they want me next week," Fagan said, with unintended irony, "they will have to send a constable after me." His outwardly energetic confidence notwithstanding, Fagan likely felt some unease, this perhaps in part due to the investigation but mostly because his health was not good. Probably while in Jersey City, waiting outside the city hall to testify, Fagan caught a cold, exacerbating other ailments. On Wednesday, May 4, Fagan was at home, at what was now his slightly more controversial house at Hudson and Tenth Streets in Hoboken, when he collapsed.[398]

Earlier in the day, Fagan dictated his last will and testament. He made his wishes known to his eldest daughter, Catherine, now about age forty. The will was drafted by hand on two sheets of letter paper. It did not name an executor. The proceeding had two official witnesses, nurses Helen Wilson and Katie Harty.[399]

I, Lawrence Fagan of the City of Hoboken, County of Hudson and State of New Jersey, being of sound and disposing mind and memory, do make, publish and declare this to be my last will and testament, as follows:

I hereby revoke all former wills made by me.

I direct that all my just debts and funeral expenses be paid and discharged as soon as convenient after my decease.

I give and bequeath unto my beloved wife Mary A. Fagan, all my estate, real and personal, everything in my name to do as she sees fit.

In witness whereof I have here unto set my hand and affixed my seal this fourth day of May in the year of our lord one thousand nine-hundred and twenty-one.

Helen Wilson

Katie Harty

LAWRENCE FAGAN

The following day, a doctor supervised a blood transfusion for Fagan, the blood supplied by a paid donor. A second transfusion was performed on Sunday, May 8. This time, the donor was his son John, now age thirty-eight and president of Fagan Iron Works. After both transfusions, there appeared a burst of new energy in Fagan, but it was ephemeral. Fagan suffered from sustained abdominal hemorrhaging, a serious condition that rapidly swallowed up any signs pointing towards recovery. Fagan died of internal bleeding while at home, the house at Hudson and Tenth Streets in Hoboken, during the early morning hours of Monday, May 9, 1921.[400]

Three days later, a funeral was held for Fagan. New Jersey Governor Edward Edwards, Hoboken Mayor Patrick Griffin, and Jersey City Mayor Frank Hague served as honorary pall-bearers. Under their guard, there was a lengthy motorcar procession, a tribute to the once energetic and independent, sometimes peculiar and unpredictable Mayor of Hoboken. Fagan's body, in a long bronze box, moved through Hoboken, then south to Jersey City. On the border of the two cities at the Holy Name Cemetery, there was a sturdy and spacious enough mausoleum already built for Fagan.[401]

By the fall of 1923, the future of the house at Hudson and Tenth Streets in Hoboken was another sealed deal. This time, there was no walking back. Mary Fagan had sold the former home of the Reiche, Crusius, and Fagan families. Notwithstanding its historical significance, the house was going to be razed from the Elysian Fields. It would be replaced by a modern elevator apartment building with commanding Hudson River views. Taking a last look at the house not too long before demolition, one newspaper reporter signaled its lost utility and wrote with reluctant nostalgia. "On the premises" of America's "original importers of animals...even the stable," which at one time "housed beautifully groomed horses," was made "a garage," the last "sign of animal life" there Fagan's Great Dane.[402]

This photo, circa 1920, shows the house at Hudson and Tenth Streets with its stable or garage. (Courtesy Fagan Album.)

With the aplomb of the Mastiff, the height of the Irish Wolfhound, and the warm disposition of the athletic Greyhound, the Great Dane, like Fagan's Hoboken, could not be ignored. So too another newspaper reporter remembered the

Fagan Mansion era, describing it a bit more fondly and actively. "Always running" up and down "the spacious grounds was a big dog, a Great Dane, whose size and mighty bark never failed to frighten the youngsters who passed the mansion on their way to 11th Street," where "open lots" still remained "to play baseball."[403]

AFTERWORD

[Fagan] was as good a fighter as Hoboken has
ever known. He was emotional—one might say,
erratic...but nevertheless, as firm in his resolutions
as the needle to the pole. His time, his talent,
and his resources were always available when
his beliefs were involved.

—"Fagan Gives Up First Fight Of His Long Career,"
unidentified newspaper eulogy in Fagan Album

MY INTEREST IN THE SUBJECT OF THIS BOOK began in the spring of 2010 after a trip to Morristown, New Jersey. My purpose there was to interview for a history teaching position at the Morristown-Beard School. The campus is located about a half-mile from the train station where William Jennings Bryan spoke in the fall of 1896, suspiciously assessing the audience there in support of him as "fashionable." Established about the same time, Morristown-Beard stands today as one of the best private, or independent, day schools in New Jersey.

Ned Farman, the father of a good friend of mine, got me the interview. Ned is one of the most intelligent and politically outspoken men I've ever met. He was not too long retired from teaching and served for many years as head of the history department at Morristown-Beard. Ned, I think, appreciated my rhetorical tenacity. That is, I was willing to take the opposing side of almost any political argument he was interested in having at the time. Aware that I had spent the last three years preparing to be a history teacher, Ned generously acted on my behalf and secured me an interview when there was a job opening at Morristown-Beard.

I would, unfortunately, let Ned down. My interview with Dr. John Mascaro, Dean of Faculty at Morristown-Beard, did not go well. For reasons without forethought, I took a temporary lull in conversation as an opportunity to share a piece of information absent, and appropriately so, from my cover letter and resume. "My great-grandfather was Mayor of Hoboken," I blurted out inexplicably. At that, Dr. Mascaro asked me two simple and very reasonable questions. First, did my great-grandfather know Frank Sinatra? Second, when was my great-grandfather Mayor of Hoboken? The interview went downhill from there, for I did not know the answer to any of his three questions. I say three questions because I had no idea Frank Sinatra was from Hoboken. In what American city did Frank Sinatra grow up? If I was asked that as a direct question back then while playing a trivia game, I probably would have guessed Las Vegas. In any case, I knew absolutely nothing about Hoboken—that is, except that my great-grandfather was once Mayor of Hoboken. I also knew absolutely nothing about my great-grandfather—that is, except that he was once Mayor of Hoboken. With this to consider, it really was ill-advised for me to volunteer such an obscure item of family history, and particularly so while interviewing to be a history teacher in New Jersey. My performance at Morristown-Beard was very poor. I not only blew any chance of teaching there but also came off as a first-class nitwit. Ned was right to be quite chippy with me the next time I saw him.

With the Morristown trip destined to serve a purpose other than its original, I began investigating Mayor Fagan and Hoboken for a short research paper at Salem State University, where I was working towards a master's degree in history. My research paper evolved into the framework for a master's thesis. As I began my research, I visited Hoboken and Jersey City several times. I rode the PATH train from Manhattan to Jersey City and the water taxi ferry-boat from Jersey City to

Manhattan. My initial visit to the microform newspaper archives at the Jersey City Public Library yielded some rich material. I was so excited to find newspaper stories about Fagan addressing crowds in front of a lamp post in Hoboken. I later headed to Hoboken in search of the correct lamp post. Unsuccessful at locating what I assumed was, or must have been, a pretty big lamp post, I inquired about it at Hoboken City Hall. There, the Municipal City Clerk, James J. Farina, and Deputy City Clerk, Jerry Lore, kindly provided a short tour of the building and, with respect to a lamp post, pointed me in the right direction. They illuminated me that I was probably not looking for an actual lamp post but rather for an old saloon or men's club. This was helpful information, for sure! In Jersey City, I explored what was the "Horseshoe" section of the city. This was, for me, a small disappointment. I think I thought I'd find myself somewhere an outsider would find foreboding, a place with a lot of angry yelling or conflicts and certainly many clear indications of dangerous waste mismanagement. None of this was so. All appeared clean and orderly, rather upscale too. The area of the Jersey City waterfront, which once would have been part of the Horseshoe, in particular, seemed only like a beautiful place to live or work, or work from home. I later came to better understand that any continuity of place had in Jersey City between the old Horseshoe and its modern-day geographical counterpart was eviscerated, at least to some large extent, during the course of construction and opening of the Holland Tunnel in the 1920s.

This photograph looks across the Hudson River from the old Horseshoe area in Jersey City to New York City. (Photo by the author, July 10, 2010.)

My unrealistic expectations for finding a Horseshoe trapped in time aside, my visits to Jersey City provided me some of the best primary source material for my history project. Cynthia Harris, manager of the New Jersey room at the Jersey City Free Public Library, kindly found for me the first year of the *Observer*, the original physical newspapers, from the way, way back of the building. The *Observers* archived there run to the early part of 1893. After that, archived issues of the *Observer*, in original physical, micro, or web digitized form, were not found by me. I likely did not look hard enough or in the right place. In any case, I found the *Observer* again in microform, in some cases digitized too, beginning with issues from July 1904.

Naturally, new primary source material consistently emerges for study on the World Wide Web. The digital archives of the Hoboken Historical Museum proved extremely helpful to me right from the get-go.

Mary Fagan, who died in 1959, kept albums that were also a great source of material. Thank you to Karen Osar and Peter Rohn, two of Fagan's great-grandchildren, for making them available to me and for sharing what knowledge they had of Fagan with me.

Thank you also to the late Arthur L. Fagan Jr. (1929–2020), who sat down with me for an interview in 2011. He had some helpful recollections and left me feeling more personally connected to this project.

In 2012, I submitted a master's thesis, which I titled "Down Manly Blood & Anxious Iron-Up, Lawrence Fagan of Hoboken & The Horseshoe." My thesis was only about sixty pages long. It did, however, contain a good deal of original research on a significant, but almost entirely under-the-radar, historical figure. As well, as these theses go, I think mine probably addressed the historiography given the period in a manner more thorough and creative than most. That said, my thesis likely lacked sufficient coherence—chronological or thematic—to be assessed as anything near a finished product, master's thesis, or otherwise. I believe my thesis advisor, Dr. Andrew Darien, excused the roughness of my presentation because he saw some genuine significance in Fagan's story. Dr. Darien also appreciated the challenges and rewards in writing a biography, or micro-history, about a significant historical figure not previously written about at all. Dr. Darien also presumed—as then did I—that my studies would continue at a larger university in a PhD program, where a formalized telling of Fagan's story would emerge in the form of a dissertation. While that ended up being a path not followed, I'm hopeful he'll be pleased to see this book and know the Fagan project first nurtured under his watch wasn't abandoned. In any case, during my thesis defense, Dr. Darien posed the question: "Ultimately, do we believe that Fagan is useful because he is a representative or exceptional figure of this era?" To that end, I began a very long and slow path of self-directed work necessary to bring some form of satisfactory conclusion to my project.

Like almost all big questions teachers ask their students, Dr. Darien's has no simple answer. Readers may choose to consider his question and reach their own conclusion about

Fagan's representative or exceptional usefulness. This book's introduction represents my best efforts at wrestling with it.

There is another question, one likely more easily comprehensible and surely more familiar to teachers and students alike, which may also be useful in thinking about Fagan. That is, did the person make the place, or did the place make the person? With this in mind, it's interesting to note how Fagan's growth in age so closely mirrored Hoboken's growth in population. Hoboken had just over twenty thousand residents in 1870. Not much later, Fagan would have finished training at Blackmore's and moved from the Horseshoe to Hoboken, settling there permanently as a man in his very early twenties. By the time Fagan was almost thirty, he had married and started a family in Hoboken, where by 1880, the population had grown to just over thirty thousand. By the time Fagan was forty, he had fathered the Hamilton County Bill, making a name for himself in politics. Meanwhile, by 1890, Hoboken's population had grown to approximately forty-four thousand residents. A decade later, Fagan, just shy of his fiftieth birthday, was serving his fourth term as Mayor of Hoboken, where, by 1900, the population had grown to approximately fifty-nine thousand residents. Mayor Fagan, as noted earlier, argued the true number was much greater. In any case, by the time Fagan was nearly sixty and making himself an influential figure in the 1910 gubernatorial race, Hoboken had seen its population grow to just over seventy thousand residents. By the time Fagan died at age seventy, Hoboken's population, tallied the year prior to his death, had atrophied slightly to approximately sixty-eight thousand residents.[404]

The entrance of the United States into the First World War, indeed, marked the end of the incredible period of growth Hoboken had experienced. The waterfront takeover and other wartime measures had an outsized and very negative impact on the city. Hoboken, so heavily steeped in German cultural identity and having an economy so heavily tied to German shipping and commercial interests, bore the burden of the war more so, probably, than anywhere else in the United States. Prospects for Hoboken waging a postwar comeback were lessened by federal immigration quotas implemented in 1921. The measures placed a yearly limit of approximately 165,000 new immigrants allowed into the country. Public historian Christina A. Ziegler-McPherson, author of *Immigrants in Hoboken: One Way Ticket, 1845–1985* (2011), writes, "Immigration had been good business for Hoboken for nearly one hundred years, but now with the [quotas] there would be far fewer immigrants passing through and settling in the city in the postwar period."[405]

The end of Hoboken's immigration business boom continued to be evident in the decline in the number of people living there. The population fell to around 59,000 residents in 1930, shrank further to around 50,000 in 1940, and remained steady at around 50,000 in 1950. The population, however, further declined to approximately 45,000 by 1970.[406] Today, as of 2020, Hoboken has a population of slightly over 60,000.[407]

A similar post-war deceleration in population was not found in Jersey City. The number of residents there rose from approximately 270,000 in 1910 to approximately 300,000 in 1920. The population tallied at slightly over 315,000 residents in 1930, dipped back modestly to around 300,000 in 1940, and remained steady at around 300,000 in 1950. A measurable decline, however, was evident by 1970, with the population then recorded at approximately 260,000.[408] Today, as of 2020, Jersey City has a population of slightly over 290,000.[409]

This postwar divergence in relative strength between Jersey City and Hoboken presumably served as one of innumerable factors making more probable the rise of an unchallengeable Jersey City leader-boss in Hudson County. That is, Jersey City Mayor Frank Hague was presumably less likely to encounter significant challenges to his authority during his near three-decade-long reign as county leader-boss coming from Hoboken, its size and stature diminishing so significantly postwar.

In any case, Fagan was certainly helpful in preventing the principal leader-bosses of his time, Dennis McLaughlin and Robert Davis, from growing their powers to anywhere near the epic proportions associated with Hague. Fagan did a great deal of damage to McLaughlin's political career in 1893. Allied with the *New York World*, amongst others, Fagan's roasting of McLaughlin broke open a giant window of opportunity for Davis to take back, and take back all for himself, the job of county leader-boss. The push and pull in the ensuing years between Davis and Fagan over control of Hoboken has been covered sufficiently in the chapters of this book. Hence, I will remark further only that no Hudson County leader-boss could ever be entirely confident of any plans, where Hoboken was a part, happening entirely as planned while Fagan was there. It was all but impossible to predict when he might just show up at the lamppost, so to speak, with an energetic plan all of his own.

Speaking to my own task, closing this telling of the story of Lawrence Fagan, his time in Hoboken, the Horseshoe too, there are a couple of last matters of business worth a quick mention. Fagan Iron Works did not remain in business very much longer after the death of its founder. The business, the large industrial facility at Coles and Fourteenth Streets in the Horseshoe section of Jersey City, took on a rather sizeable mortgage in October of 1927. At a juncture not too long thereafter, the business defaulted on the loan, a sum of just over $230,000.00 remaining due. In August of 1931, the facility was sold under foreclosure, with the Hoboken Land and Improvement Company taking title to the plant. Early in 1937, the Hoboken Land and Improvement Company sold the property to the Continental Can Company.[410] The *Observer* fared much better. The newspaper, under management of Arthur. L. Fagan, my grandfather, continued to be a very steady and successful business through the end of the Second World War. Arthur Fagan's death at age forty-seven in 1946, however, brought great uncertainty to the future of the publication. Not long after his death, the Fagan and Seide families sold the *Observer* to the Newhouse media group. Newhouse, which had also acquired the *Jersey Journal*, merged the *Observer* into the *Journal*. The *Journal* officially ceased to exist, no longer published in any form, print or digital, in February of 2025.[411]

Thank you kindly for reading all or some portion of this book about Hoboken and the Horseshoe's Lawrence Fagan and the gilded, manly age of disorderly industrial Armageddon and progressive urban reform in which he lived—moving both top down and bottom up with a most peculiar energy. If you enjoyed this book, please consider leaving an online review. It's my understanding that doing so will assist in making the book discoverable to more readers, potentially allowing it to rise out of complete and total obscurity.

In researching and writing this history, I have interpreted all information, actions, and views to the best of my abilities. All mistakes, from ignorant or unconventional interpretation, to information suspiciously or conspicuously absent in presentation, or in lackadaisical or otherwise erroneous citation, are my own.

— **Barrington, Rhode Island**

July 2025

ACKNOWLEDGEMENTS

GREAT THANKS TO:

Claudia Rodríguez Arrieta—for loving me and letting me love her for all of space and time; for her editing and formatting assistance and belief in my ability to finish this project.

Connie Dealy—for her love and for being a terrific mother; for her diligent work and creativity in providing editing assistance during the early stages of this project.

John Dealy (1938–2014)—for his love and for being a terrific father.

Meg and Bob Ackerman—for their love and long support; for reading this manuscript in its final stage, subsequent suggestions and editing assistance.

Kizzy-Hutton (2011–2024) and **Ellie-Bear**— for their devotion and love; for giving structure, motivation, and fun.

Vincent Cannato—for being an inspiring history professor and author; for reading this manuscript in its final stage, and giving encouragement and advice on how to best finish it.

Gayle Fischer—for her skillful work on my thesis committee, and later providing resources and encouragement valuable to finishing this project.

Andrew Darien—for being a superb professor and thesis advisor.

Emerson Baker—for serving on my thesis committee.

The Jersey City Free Public Library; the NJ Room's Cynthia Harris and John Beekman; Jerry Lore, James Farina and all at Hoboken City Hall; Susan Brosnan at the Museum of the Knights of Columbus, New Haven; the Portsmouth (RI) Free Public Library; New Jersey Archives; Salem State University Library; UMass Boston Library; USC Library; Brandeis University Library; Hoboken Historical Museum; Englewood (NJ) Free Public Library; Phi Alpha Theta; Alex Kyrou; Alice Bianchi; Elizabeth Kenny; Chris Mauriello; Howard Chudacoff; Fagan, Dahlberg, Haverstick, Rohn, Osar, Talbot and Rodríguez Arrieta Families; Nancy Kreisler; Kate & Bill Miller; Deborah McCain; Bob Branham; Charles Nero; Tommaso Whitney; Kevin Bowe; Handsome Johnny; Max Bauer; Todd Sinclair; John Walters; Walter Kowalski; Mike Hollow; Rich Palladino; Jamie Jamitkowski; Randy Miller; Ben Lentini; Gary Cappetta; Tom Prichard; Tom Laughlin; Stevie Richards; Bill DeMott; Mike Crockett; Farman, Piandes, Palmer, Fortin, Anderson and Reynolds Families; Cil Bloomfield; Wyatt Courtney; Julie Kahn; Bill Emmet; Philip Hall; Steve Middleton; Dave Schragger; Ed Stehle; Regan Kerney; Lorin Maloney; Chris Kurhajetz; Vance Garry; Peter Schieffelin; Lainie Rutkow; Maggie Martinez; Ashley Martin; Kellie Tabor-Hann; Melanie McCormack; Anne-Marie & Charles Herndon; Carolyn Booth; Nick Walker; Jenna Graham; Preston Bassinder; Ariana Cabral; Alexander Carrellas; Ryan Fitzmorris; Ann Boyer, Erica Marsden, Robin Schroffel, Kimberly Martin for editing assistance; Spike Katz for recording assistance.

BIBLIOGRAPHY

Adamic, Louis. *Dynamite: The Story of Class Violence in America* [1934]. Oakland and Edinburgh: AK Press, 2008.

Anbinder, Tyler. *Five Points: The 19th-Century New York City Neighborhood That Invented Tap Dance, Stole Elections, and Be-came the World's Most Notorious Slum.* New York and London: Penguin Group, 2002.

Beatty, Jack. *The Rascal King: The Life and Times of James Michael Curley 1874–1958.* United States: Da Capo Press, 2000.

Bernstein, Iver. *The New York City Draft Riots: Their Significance for American Society in the Age of the Civil War.* New York and Oxford: Oxford University Press, 1990.

Cahill, Thomas. *How The Irish Saved Civilization: The Untold Story of Ireland's Heroic Role from the Fall of Rome to the Rise of Medieval Europe.* New York and London: Doubleday, 1995.

Cannato, Vincent J. *American Passage: The History of Ellis Island.* New York: HarperCollins, 2009.

———. *The Ungovernable City: John Lindsay and His Struggle to Save New York.* New York: Basic Books, 2001.

Caro, Robert A. *The Power Broker: Robert Moses and the Fall of New York.* New York: Vintage Books, 1975.

Cavanaugh, Jack. *Tunney: Boxing's Brainiest Champ and His Upset of The Great Jack Dempsey.* New York: Ballantine Books, 2006.

Chernow, Ron. *Alexander Hamilton.* New York: Penguin Books, 2004.

———. *Titan: The Life of John D. Rockefeller, Sr.* [1998]. New York: Vintage eBooks, 2004.

———. *The House of Morgan: An American Banking Dynasty and the Rise of Modern Finance* [1990]. New York: Grove Press, 2010.

Chudacoff, Howard P. *The Age of the Bachelor: Creating an American Subculture.* Princeton: Princeton University Press, 1999.

Chudacoff, Howard P., and Smith, Judith E. *The Evolution of American Urban Society* (Sixth Edition). Upper Saddle River, NJ: Pearson Prentice Hall, 2005.

Clark, Dennis. *The Irish in Philadelphia: Ten Generations of Urban Experience.* Philadelphia: Temple University Press, 1973.

Clymer, Jeffory A. *America's Culture of Terrorism: Violence, Capitalism, and the Written Word.* Chapel Hill and London: University of North Carolina Press, 2003.

Collins, Gail. *America's Women: 400 Years of Dolls, Drudges, Helpmates, and Heroines*. New York: HarperCollins, 2003.

Colrick, Patricia Florio. *Images of America: Hoboken*. Charleston and Chicago: Arcadia, 1999.

Connors, Richard J. *A Cycle of Power: The Career of Jersey City Mayor Frank Hague*. Metuchen: Scarecrow Press, Inc., 1971.

Cookson, Peter W., and Persell, Caroline Hodges. *Preparing For Power: America's Elite Boarding Schools*. United States: Perseus Books, 1985.

Czachowski, Joe. *Remembering Hoboken*. Nashville: Turner Publishing, 2010.

Darien, Andrew T. *Becoming New York's Finest: Race, Gender, and the Integration of the NYPD, 1935–1980*. New York: Palgrave MacMillan, 2013.

Dolan, Jay P. *The Irish Americans: A History*. New York and Berlin: Bloomsbury Press, 2008.

Douglas, George H. *The Golden Age of the Newspaper*. Westport and London: Greenwood Press, 1999.

Edwards, Rebecca. *New Spirits: Americans in the Gilded Age, 1865–1905*. New York: Oxford University Press, 2006.

Erie, Steven P. *Rainbow's End: Irish Americans and the Dilemmas of Urban Machine Politics, 1840–1985*. Berkeley and Los Angeles: University of California Press, 1988.

Fabian, Ann. *Card Sharps and Bucket Shops: Gambling in Nineteenth-Century America*. New York: Routledge, 1999.

Fischer, Gayle V. *Pantaloons and Power: A Nineteenth-Century Dress Reform in the United States*. Kent, OH: Kent State University Press, 2001.

Fleming, Thomas. *Mysteries of My Father: An Irish-American Memoir*. Hoboken: Wiley & Sons, 2005.

———. *New Jersey: A History*. New York: W.W. Norton & Company, 1977.

Flint, Anthony. *Wrestling with Moses: How Jane Jacobs Took on New York's Master Builder and Transformed the American City*. New York: Random House, 2011.

Foner, Eric. *Who Owns History? Rethinking the Past in a Changing World*. New York: Hill and Wang, 2002.

Foner, Eric, and Lisa McGirr, eds. *American History Now*. Philadelphia: Temple University Press, 2011.

Foster, Mark S. "The Early Career of Mayor Frank Hague." Master's thesis, University of Southern California, 1968.

Gabrielan, Randall. *Jersey City in Vintage Postcards*. Charleston and Chicago: Arcadia, 1999.

———. *Hoboken History & Architecture at a Glance*. Atglen, PA: Schiffer Publishing, 2010.

Gage, Beverly. *The Day Wall Street Exploded: A Story of America in Its First Age of Terror*. Oxford and New York: Oxford University Press, 2003.

Gilfoyle, Timothy J. *City of Eros: New York City, Prostitution, and the Commercialization of Sex, 1790–1920*. New York and London: W.W. Norton & Company, 1992.

Gladwell, Malcolm. *Outliers: The Story of Success*. New York: Hachette Book Group, 2008.

Glazier, Michael, ed. *The Encyclopedia of the Irish in America*. Notre Dame, IN: University of Notre Dame Press, 1999.

Goodwin, Doris Kearns. *The Bully Pulpit: Theodore Roosevelt, William Howard Taft, and the Golden Age of Journalism*. New York: Simon & Schuster, 2013.

Gordon, Michael A. *The Orange Riots: Irish Political Violence in New York City, 1870 and 1871*. Ithaca and London: Cornell University Press, 1993.

Gordon, Robert. "The Great Harbor Fire: The North German Lloyd Disaster of 1900." New Jersey History 100 (Fall/Winter 1982): 1–13.

Gorn, Elliot J. *The Manly Art: Bare-Knuckle Prize Fighting in America*. Ithaca: Cornell University Press, 1986.

Greeley, Andrew M. *The Irish Americans: The Rise to Money and Power*. New York: Warner Books, 1981.

Guglielmo, Jennifer. *Living The Revolution: Italian Women's Resistance and Radicalism in New York City, 1880–1945*. Chapel Hill: University of North Carolina Press, 2010.

Harris, Cynthia, and Yost, Leon. *Changing Jersey City: A History in Photographs*. Atglen, PA: Schiffer Publishing, 2009.

Hartog, Hendrik. *Public Property and Private Power: The Corporation of the City of New York in American Law, 1730–1870*. Ithaca and London: Cornell University Press, 1989.

Hartshorn, Peter. *I Have Seen The Future: A Life of Lincoln Steffens*. Berkeley: Counterpoint, 2011.

Heaney, John J. *The Bicentennial Comes To Hoboken*. Trenton: New Jersey Historical Society, 1976.

Hirst, David W. *Woodrow Wilson: Reform Governor—A Documentary Narrative*. New York: D. Van Nostrand Company, 1965.

Hofstadter, Richard. *The Age of Reform: From Bryan to F.D.R.* New York: Random House, 1955.

———. *The American Political Tradition: And The Men Who Made It* [1948]. New York: Vintage Books, 1989.

Hoganson, Kristin L. *Fighting for American Manhood: How Gender Politics Provoked The Spanish-American and Philippine-American Wars*. New Haven and London: Yale University Press, 1998.

Holli, Melvin G. *The American Mayor: The Best & the Worst Big-City Leaders*. University Park, PA: Pennsylvania State University Press, 1999.

———. *Reform in Detroit: Hazen S. Pingree and Urban Politics*. New York: Oxford University Press, 1969.

Ignatiev, Noel. *How the Irish Became White* [1995]. New York and London: Routledge Classics, 2009.

Ingham, John N., *The Iron Barons: A Social Analysis of an American Urban Elite 1874–1965*. Westport, CT: Greenwood Press, 1978.

Isenberg, Michael T. *John L. Sullivan and His America*. Urbana and Chicago: University of Illinois Press, 1994.

Jacobson, Matthew Frye. *Barbarian Virtues: The United States Encounters Foreign Peoples at Home and Abroad, 1876–1917*. New York: Hill and Wang, 2000.

———. *Whiteness of a Different Color: European Immigrants and the Alchemy of Race*. Cambridge and London: Harvard University Press, 1998.

Kaplan, Justin. *Lincoln Steffens: A Biography* [1974]. New York: Simon & Schuster, 2004.

Kazin, Michael. *A Godly Hero: The Life of William Jennings Bryan*. New York: Anchor Books, 2007.

Kelly, Kitty. *His Way: The Unauthorized Biography of Frank Sinatra*. New York: Bantam Books, 1986.

Kenny, Kevin. *Making Sense of the Molly Maguires*. New York and Oxford: Oxford University Press, 1998.

———. *The American Irish: A History*. New York: Pearson Education Inc., 2000.

———. *New Directions in Irish-American History*. Madison: University of Wisconsin Press, 2003.

Kerney, James. *The Political Education of Woodrow Wilson*. New York and London: Century Company, 1926.

Larson, Erik. *Thunderstruck*. New York: Three Rivers Press, 2006.

Leach, Bob. *Young Frank Hague and the Lucky Horseshoe*. Jersey City: Minuteman Press, 2009.

Lepore, Jill. "Historians Who Love Too Much: Reflections on Microhistory and Biography." The Journal of American History 88, no. 1 (June 2001): 129–144.

Link, Arthur S. *Wilson: The Road to the White House* [1947]. Princeton: Princeton University Press, 1965.

———. *The Papers of Woodrow Wilson Volume 21 – 1910*. Princeton: Princeton University Press, 1976.

Lord, Walter. *The Good Years: From 1900 to the First World War*. New York: Harper & Brothers, 1960.

Maddux, Brenda. "Introduction." In *The Dubliners,* by James Joyce [2005 Edition]. New York: Bantam Classics.

Maier, Thomas. *The Kennedys: America's Emerald Kings.* New York: Perseus Books, 2003.

Maynard, W. Barksdale. *Woodrow Wilson: Princeton to the Presidency.* New Haven and London: Yale University Press, 2008.

McGerr, Michael. *A Fierce Discontent: The Rise and Fall of the Progressive Movement in America,* 1870–1920. New York: Oxford University Press, 2005.

———. *The Decline of Popular Politics: The American North, 1865–1928.* New York: Oxford University Press, 1986.

McIntosh, Peggy. *On Privilege, Fraudulence, and Teaching as Learning.* New York: Routledge, 2020.

McKean, David Dayton. *The Boss: The Hague Machine in Action.* Boston: Houghton Mifflin, 1940.

Meagher, Timothy J. *The Columbia Guide to Irish American History.* New York: Columbia University Press, 2005.

Melosi, Martin V. *Garbage in the Cities: Refuse, Reform, and the Environment.* Pittsburgh: University of Pittsburgh Press, 2005.

Merchant, Carolyn. *American Environmental History.* New York: Columbia University Press, 2007.

Metz, Holly. City Animals: *A History of Our Changing Relationship with Other Hoboken Residents.* Hoboken: Hoboken Historical Museum Publications, 2004.

Miller, Kirby A. *Emigrants and Exiles: Ireland and the Irish Exodus to North America.* New York: Oxford University Press, 1985.

Miller, Zane L. Boss Cox's Cincinnati: *Urban Politics in the Progressive Era* [1968]. Columbus: Ohio State University Press, 2000.

Morris, Edmund. *The Rise of Theodore Roosevelt* [1979]. New York: Random House, 2010.

Murphy, Kevin P. *Political Manhood: Red Bloods, Mollycoddles, & the Politics of Progressive Era Reform.* New York: Columbia University Press, 2008.

Noble, Ransom. *New Jersey Progressivism before Wilson.* Princeton: Princeton University Press, 1946.

Okrent, Daniel. *Last Call: The Rise and Fall of Prohibition.* New York: Scribner, 2010.

Painter, Nell Irvin. *Standing at Armageddon: The United States, 1877–1919* [1987]. New York and London: W.W. Norton & Company, 2008.

———. *The History of White People.* New York and London: W.W. Norton & Company, 2010.

Peiss, Kathy. *Cheap Amusements: Working Women and Leisure in Turn-of-the Century New York.* Philadelphia: Temple University Press, 1986.

Pestritto, Ronald, and Atto, William, eds. *American Progressivism: A Reader*. New York: Rowman & Littlefield, 2008.

Phillips, Michael. *White Metropolis: Race, Ethnicity, and Religion in Dallas, 1841–2001*. Austin: University of Texas Press, 2006.

Pollan, Michael. *The Botany of Desire: A Plant's-Eye View of The World*. New York: Random House, 2002.

Procter, Ben. *William Randolph Hearst: The Later Years, 1911–1951*. New York: Oxford University Press, 2007.

Procter, Mary, and Matuszecki, Bill. *Gritty Cities: A Second Look At: Allentown; Bethlehem; Bridgeport; Hoboken; Lancaster; Norwich; Paterson; Reading; Trenton; Troy; Waterbury; Wilmington*. Philadelphia: Temple University Press, 1978.

Quinn, Dermott. *The Irish in New Jersey: Four Centuries of American Life*. New Brunswick and London: Rutgers University Press, 2006.

Rafferty, Matthew Taylor. "Political Ethics and Public Style in the Early Career of Jersey City's Frank Hague." New Jersey History 124, no. 1 (2009): 29–56. http://njh.libraries.rutgers.edu/index.php/njh/index.

Rapport, George C. *The Statesman and the Boss. New York and Washington*: Vantage Press, 1961.

Rasenberger, Jim. America 1908: *The Dawn of Flight, the Race to the Pole, the Invention of the Model T, And The Making of a Modern Nation*. New York: Scribner, 2007.

Rodgers, Daniel T. *Atlantic Crossings: Social Politics in a Progressive Age*. Cambridge and London: Harvard University Press, 1998.

———. *Contested Truths: Keywords In American Politics Since Independence*. New York: Basic Books, 1987.

———. "In Search of Progressivism." *Reviews in American History* 10, no. 4 (December 1982): 113–132.

Ross, Steven J. *Workers on the Edge: Work, Leisure, and Politics in Industrializing Cincinnati, 1788–1890*. New York: Columbia University Press, 1985.

Russell, Thaddeus. *A Renegade History of the United States*. New York: Free Press, 2010.

Sandweiss, Martha A. *Passing Strange: A Gilded Age Tale of Love and Deception across the Color Line*. New York: Penguin Books, 2009.

Schudson, Michael. *Discovering the News: A Social History of American Newspapers. United States*: Perseus Books, 1978.

Shannon, William V. *The American Irish: A Political and Social Portrait*. New York: MacMillan, 1964.

Silcox, Harry C. *Philadelphia Politics from the Bottom Up: The Life of Irishman William McMullen, 1824–1901*. Philadelphia: Balch Institute Press, 1989.

Stahlkuppe, Joe. *Great Danes*. Hauppauge, NY: Barron's Educational Series, 2002.

Starr, Paul. *The Creation of the Media: Political Origins of Modern Communications*. New York: Perseus Books, 2004.

Steinberg, Jonathan. *Bismarck: A Life*. New York: Oxford University Press, 2011.

Tobin, Eugene Marc. "Mark Fagan and the Politics of Urban Reform, Jersey City 1900–1917." Ph.D. diss., Brandeis University, 1972.

Treese, Lorett. *Railroads of New Jersey: Fragments of the Past in the Garden State Landscape*. Mechanicsburg, PA: Stackpole Books, 2006.

Tuchman, Barbara W. *Practicing History*. New York: Random House, Inc., 1981.

Tunney, Jay R. *The Prizefighter and the Playwright: Gene Tunney and Bernard Shaw*. Ontario: Firefly Books, 2010.

Von Drehle, David. *Triangle: The Fire That Changed America*. New York: Grove Press, 2003.

Wiebe, Robert H. *The Search for Order, 1877–1920*. New York: Hill and Wang, 1967.

Willrich, Michael. *Pox: An American History*. New York: Penguin Press, 2011.

Zacks, Richard. *Island of Vice: Theodore Roosevelt's Doomed Quest To Clean Up Sin-Loving New York*. New York: Random House, 2012.

Ziegler-McPherson, Christina A. *Immigrants in Hoboken: One-Way Ticket, 1845–1985*. Charleston: The History Press, 2011.

Zinn, Howard. *A People's History of the United States 1942–Present* [1980]. New York: HarperCollins, 1999.

NOTES

ABBREVIATIONS USED IN NOTES

Ancs.cf	Ancestry.com
FA	Fagan album*
OBS	The Observer**
JJ	The Jersey Journal
JCN	The Jersey City News
NYDT	The New York Daily Tribune
NYS	The New York Sun
NYT	The New York Times
NYW	The New York World
TET	The Trenton Evening Times
WWP	Woodrow Wilson papers**

*Collection of letters, photographs, and newspaper clippings which belonged to Mary A. [Foley] Fagan.

**Fagan's newspaper, first known as *The Observer*; subsequently as *The Observer of Hudson County*, *The Hoboken Observer*, *The Hudson Observer*, and *The Jersey Observer*.

***Arthur S. Link, ed., *The Papers of Woodrow Wilson Volume 21–1910* (Princeton: Princeton University Press, 1976).

Introduction

[1] "Fagan Family Closes House on Hudson Street, Hoboken—Property at Tenth Street to be Site for Elevator Apartment," {newspaper clipping}, FA, likely from late September 1923. For the house, see also "Fagan Mansion in Hoboken Sold; To Be Razed for Big Apartment—Ten-Story Million Dollar Building Will Be Reared on Site of Famous House—Fagan Home for Years Taken Over By Syndicate," *Hudson Dispatch*, September 21, 1923.

[2] Charles F. Holden, *Holden's Book on Birds: Little Dewdrops of Celestial Melody* (New York: Charles Reiche & Brother, 1873), page 3 in advertisement section. For the Reiche family's animal importing, see also "An Elephant for

the City: A Proposition to Buy the Largest One in America For Central Park," *NYT*, March 20, 1882; "Selling A Big Elephant: A Curious Auction Sale at Hoboken Yesterday Afternoon," *NYT*, March 26, 1882; "Henry Reiche Dead," *NYT*, June 17, 1887. The *Hudson Dispatch*, September 21, 1923, identifies the house's first owner as the exotic animal importer "Reichert." The same moniker is also ascribed to a figure who performed experiments on snake venom and lizard saliva; see "Scientific Gossip," *NYT*, July 1, 1883 and August 26, 1883.

[3] Census data shows Fagan in Jersey City, occupation listed as "white-smith," residing in dwelling 511, Ward 2; see *Ancs.cf*: United States Federal Census, 1870. References to Fagan at Blackmore's appear in state government profiles of William D. Daly. For example, see T.F. Fitzgerald, comp., ed., *Manual of the Legislature of New Jersey*, 121st Session, 1897 (Trenton, NJ: 1897), 239. For Daly, see Part Five. The address, 60 R.R. Ave., Jersey City, under the heading "Iron Founder, Forges, &c.," is given for James L. Blackmore in *A New Jersey State Business Directory for 1866* (New York: Talbott and Blood, 1866), 150.

[4] Eric Foner, *Who Owns History? Rethinking the Past in a Changing World* (New York: Hill & Wang, 2002), xvi. For "lifeblood" as a metaphor for manuscript reviewing, see Barbara Young Welke, "The Art of Manuscript Reviewing: 10 Guidelines from Peggy Pascoe, a Master of the Art," *Perspectives on History* (September 2011): 38–41. "Beyond acknowledgements in books and articles," notes Welke, "[historians] have few professional outlets to recognize the largely invisible work that is the lifeblood of our profession — manuscript reviewing" (38).

[5] A helpful extended obituary of Lawrence Fagan was published in 1921: American Historical Society, ed., pub., *American Biography: A New Cyclopedia*, Vol. 9 (New York: 1921), 293–295. Fagan is mentioned once in Walter Lord's *The Good Years: From 1900 to the First World War* (New York: Harper & Brothers, 1960), 5. Also, Fagan is mentioned once in Robert Gordon's "The Great Harbor Fire: The North German Lloyd Disaster of 1900," *New Jersey History* 100, no. 3–4 (1982): 1–13 (11). Lawrence Fagan is identified by name in one footnote in Eugene Tobin's "Mark Fagan and the Politics of Urban Reform, Jersey City 1900–1917" (Ph.D. diss., Brandeis University, 1972), 365. No evidence has been found to suggest that Jersey City Mayor Mark Fagan and Lawrence Fagan were related; the Irish surname "Fagan" was far more common in America circa 1877–1917 than it is today. By name, Lawrence Fagan is also identified in two footnotes in *WWP*, 23, 27.

[6] Fagan's newspaper was first known as *The Observer*; subsequent names included *Observer of Hudson County*, *Hoboken Observer*, *Hudson Observer*, and *Jersey Observer*.

[7] Joseph P. Tumulty, *Woodrow Wilson As I Know Him* (Garden City, NY: Doubleday, 1921), 19.

[8] "Ex-Mayor Fagan Dead," *Wall Street Journal*, May 10, 1921.

[9] Jill Lepore, "Historians Who Love Too Much: Reflections on Microhistory and Biography," the *Journal of American History* 88, no. 1 (June 2001): 129–144 (133).

[10] Barbara W. Tuchman, *Practicing History* (New York: Random House, 1981), 65.

[11] For broad perspectives on the period 1877–1917, its nomenclature, and historiography, see Daniel T. Rodgers, "In Search of Progressivism," *Reviews in American History* 10, no. 4 (December 1982): 113–132; Glenda Elizabeth Gilmore, *Who Were the Progressives?* (Boston and New York: Bedford/St. Martin's, 2002); Robert D. Johnston, "The Possibilities of Politics: Democracy in America, 1877–1917," in Eric Foner and Lisa McGirr, eds., American Historical Association, *American History Now* (Philadelphia: Temple University Press, 2011), 96–124. For broader histories of the period, see Richard Hofstadter, *The Age of Reform: From Bryan to F.D.R.* (New York: Random House, 1955); Robert H. Wiebe, *The Search for Order, 1877–1920* (New York: Hill and Wang, 1967); Nell Irvin Painter, *Standing at Armageddon: A Grassroots History of the Progressive Era* (1987), 2008 ed. (New York: W.W. Norton & Company); *Manliness & Civilization: A Cultural History of Gender and Race in the United States, 1880–1917* (Chicago and London: University of Chicago Press, 1995); Michael McGerr, *A Fierce Discontent: The Rise and Fall of the Progressive Movement in America, 1870–1920* (New York: Oxford University Press, 2003); Jackson Lears, *Rebirth of a Nation: The Making of America, 1877–1920* (New York: HarperCollins, 2009).

[12] "Accident on a Car Elevator: Horses Back a Wagon Off—The Machinery Stopped in the Nick of Time," *NYS*, May 12, 1897.

[13] Mary Proctor and Bill Matuszecki, *Gritty Cities: A Second Look At: Allentown; Bethlehem; Bridgeport; Hoboken; Lancaster; Norwich; Paterson; Reading; Trenton; Troy; Waterbury; Wilmington* (Philadelphia: Temple University Press, 1978), 4, 91.

[14] "Morgue Keepers Quarrel," *NYS*, July 3, 1900. On the dispute, see also "Strife over the Corpses," *NYDT*, July 2, 1900.

[15] For helpful works on the Horseshoe, see Bob Leach, *Young Frank Hague and the Lucky Horseshoe: How a Neighborhood Forged a Political Boss* (Jersey City: Minuteman Press, 2009); William Edgar Sackett, *Modern Battles of Trenton: Being a History of New Jersey's Politics and Legislation from the Year 1868 to the Year 1894* (Trenton, NJ: John L. Murphy, 1895), 24–48; Dayton David McKean, *The Boss: The Hague Machine in Action* (Boston: Houghton Mifflin, 1940), 1–45; Mark S. Foster, "The Early Career of Mayor Frank Hague" (master's thesis, University of Southern California, 1968); Richard J.

Connors, *A Cycle of Power: The Career of Jersey City Mayor Frank Hague* (Metuchen, NJ: Scarecrow Press, 1971); Thomas Fleming, *Mysteries of My Father: An Irish American Memoir* (Hoboken: Wiley & Sons, 2005); Matthew Taylor Raffety, "Political Ethics and Public Style in the Early Career of Jersey City's Frank Hague," *New Jersey History* 124, no. 1 (2009): 29–56, http://njh.libraries.rutgers.edu/index.php/njh/issue/archive.

[16] "Horseshoe Taxpayers Hold an Angry Mass Meeting on the Sewer Nuisance—Threats Made to Arise in the Spirit of '76 and Plug Up the Offending Drain—Many a Child Made Ill, Principal Mackey Says," *OBS*, July 19, 1904; "Will Cost $150,000 to Relieve Horseshoe," *OBS*, July 20, 1904. For insights on the period 1877–1917, as urban environmental history, see Carolyn Merchant, *American Environmental History* (New York: Columbia University Press, 2007), 110–128; Martin Melosi, *Garbage in the Cities: Refuse, Reform, and the Environment* (Pittsburgh: University of Pittsburgh Press, 2005), 1–189; Sarah T. Phillips, "Environmental History," in Foner and McGirr, *American History Now*, 285–286, 298–300, 303–304.

[17] Leach, *Young Frank Hague*, 6.

[18] Ibid.

[19] For perspectives on bottom up and top down see Foner, *Who Owns History?*, ix–xix; Kevin Kenny, ed., auth., "General Introduction," *New Directions in Irish-American History* (Madison, WS: University of Wisconsin Press, 2003), 1–10; Thaddeus Russell, *A Renegade History of the United States* (New York: Free Press, 2010), ix–xiii; Lawrence Glickman, "The 'Cultural Turn,'" in Foner and McGirr, *American History Now*, 221–241.

[20] Some additional works, which might be cautiously characterized as top-down or bottom-up history in an American historiography framework, were helpful in researching and providing context for this project. [Top Down]: James Kerney, *The Political Education of Woodrow Wilson* (New York and London: Century Company, 1926); Connors, *A Cycle of Power* (1971); John Ingham, *The Iron Barons: A Social Analysis of an American Urban Elite, 1874–1965* (1978); Ron Chernow, *Titan: The Life of John D. Rockefeller, Sr.* [1998] (New York: Vintage ebooks, 2004). [Bottom-Up]: Dennis Clark, *The Irish in Philadelphia: Ten Generations of Urban Experience* (Philadelphia: Temple University Press, 1973); Howard Zinn, "Robber Barons and Rebels," in *A People's History of the United States: 1492–Present* [1980] (New York: HarperCollins, 1999); Kerby A. Miller, *Emigrants and Exiles: Ireland and the Irish Exodus to North America* (New York: Oxford University Press, 1985); Kathy Peiss, *Cheap Amusements: Working Women and Leisure in Turn-of-the-Century New York* (Philadelphia: Temple University Press, 1986); Harry C. Silcox, *Philadelphia Politics from the Bottom Up: The Life of Irishman William McMullen, 1824–1901* (Philadelphia: Balch Institute Press, 1989).

[21] Kevin Kenny, "Labor and Organizations," in J.J. Lee and Marion Casey, eds., *Making the Irish American: History and Heritage of the Irish in the United States* (New York: New York University Press, 2006), 354–363. See also Timothy Meagher, *The Columbia Guide to Irish American History* (New York: Columbia University Press, 2005), 95–104.

[22] William V. Shannon, *The American Irish: A Political and Social Portrait* (New York: MacMillan, 1964), 86. Also, on the overall lack of Irish Catholic representation in the category of "urban iron baron," see charts and tables throughout John N. Ingham, *The Iron Barons: A Social Analysis of an American Urban Elite, 1874–1965* (Westport, CT and London: Greenwood Press, 1978).

[23] "New Club House for Independents: Knights of Columbus Club Will Probably Be Leased by Them—More Assurances That Fagan Will Make a Run," *JJ*, June 5, 1903.

[24] Tumulty, *Woodrow Wilson*, 1–9.

[25] Ibid., 3.

[26] Ibid.

[27] H.E. Alexander to Wilson: Trenton, NJ, July 23, 1910, *WWP*, 22–23.

[28] On "manly" themes, see Elliot Gorn, *The Manly Art: Bare-Knuckle Prize Fighting in America* (Ithaca: Cornell University Press, 1986); Michael Isenberg, *John L. Sullivan and His America* (Chicago: University of Illinois Press, 1988); George Chauncey, *Gay New York: Gender, Urban Culture, and the Making of the Gay Male World 1890–1940* (New York: Basic Books, 1994).

[29] See Gail Bederman, *Manliness & Civilization: A Cultural History of Gender and Race in the United States, 1880–1917* (Chicago and London: University of Chicago Press, 1995), especially 77–120, 170–215; Kristin L. Hoganson, *Fighting for American Manhood: How Gender Politics Provoked the Spanish-American and Philippine-American Wars* (New Haven and London: Yale University Press, 1998), especially 15–42; see also Jeffry A. Clymer, *America's Culture of Terrorism: Violence, Capitalism, and the Written Word* (Chapel Hill: University of North Carolina Press, 2003), 69–99, 134–170. On male anxieties and immigration policy, see Vincent J. Cannato, *American Passage: The History of Ellis Island* (New York: HarperCollins, 2009), 95–106.

[30] See Kevin P. Murphy, *Political Manhood: Red Bloods, Mollycoddles, & the Politics of Progressive Era Reform* (New York: Columbia University Press, 2008), especially 38–67; see also Raffety, "Political Ethics and Public Style," (2009).

[31] "Mayor Fagan Thanked: His Administration Indorsed By the Citizens' Association," *NYW*, September 23, 1893.

[32] "$47 For Punching a Delegate: Former Mayor of Hoboken For Punishing a Strike Agitator," *NYS*, August 19, 1903.

[33] David Kennedy, as quoted in Daniel T. Rodgers, *In Search of Progressivism*, 114.

[34] For discussion of this historiography, see Mark S. Foster's "The Early Career of Mayor Frank Hague" (1968), and "Frank Hague of Jersey City: The 'Boss' as Reformer," *New Jersey History* 86, no. 2 (1968): 106–117; see also Melvin G. Holli, "The Reformer as Machine Politician," in Bruce M. Stave, ed., *Urban Bosses, Machines, and Progressive Reformers* (Lexington, MA: D.C. Heath and Company, 1972), 99–102; David R. Colburn and George E. Pozetta, "Bosses and Machines: Changing Interpretations in American History," *The History Teacher* 9, no. 3 (May 1976): 451–473.

[35] Gilmore, *Who Were The Progressives?*, 18.

[36] Ronald J. Pestritto and William J. Atto, eds., *American Progressivism: A Reader* (New York: Rowman & Littlefield, 2008), 2.

Part 1: 1851–1887

[37] Miller, *Emigrants and Exiles*, 280–344; Jay P. Dolan, *The Irish Americans: A History* (New York: Bloomsbury Press, 2008), 67; Michael Pollan, *The Botany of Desire: A Plant's-Eye View of The World* (New York: Random House, 2002), 205–206.

[38] Irish emigrant, as quoted in Miller, *Emigrants and Exiles*, 281.

[39] Miller, *Emigrants and Exiles*, 346–353; Kenny, *New Directions*, 7.

[40] Frederick Douglass, as quoted in Nell Irvin Painter, *The History of White People* (New York: W.W. Norton, 2010), Kindle Electronic Edition: Chapter 9, loc. 2418–2424. On Douglass in Ireland, see also Fionnghuala Sweeney, "'The Republic of Letters:' Frederick Douglass, Ireland, and the Irish Narratives," in Kenny, *New Directions*, 122–139.

[41] Thomas Carlyle, as quoted in Painter, *History of White People*, Chapter 9, loc. 2271–2282.

[42] Dolan, *Irish Americans*, 37–38, 76–78.

[43] The birth date January 1, 1851, appears in contemporaneous reference sources, earliest in T.F. Fitzgerald, comp., ed., *Manual of the Legislature of New Jersey*, 113th Session, 1889 (Trenton, NJ: 1889), 218. Fagan's age is recorded in census data; see *Ancs.cf*: United States Federal Census, 1860, 1870, 1880, 1900, 1910. Lawrence Fagan's great-grandson, Peter Rohn, recalled being told that Fagan landed in Maine; however, Rohn was uncertain whether this memory referred to his arrival as an infant or a teenager (conversations with the author, May 2010). In an 1858–1859 Portland city directory, a blacksmith named James Fagan (a moulder), N.K. Fagan, and Thomas Fagan (a steam engineer) are listed at 8 York Street. See S.B. Beckett, *The Portland Directory and Reference Book for 1858–9* (Portland: Brown Thurston, 1858), 78. Evidence suggesting Fagan's 1852 arrival occurred in Pennsylvania—likely through Philadelphia—includes a document dated October 8, 1852, in Allegheny County, PA: a petition to naturalize a Lawrence Fagan, submitted

on his behalf by Daniel Fagan; see *Ancs.cf: Selected U.S. Naturalization Records – Original Documents, 1790–1974.*

[44] On the popularity of Pennsylvania for Irish immigrants, see Clark, *Irish in Philadelphia,* 29–34.

[45] Dolan, *Irish Americans,* 37–39; Dennis Clark, *Irish in Philadelphia,* 61–73.

[46] *Documents Relating to the Manufacture of Iron in Pennsylvania,* published on behalf of the Convention of Iron Masters (Philadelphia: The General Committee, 1850), 14–16.

[47] Ibid., 26.

[48] See *Ancs.cf:* 1860 United States Federal Census.

[49] On New York City tenements, see James D. McCabe, *Lights and Shadows of New York Life; or, the Sights and Sensations of the Great City* (Philadelphia: National Publishing Company, 1872), Kindle Electronic Edition: Chapter 60, loc. 9396–9527; Eric Homberger, *The Historical Atlas of New York City: A Visual Celebration of 400 Years of New York City's History* (1994), revised and updated ed. (New York: Holt Paperbacks, 2005), 84–85; Tyler Anbinder, *Five Points: The 19th-Century New York City Neighborhood That Invented Tap Dance, Stole Elections, and Became the World's Most Notorious Slum* (New York: Penguin Group, 2001), 72–80; Timothy J. Gilfoyle, *City of Eros: New York City, Prostitution, and the Commercialization of Sex* (New York: W.W. Norton & Company, 1992), 35–51, 329; Russell Shorto, foreword to Herbert Asbury's *The Gangs of New York: An Informal History of the Underworld* (1928), 2008 ed. (New York: Vintage Books), xi–xv.

[50] In addition to *Lights and Shadows of New York Life,* McCabe also wrote *The Life and Campaigns of General Robert E. Lee* (1866) and *Paris by Sunlight and Gaslight* (1869).

[51] McCabe, *Lights and Shadows of New York Life,* Chapter 60, loc. 9505–9511.

[52] See *Ancs.cf:* 1860 United States Federal Census.

[53] For likely curriculum, see McCabe, *Lights and Shadows,* Chapter 56, loc. 9217–9226.

[54] Memo to Hoboken City Council, unspecified date in 1896. Lawrence Fagan, as quoted in "Visitor from Another Time," *Hoboken Reporter,* January 24, 1993.

[55] On the Draft Riots, see Iver Bernstein, *The New York City Draft Riots: Their Significance for American Society and Politics in the Age of the Civil War* (New York and Oxford: Oxford University Press, 1990).

[56] See *Ancs.cf:* 1861 England Census.

[57] T. Webster and Mrs. Parkes, *The American Family Encyclopedia of Useful Knowledge* (New York: J.C. Derby, 1856), 65.

[58] See *Ancs.cf:* 1861 England Census.

[59] Meagher, *Columbia Guide to Irish American History,* 75.

[60] In 1852, the address of 18 Great Brunswick Street is given for William Morrissey, "Manufacturer and Housesmith," in *Thom's Irish Almanac* (Dublin: 1852), 759. In 1857, the same address appears in an advertisement for James Fagan & Sons, "Housesmiths and Bellhangers," in *Thom's Irish Almanac* (Dublin: 1857), 58. On Lawrence's relation to James Fagan, see the 18 Great Brunswick Street address noted in John Fagan [letter] to "Cousin" Lawrence Fagan, Dublin, Ireland, March 14, 1905, in *FA*.

[61] Webster and Parkes, *American Family Encyclopedia*, 65.

[62] On the uncertain, unfavorable circumstances, see Miller, *Emigrants and Exiles*, 367–368; see also George F. Shaw, "On the Use and Abuse of Apprenticeship" [Read, March 18, 1861], *Journal of the Statistical and Social Inquiry Society of Ireland*, Vol. III, no. XVIII–XXV (January 1861–December 1863): 93–100.

[63] For likely courses of study, see Henry Kiddle and Alexander J. Schem, eds., *The Cyclopedia of Education: A Dictionary of Information for the Use of Teachers, School Officers, Parents and Others*, 3rd ed. (New York: E. Steiger & Co., 1883), 649; McCabe, *Lights and Shadows of New York Life*, Chapter 56, loc. 9221–9231.

[64] On Tweed's 1870 consolidation of power and related outcomes, see McCabe, *Lights and Shadows of New York Life*, Chapter 56, loc. 9193–9202; see also M.R. Werner, *Tammany Hall* (1928), 1968 ed. (New York: Greenwood Press), 171–275.

[65] On the Orange Riots, see Michael A. Gordon, *The Orange Riots: Irish Political Violence in New York City, 1870 and 1871* (Ithaca: Cornell University Press, 1993).

[66] Hofstadter, *The Age of Reform*, 174.

[67] Statistics from the University of Virginia Geospatial and Statistical Data Center: http://mapserver.lib.virginia.edu; and the Population Division of the U.S. Census Bureau: http://www.census.gov/population/www/documentation/twps0027/twps0027.html [both accessed July 25, 2010]. Helpful and detailed analysis of Hoboken census data can also be found in Christina A. Ziegler-McPherson, *Immigrants in Hoboken: One Way Ticket, 1845–1985* (Charleston and London: History Press, 2011).

[68] Howard P. Chudacoff and Judith E. Smith, *The Evolution of American Urban Society*, 6th ed. (Upper Saddle River, NJ: Pearson, 2005), 152. Also, for an overview of these themes in New Jersey, see Thomas Fleming, *New Jersey: A History* (New York: W.W. Norton & Company, 1977), 126–145.

[69] Miller, *Emigrants and Exiles*, 356; Dolan, *Irish Americans*, 78–79.

[70] Robert Rieser and Robert R. Stinson, eds., *Hudson County Today: Its History, People, Trades, Commerce, Institutions and Industry* (Union, NJ: Hudson Dispatch, 1914), 25.

71 See "History" of Stevens Institute of Technology: http://www.stevens.edu/sit/about/history.cfm.

72 For an account of Hoboken's past as a destination for recreation, see Winfield, Charles H., *Hopoghan Hackingh: Hoboken, a Pleasure Resort for Old New York* (New York: Caxton Press, 1895).

73 Ziegler-McPherson, *Immigrants in Hoboken*, 45; Winfield, *Hopoghan Hackingh*, 72–76; Rieser and Stinson, *Hudson County Today*, 22–26.

74 Kevin Kenny, *The American Irish: A History* (New York: Pearson Education Inc., 2000), 78–79.

75 On the clash between Protestant temperance and German custom, see Morris, *Rise of Theodore Roosevelt*, 513, 526–527; Richard Zacks, *Island of Vice: Theodore Roosevelt's Doomed Conquest To Clean Up Sin-Loving New York* (New York: Doubleday, 2012), 118–120, 167–174; Ziegler-McPherson, *Immigrants in Hoboken*, 45, 53–54; Kenny, *American Irish*, 79.

76 Ziegler-McPherson, *Immigrants in Hoboken*, 32, 44–45.

77 On animals to Hoboken, see "Selling A Big Elephant: A Curious Auction Sale at Hoboken Yesterday Afternoon," *NYT*, March 26, 1882; "Animals for Hagenbeck's—A Large Consignment from Hamburg on the Scandia," *NYT*, September 2, 1894; *Hudson Dispatch*, September 21, 1923; Holly Metz, *City Animals: A History of Our Changing Relationship with Other Hoboken Residents* (Hoboken: A Hoboken Historical Museum Publication, 2004).

78 "Ugly but Costly Fatima—The Docile Hippopotamus Who Is Now at Central Park," *NYT*, October 17, 1886.

79 Hofstadter, *Age of Reform*, 188.

80 On identity politics and the "invisible knapsack," see Peggy McIntosh, *On Privilege, Fraudulence, and Teaching as Learning* (New York: Routledge, 2020).

81 Martha A. Sandweiss, *Passing Strange: A Gilded Age Tale of Love and Deception Across the Color Line* (New York: Penguin Books, 2009), 185, 340.

82 American Historical Society, *American Biography*, 293–295.

83 International Publishing Company, comp., pub., *A Quarter Century's Progress of New Jersey's Leading Manufacturing Centres* (New York: 1887), 167.

84 Ibid.

85 Ibid.

Part 2: 1888–1893

86 For background on the Second National Bank, see "The Claims of Hoboken as an Ideal Town for Factory Sites and of West Hoboken as a Residence Station," *NYDT*, December 28, 1902; "Hoboken Illustrated," *New York Dawn Special Edition*, January 1909; Rieser and Stinson, *Hudson County Today*, 26–

27; John J. Heaney, *The Bicentennial Comes to Hoboken* (Trenton: New Jersey Historical Society, 1976), 75.

[87] "Hudson County Politics: Colored Voters Parade—Lawrence Fagan for Assemblyman," *NYS*, October 9, 1888.

[88] For Jersey City's African-American residents, see Tobin, "Mark Fagan," (6–7). For Hoboken's African-American residents, see Ziegler-McPherson, *Immigrants in Hoboken*, 35.

[89] *NYS*, October 9, 1888.

[90] Volunteer firefighting as having been the impetus for Fagan's entry into politics is noted in obituary, "Ex-Mayor Fagan Dies at 70: Hoboken Politician and Iron Manufacturer Began Career as Blacksmith," *NYT*, May 10, 1921.

[91] On volunteer firefighting and urban politics, see Silcox, *Philadelphia Politics from the Bottom Up*, 20–23, 37–38, 65–70.

[92] See T.F. Fitzgerald, comp., ed., *Manual of the Legislature of New Jersey*, 115th Session, 1891 (Trenton, NJ: 1891), 213.

[93] *NYS*, October 9, 1888.

[94] For background on Letts, see T.F. Fitzgerald, comp., ed., *Manual of the Legislature of New Jersey*, 112th Session, 1888 (Trenton, NJ: 1888), 210.

[95] Fagan received 2,110 votes; Letts received 1,372 votes; see figures in "New Jersey: She Has Stood Nobly by the Democratic Nominees—The Next Legislature Will Be Democratic," *NYW*, November 7, 1888.

[96] On the fire and new build, see Fitzgerald, *Manual of the Legislature of New Jersey*, 112th Session, 1888, 5–6.

[97] On Fagan's Hamilton County Bill, see "Another Deadlock Stops Work," *New Brunswick Daily News*, March 27, 1889; "The New County of Hamilton," *TET*, April 19, 1889; "Adjourned Sine Die: 113TH Legislature Is No Longer In Existence," *TET*, April 20, 1889; "New-Jersey's Statesman—A Forecast of the Legislature's Work," *NYT*, January 13, 1890; "New City in New Jersey: Plan Is To Consolidate Hoboken and North Hudson Townships," *NYDT*, January 4, 1901.

[98] Ron Chernow, *Alexander Hamilton* (New York: Penguin Books, 2004), 652.

[99] Hendrik Hartog, *Public Property and Private Power: The Corporation of the City of New York in American Law, 1730–1870* (Ithaca and London: Cornell University Press, 1989), 115–117.

[100] Rieser and Stinson, *Hudson County Today*, 3.

[101] Lord, *The Good Years*, 5–6. Lord also wrote on the sinking of the Titanic, *A Night to Remember* (1955), and *Day of Infamy: The Bombing of Pearl Harbor* (1957).

[102] "The County Divide: Reasons Which Will Prompt Various People to Vote for the Hamilton Scheme," *JCN*, April 4, 1889.

[103] "What Is Caught With the Camera Around the Statehouse," *TET*, March 20, 1889; *TET*, April 20, 1889; "Hamilton County in the Soup," *JCN*, April 9, 1889. For discord between the assemblymen, see "House Committees;" "Joint Committees," *TET*, January 15, 1889.

[104] Fagan got 2,597 votes; Republican Mr. Hudlick got 1,471 votes; third-party progressive candidate Mr. Boldover got 38 votes. See figures in T.F. Fitzgerald, comp., ed., *Manual of the Legislature of New Jersey*, 114th Session, 1890 (Trenton, NJ: 1890), 228.

[105] See description of Fagan's political interests in "A Very Quiet Wedding— Assemblyman Fagan and Miss Mamie [sic] A. Foley Are Married," {newspaper clipping}, *FA*, 1891.

[106] See *Ancs.cf*: 1880 United States Federal Census.

[107] Address noted in *Gopsill's Jersey City, Hoboken, West Hoboken, Union Hill, and Weehawken Directory* 1890–91 (Washington: Andrew Boyd Publishing, 1890), 199.

[108] No headline, {newspaper clipping}, *FA*, 1891.

[109] "A Very Quiet Wedding;" {newspaper clipping}, *FA*, 1891; "Fagan-Foley: Hoboken's Ex-Assemblyman Married—A Very Quiet Event," *JCN*, September 10, 1891. Additional background on the Foley family provided by Joan [Fagan] Rohn, granddaughter of Lawrence Fagan, and Karen [Rohn] Osar, great-granddaughter of Lawrence Fagan, conversation with author, Danbury, CT, February 17, 2012.

[110] New Jersey Secretary of State, comp., *Corporations of New Jersey: List of Certificates Filed 1846–1891* (Trenton: 1892), 84.

[111] "Mansfield Gets One Year—Sensation for the 'Sporting Fraternity' of Hudson County—Strong Influence Was Brought to Bear and His Friends Thought He Would Get Off With a Fine, He May Turn State's Evidence," *NYDT*, May 22, 1896.

[112] George E. Mott was one of the partners.

[113] "Our Salutation," *OBS*, February 6, 1892.

[114] "Reform Is Needed Here," *OBS*, February 27, 1892. For additional criticism of the police department, see "Summary of Local News," *OBS*, February 13, 1892.

[115] For a photographic shot of Coyle's saloon, see Joe Czachowski, *Remembering Hoboken* (Nashville: Turner Publishing, 2010), 28.

[116] "One Man Three Offices," *OBS*, March 5, 1892. For additional criticism of multiple office holders, see "Another Antique System," *OBS*, March 19, 1892; see also "An Elastic Charter," *OBS*, December 31, 1892.

[117] "Question of Honor," *OBS*, April 30, 1892.

[118] Steven P. Erie, *Rainbow's End: Irish Americans and the Dilemmas of Urban Machine Politics, 1840–1985* (Berkeley and Los Angeles: University of California Press, 1988), 2.

[119] "After the Battle," *OBS*, April 16, 1892; *OBS*, December 31, 1892; "Young Men in Political Life," *OBS*, January 7, 1893.

[120] "Hoboken's Nominees: 'Larry Fagan' Heads the Ticket with the Mayoralty Nomination," *Jersey City News*, March 28, 1893.

[121] "Fagan Courts a Fight: Declares He Is Not Afraid of Seide, Stanton and Coyle—Does Not Recognize McLaughlin as the Party Leader," *NYW*, March 27, 1893. On the *NYW*, see Douglas, *Golden Age of the Newspaper*, 95–105.

[122] *NYW*, March 27, 1893.

[123] Leach, *Young Frank Hague*, 9.

[124] Sackett, *Modern Battles of Trenton*, 305–306.

[125] On Sackett, see Charles H. Weygant, *The Sacketts of America: Their Ancestors and Descendants 1630–1907* (Newburgh: Journal Print, 1907), 397–398.

[126] Sackett, *Modern Battles of Trenton*, 305–306.

[127] According to "Guttenberg Must Go—The Track Backed By The Notorious Hudson County Ring—Ministers Denounce The Gambling Resort, Concerted Action To Be Taken," *NYDT*, April 13, 1891, the shareholders in the venture, as of June 23, 1890, were: Gottfried Walbaum [300 shares], Dennis McLaughlin [255], Peter Wilkins [210], John Crusius [205], John C. Carr [170], William Lovell [70], A.G. Lackman [56], O.H. Meyer [51], Lawrence Fagan [44], John P. Feeney [10], E.J. Paxton [10], and some smaller shareholders.

[128] On opposition to race track gambling, see *NYDT*, April 13, 1891; Sackett, *Modern Battles of Trenton*, 383–386; *Modern Battles of Trenton, Volume II: From Werts to Wilson* (New York: Neale Publishing, 1914), 27–29.

[129] *Hoboken Evening News* as quoted in "What The Other Side Says—Fagan's Enemy Wall Says McLaughlin Is For Fagan," *NYW*, March 26, 1893.

[130] On Roosevelt legislating, teased as "Teddy," see Edmund Morris, *The Rise of Theodore Roosevelt* (1979), 2010 Edition (New York: Random House), 140–186.

[131] On Wall, see "Obituary," *The Editor and Publisher Journalist*, April 30, 1910. On Seide, see "Publisher Dies at Jersey City—Elks Service Tomorrow For Gustav Seide," *Bergen Evening Record*, December 7, 1936. *The News* had supported German Democratic candidate Colonel Erlenkoetter for mayor.

[132] *The News* was founded in 1870. *The Observer* entered 1893 as a weekly publication and ended the year as a daily, except Sunday, publication, see Rowell & Company, ed., pub., *American Newspaper Directory* (New York, 1894), 475. According to the newspaper article, "Fagan Will Bolt—He Will Support Toffey and Work For His Election," *JCN*, October 16, 1893, *The Observer* was scheduled to start publishing daily during the week of October 23, 1893.

133 "Hoboken's New Mayor," *NYW*, December 22, 1892; "Ring Rule in Hoboken," *NYT*, December 27, 1892; *OBS*, December 31, 1892.

134 *NYW*, March 27, 1893.

135 "Qualified Denial—Mr. Fagan Should Speak Plainer as to His Attitude Toward Mr. McLaughlin," *JCN*, March 27, 1893.

136 "Red Hot In Hoboken—Mr. Fagan's Hostility to Dennis McLaughlin Stirring up Bad Blood," *JCN*, March 28, 1893; "Dennis McLaughlin Angry—Mr. Fagan Fails To Pacify Him By Denying He Ever Called Him A Stuffed Pig," *NYS*, March 29, 1893.

137 For election result, see "Fagan Wins: The Vote was Close and Kept the Politicians Guessing," *JCN*, April 12, 1893; "New Jersey Elections: A Still Hunt by the People for the Jersey City Ring," *NYT*, April 12, 1893.

138 "Election Day In Jersey—Ring Rule In Hoboken Is Upset By Mr. Fagan's Victory," *NYW*, April 12, 1893.

139 "Stray Notes Here And There," *NYDT*, April 18, 1893.

Part 3: 1893–1899

140 "News From New Jersey;" "Mayor Fagan Is Vigorous," *NYS*, May 2, 1893; "Mayor Fagan's Message: Praises the Public School and Arraigns Police Departments," *JCN*, May 1, 1893.

141 "Editorial Comment," *JCN*, May 2, 1893.

142 "The News This Morning," *NYDT*, May 2, 1893. On the *NYDT*, see George H. Douglas, *The Golden Age of the Newspaper* (Westport, CT and London: Greenwood Press, 1999), 86–88.

143 "Mayor Fagan's Crusade—He Wields the Pruning Knife of Reform with Telling Effect," *JCN*, May 3, 1893; "Mayor Fagan's Word Goes—The Station Lounging House Closed and a New Chief of Detectives Appointed," *NYS*, May 3, 1893; "Mayor Fagan's Active Beginning," *TET*, May 3, 1893; "Mayor Fagan's War On Policy Dealers," *NYS*, May 4, 1893; "News From New Jersey—Democrats Have A Lively Meeting," *NYDT*, May 14, 1893. For discussion helpful in defining policy slips and green goods, see "To Wage War on Gamblers—Judge Lippincott's Charge to the Hudson County Grand Jury," *NYW*, April 4, 1893.

144 "Policy Spotter Caught," *JCN*, May 5, 1893; "Green Goods Men Leave Hoboken," *JCN*, May 6, 1893; "Caught A Policy Dealer—He Was Working From House With Gigs in His Pocket," *JCN*, June 8, 1893; "Flim Flammers in Hoboken," *JCN*, November 11, 1893.

145 "Guilty Policy Men—A Sensational Charge: One of the Policy Men Says He Paid Hoboken Officers for Protection," *JCN*, July 5, 1893; "Gallagher Suspended—The Shrewd Hoboken Detective Charged With Extortion by a Policy Dealer," *JCN*, July 6, 1893. The police board ultimately dismissed the

protection charges against Gallagher when he provided witness testimony that, on some of the occasions in which he was alleged to have received money from the policy broker, he had been out of the city while he was supposed to be on duty. The Board voted against his termination but fined him fifteen days' pay for the fifteen days it determined that he had been absent without leave. Fagan's vote opposed the resolution, see "Gallagher Fined," *JCN*, August 15, 1893.

[146] Douglas, *Golden Age of the Newspaper*, 95–105.

[147] See *NYW* stories: "How Hudson's Sheriff Feels in Regard to Pool-Rooms and Policy," *NYW*, May 26, 1893; "New Jersey—Policy Men Sentenced," *NYW*, July 14, 1893; "Grand Jury Scored—Because They Ignored The World's Evidence of Jersey City Crimes," *NYW*, July 19, 1893; "Green Goods Victims: Two Jerseymen Pay $200 for an Old Tin Box," *NYW*, July 21, 1893; "Grand Juror A Policy Man: Judge Lippincott Discloses A Strange Story in Jersey City," *NYW*, July 28, 1893; "Fixed Up For Stanton—Davis And McLaughlin Named The Grand Jury," *NYW*, September 9, 1893; "Stanton Men Chosen: Primaries in Hudson County Cooked to Suit the Old Bosses," *NYW*, October 5, 1893.

[148] "Pastors For Toffey: They Think He Should Be the Next Sheriff—Time That the Domineering Ring should be Throttled," *NYW*, October 23, 1893.

[149] "Pulpit in Politics," *JJ*, October 30, 1893.

[150] "Democrats To Colonize In Hoboken," *NYDT*, October 21, 1893.

[151] "Violence Is Feared: Startling Rumours Flying About The County—Hoboken Especially," *JJ*, November 6, 1893

[152] Ibid.

[153] For the election, see "Stanton's Men Working Hard: If He Is Elected It May Be by a Small Margin," *NYW*, November 7, 1893; "A Ring-Smashing Day: Hudson County Rises Up And Declares Itself," *NYDT*, November 8, 1893; "Republicans Make Great Gains in New Jersey," *NYS*, November 8, 1893; "Mayor Fagan Still A Democrat—He Carried Hoboken Against Stanton," *NYW*, November 8, 1893; "The Victory In Hoboken: A Great Triumph for Mayor Fagan and Reform," *JJ*, November 8, 1893; "Victory And Rejoicing in Hudson County: The Overthrow of The Ring Complete," *NYDT*, November 9, 1893.

[154] *JJ*, November 8, 1893.

[155] For Stanton's indictments, see "Indictments Found—Against the Hoboken 'Observer,' 'World' and Detective Goode," *JCN*, November 15, 1893; "New Jersey's Corrupt Political Gang Seeks Vengeance on The World—Hurled from Power, They Strike at the Cause of Their Downfall," *NYW*, November 16, 1893; "Hot For Revenge," *NYW*, November 17, 1893; "A Queer Grand Jury: Now The World May Be Presented For Criticizing Its Actions—What The Ring Itself Is Doing," *NYW*, November 20, 1893.

[156] After losing the election for sheriff in 1893, Stanton later spent a period of time in office as county recorder.

[157] For background on Davis, see Sackett, *Modern Battles of Trenton*, 306–310; "Bob Davis Dies After Long Illness: In Politics Before He Could Vote and Became Democratic Leader of Hudson County—Bride Of A Week With Him—His Estate Said to be Worth $1,000,000," *NYT*, January 10, 1911; Tumulty, *Woodrow Wilson*, 8–10.

[158] "Another Antique System," *OBS*, March 19, 1892.

[159] See discussion in *NYW*, March 27, 1893.

[160] "'Bob' Davis Speaks—Things That Democrats Will Not Like to Hear: He Says He Is No Boss, And Has Not Been in Some Time—Warned McLaughlin of Defeat," *JJ*, November 11, 1893.

[161] "Dennis McLaughlin Ill—The Race Track 'Boss' is Suffering with Pneumonia," *NYW*, November 15, 1893.

[162] *NYW*, November 16, 1893.

[163] McKean, *The Boss*, 26–29; Leach, *Young Frank Hague*, 67–72.

[164] John Paul Bocock, "The Irish Conquest of Our Cities," *Forum*, April 1894.

[165] Ibid.

[166] "For Irish Prisoners—Enthusiastic Amnesty Meeting in Hoboken," *JCN*, April 9, 1896; "City and Vicinity—Jersey City," *NYT*, April 9, 1896.

[167] Fagan, as quoted in Melissa Melms, "The Hoboken Public Library," *hMag.com*, October 3, 2011: http://www.hmag.com/2011/10/the-hoboken-public-library/. For discussion of locating library at city hall, see *NYS*, May 2, 1893; "Hoboken's Armory Closed," *NYT*, May 6, 1893. For the library groundbreaking, see "Hoboken's New Public Library: The Cornerstone Laid Yesterday by Mrs. Martha B. Stevens," *NYT*, April 21, 1896; "Hoboken's Free Public Library—The Cornerstone of the New Building Laid by Mrs. Martha B. Stevens," *NYDT*, April 21, 1896.

[168] On the recession, see Painter, *Standing at Armageddon*, 110–140; Lears, *Rebirth of A Nation*, 167–221.

[169] See "Jersey City 206,433, Hoboken 59,364—Increase in Ten Years Declared to Be 43,430 and 15,716 Respectively," *NYW*, August 24, 1900.

[170] Ziegler-McPherson, *Immigrants in Hoboken*, 85–86.

[171] On financial trusts in New Jersey and circumstances surrounding their proliferation, see Christopher Grandy, "New Jersey Corporate Charter Mongering, 1875–1929," *Journal of Economic History* 49, no. 3 (September 1989): 677–692.

[172] Ron Chernow, *Titan: The Life of John D. Rockefeller, Sr.* (1998), 2004 Edition (New York: Vintage Books), Kindle Electronic Edition: Chapter 18, Location 7094–7122.

[173] George Werts, as quoted in Grandy, "New Jersey Charter Mongering," 683.

[174] "Hoboken's Mayor Congratulated," *NYS*, April 14, 1895. On the primary and general election, see "New Jersey Notes—Hoboken," *NYDT*, March 9, 1895; "Fagan's Walkover—Easily Defeats August Grassman for Hoboken's Mayoralty Nomination," *JCN*, March 26, 1895; "Fagan Carries Hoboken—The Election Very Quiet and Few Demonstrations During the Evening While the Count Was in Progress," *JCN*, April 10, 1895; "Fighting Ground," *NYW*, April 10, 1895.

[175] The election had 7,135 total votes cast. Democratic candidate Fagan got 5,052 votes (just under 71%). Independent Democratic candidate August M. Bruggemann got 1,216 votes (approximately 17%). Republican candidate Clement Leonard got 867 votes (approximately 12%). See "Fagan Wins—The Vote in Hoboken Surprisingly Heavy," *JCN*, April 14, 1897.

[176] The Trust Company of New Jersey., *History of Hudson County and of the Old Village of Bergen: Being a Brief Account of the Foundation and Growth of What Is Now Jersey City and of the Many Advantages Now Offered the Inhabitants Thereof in the Newly Constructed Building of the Trust Company of Jersey City* (New York: Bartlett Orr Press, 1921), 52–55. For building description, see "12 Hudson Place—Stunning Historic Landmark—Across From Path," *Meridian Properties* advertisement, January 26, 2012: http://12hudson-place.isforlease.com/.

[177] The Spectator Company, comp., *Charters of American Life Insurance Companies* (New York: 1895), supplement pg. 15. On founding of Colonial Life Insurance Company, see also Ernest J. Heppenheimer {letter} to Mary Fagan: Jersey City, NJ, May 21, 1921, FA.

[178] Information on Jackson Street Bridge from a report compiled by the firms of Goodkind & O'Dea, Inc. and Raber & Associates for the NJ Dept. of Trans., 1985, see Library of Congress Collection: *Historic American Engineering Record* NJ-54, No. 7–NEARK, 18. A 1991 rehabilitation of the structure is noted by Bridgehunter.com: http://bridgehunter.com/nj/essex/700H02/. On the Newark Riots, see "Police Battle Snipers—Seal Off Riot Area," *Newark Star-Ledger*, July 15, 1967.

[179] Sackett, *Modern Battles of Trenton*, 384. For Crusius's stake in Guttenberg, see part two's footnotes on Fagan's ties to McLaughlin. For background on the house, see introduction.

[180] Metz, *City Animals*, 33–34.

[181] For Crusius's difficulties, see "Race-Track Men Indicted," *NYT*, January 4, 1894; "Big Four Sentenced—One Year's Imprisonment in the Penitentiary and a Fine of $500," *JCN*, February 15, 1895.

[182] Hazen Pingree, as quoted in Melvin G. Holli, *The American Mayor: The Best & The Worst Big-City Leaders* (University Park, PA: Pennsylvania State University Press, 1999), 35. On Pingree, see also Holli, *Reform in Detroit: Hazen S. Pingree and Urban Politics* (New York: Oxford University Press, 1969).

[183] On Samuel "Golden Rule" Jones, see Holli, *The American Mayor: The Best & The Worst*, 44–52.

[184] From 1890–1900, Toledo's population rose from 81,434 to 131,822; Detroit's from 205,876 to 285,704, see Population Division of U.S. Census Bureau.

[185] *NYW*, August 24, 1900.

[186] See "Jewish Subscription Dance—Hoboken Hebrews Have an Enjoyable Ball," *JCN*, April 4, 1895; "Jewish Celebration in Hoboken," *JCN*, October 23, 1894; "Object to Ahlwardt—Hoboken Jews Ask the Acting Mayor to Stop His Lecture," *JCN*, February 5, 1896; "Hebrew Democrats," *JCN*, October 22, 1898; "Independent Hebrews Meet," *JCN*, October 24, 1898; "Hebrews for Democracy," *JCN*, October 31, 1898.

[187] "Laying a Synagogue's Cornerstone: Mayor Fagan and Attorney Minturn Perform the Ceremony," *NYDT*, August 11, 1899. On the ceremony, see also "Hebrew Cornerstones Laid—Collection of Rare Coins Placed in One Box," *JCN*, August 10, 1899.

[188] "Want Good Roads—Citizens of Hoboken Form Association," *JCN*, January 29, 1897; "Hoboken Needs Good Roads—There Is No Suitable Avenue of Escape to Jersey City," *NYS*, January 30, 1897.

[189] On the Hexamer family, see American Historical Society, ed., pub., *American Biography: A New Cyclopedia* Vol. 16 (New York: 1924), 168–170.

[190] Zacks, *Island of Vice*, 118; Ziegler-McPherson, *Immigrants in Hoboken*, 45, 47, 53.

[191] Ziegler-McPherson, *Immigrants in Hoboken*, 38, 45, 47, 52, 62–63, 85, 161, 164; Kenny, *American Irish*, 79, 201–204.

[192] Howard Chudacoff, *The Age of the Bachelor: Creating an American Subculture* (Princeton: Princeton University Press, 1999), 40–46, 106–115; Madelon Powers, *Faces Along the Bar: Lore and Order in the Workingman's Saloon, 1870–1920* (Chicago and London: University of Chicago Press, 1998), 34–35, 141–149; Leach, *Young Frank Hague*, 6, 46–53; Erie, *Rainbow's End*, 3–4.

[193] "New-Jersey News," *NYDT*, May 26, 1896.

[194] For an example, see "High Officials Were Indicted—But the Grand Jury in Jersey City Reconsidered Its Action," *NYT*, December 7, 1893.

[195] On Roosevelt and the Raines Law in New York City, see Zacks, *Island of Vice*, 244–262.

[196] "Raines Law Helps Hoboken," *NYS*, April 6, 1896; see also "New Jersey News," *NYDT* April 7, 1896.

[197] "Plenty to Drink in Hoboken—A Rumor of Spies in Jersey City Closes Some Front Doors and Frightens the Police," *NYDT*, April 13, 1896.

[198] Ibid.

[199] "As Viewed by a Preacher—The Rev. J.L. Scudder Arraigns," *NYDT*, April 13, 1896.

[200] "Dr. Scudder's Stirring Address," *NYDT* April 28, 1896.

[201] "Temperance Women in Hoboken—They Think That City a Promising Field for Work," *NYDT*, April 24, 1896.

[202] For the Grand Jury, see "It May Be a Dry Sunday—Hudson County Grand Jury Takes Up the Liquor Question with a Vengeance," *NYDT*, April 22, 1896; "Jersey City and Hoboken Will Come to New York for Drink on Sunday," *NYS*, April 22, 1896.

[203] "How to Observe Sunday—Hoboken Saloonkeepers Warned to Have Front Doors Shut and Blinds Drawn," *NYDT*, April 24, 1896.

[204] "Jersey Towns Were Dry—Even Hoboken Liquor-Sellers Were Compelled to Do a Side-Door Business," *NYDT*, April 27, 1896.

[205] "Must Keep Saloons Closed—Hudson County (N.J.) Police Instructed to Enforce the Law," *NYT*, May 3, 1896.

[206] Zacks, *Island of Vice*, 256–262.

[207] "His Action Causes a Sensation—Mayor Fagan Declared That Alderman Capelli Was 'Not Fit to Be a Councilman or Even a Saloonkeeper,'" *NYDT*, July 1, 1897.

[208] Ibid.

[209] "Wants All the Stores Closed: Mrs. Bush Objects to the Sale of Milk or Meat on Sunday, and as for Beer...," *NYS*, July 5, 1897.

[210] Douglas, *Golden Age of the Newspaper*, 73–74.

[211] *NYS*, July 5, 1897.

[212] Ibid.

[213] Ibid.

[214] On the factory fire, see "A Big Blaze in Hoboken: Fire Destroys a Large Factory and Tenement Houses—One Hundred and Thirty Families Made Homeless," *NYDT*, May 21, 1897; "A Big Fire in Jersey—The Destruction of R.H. Macy's Factory in Hoboken—Other Buildings Destroyed—Many People Were Rendered Homeless by the Rapid Spread of the Flames, and Some Have Narrow Escapes—Loss Is Very Large," *TET*, May 21, 1897; "Hoboken Scorched—Blocks in Ashes and One Hundred and Forty Families Homeless," *Syracuse Evening Herald*, May 21, 1897.

[215] *TET*, May 21, 1897.

[216] Annual Message to Hoboken City Council, unspecified date in 1898, Lawrence Fagan as quoted in "Visitor from Another Time," *Hoboken Reporter*, January 24, 1993.

[217] "Batch of Indictments: The Hudson Grand Jury Completes Its Work—Many Evils Dealt With," *NYDT*, December 12, 1899; "Hoboken's Mayor Indicted—Hudson County Is Excited," *NYT*, December 12, 1899.

[218] "Theatres May Open Sunday—Judge Blair So Decides in Dismissing Indictments Against Hoboken Officials," *NYDT*, November 23, 1901.

Part 4: 1899–1901

219 "As a Jerseyman Sees It," *NYDT*, March 13, 1899.

220 "Fagan Squarely Arraigned—Ex-Judge Skinner Wants to Know Whether Hoboken Wants Two More Years of Him," *NYDT*, March 30, 1899.

221 The votes in the mayoral election tallied: Fagan [4,313]; Stuhr [3,268]; Schell [275]. Candidate William A. Schell ran as a Republican but had fallen out of favor with Republican Party leaders, see "New Jersey Elections," *NYT*, April 12, 1899; "Fagan's Plurality—Schell Finishes a Poor Third," *NYDT*, April 13, 1899.

222 "Russ Is Not a Puppet: Therefore He Resigns from the Hoboken School Commission—Fagan Appoints Four Members," *NYDT*, April 18, 1899; "Russ Rebukes Fagan—Hoboken Schools Made to Aid the Democratic Machine," *NYDT*, April 19, 1899.

223 Adding to Russ's disenchantment with Fagan was the fact that a new fee had recently been levied on employees of the School Board and that the job of overseeing the city's census, which in the past had been granted to the Commission of Public Instruction, was granted to another department.

224 *NYDT*, April 19, 1899.

225 Ibid.

226 See "Stuhr Succeeds Russ—Mayor Fagan Appoints His Opponent a Commissioner of Public Instruction," *NYDT*, April 25, 1899.

227 See "Principal Resigns in Hoboken," *NYDT*, February 8, 1900.

228 "Fagan Vents His Wrath—Dismisses Banta as Superintendent of the Police Telegraph System," *NYDT*, June 2, 1899. See also "Mayor Fagan Removes Banta," *NYT*, June 2, 1899.

229 "Not Transferred to Fagan's Banks—City Treasurer Smith Refuses to Draw Hoboken's Deposits from the First National Bank," *NYDT*, June 2, 1899.

230 Willa Cather, as quoted in Michael Kazin, *A Godly Hero: The Life of William Jennings Bryan* (New York: Anchor Books, 2006), 101.

231 Bryan's big ideas are well summarized in his "Cross of Gold" speech. See William Jennings Bryan, *Speeches of William Jennings Bryan*, Vol. I (New York: Funk & Wagnalls, 1909), 238–249. On Bryan's oratory and arguments related to capitalism in the 1896 campaign, see Kazin, *A Godly Hero*, 45–79.

232 Bryan, *Speeches*, Vol. I, 248.

233 Ibid., 241.

234 William Jennings Bryan, *The First Battle: A Story of the Campaign of 1896* (Chicago: W.B. Conkey Co., 1896), 478–479. For stops in New Jersey and Pennsylvania, see also "Bryan Traverses New Jersey—Greeted at Many Points on His Trip from Philadelphia," *NYT*, September 24, 1896.

[235] For Daly's efforts on behalf of Bryan, see Bryan, *First Battle*, 478–479; Sackett, *Modern Battles of Trenton*, Vol. II, 75–80; see also "Senator Smith Is Out—But Will Contribute to Bryan Cause in New Jersey," *NYT*, September 25, 1896; "The New Jersey Campaign—The Democrats Ready to Begin in Earnest at Last," *NYT*, September 27, 1896.

[236] "Politics in New-Jersey—Congressman Daly Talks About Probable Democratic National Convention Delegates," *NYDT*, April 9, 1900.

[237] Daly's support was instrumental in helping Fagan secure the Democratic nomination for mayor in 1893, see *NYW*, March 27, 1893.

[238] For general background on Daly, see "Washington Mourns Daly," *NYDT*, August 2, 1900; *The Fifty-Sixth Congress of the United States, Second Session, Memorial Addresses on the Life and Character of William D. Daly, Late a Representative from New Jersey* (Washington, DC: Government Printing Office, 1901).

[239] "Bryan Will Visit Jersey City," *NTY*, January 21, 1900; "Jersey Will Give a Royal Welcome," *NYW*, January 24, 1900.

[240] "Boy Orator At It Again—Speeches by Bryan Yesterday in Connecticut and Jersey," *NYS*, January 25, 1900; "Bryan in Jersey City—Disregards 'Boss' Davis' Wish and Talks About Silver," *NYDT*, January 25, 1900; "Mr. Bryan in Jersey City—Entertained at Dinner and Afterward Addresses a Meeting," *NYT*, January 25, 1900.

[241] *NYT* account suggests Fagan attended the dinner honoring Bryan; *NYS* and *NYDT* accounts suggest Fagan did not.

[242] Abraham Lincoln to H.L. Pierce, Springfield, IL, April 6, 1859, in John G. Nicolay and John Hay, eds., *Complete Works of Abraham Lincoln*, Vol. 5 (Harrogate, TN: Lincoln Memorial University Press, 1894), 124–127. Lincoln was writing to Republicans in Boston celebrating Thomas Jefferson's birthday.

[243] *NYS*, January 25, 1900; *NYDT*January 25, 1900; *NYT*, January 25, 1900.

[244] See "Lincoln on Wealth," {newspaper clipping}, *FA*. The quote originates from an 1864 letter by Lincoln to the New York Workingmen's Democratic Association.

[245] "Mayor Fagan's Last Term—Announces That He Is Not a Candidate for Re-Election in Hoboken," *NYDT* February 4, 1900.

[246] Information on stillborn twins from Joan [Fagan] Rohn and Karen [Rohn] Osar, conversation with author, Danbury, CT, February 17, 2012.

[247] "Offers to Light Hoboken: Congressman Daly Makes a Bid on Behalf of a New Company," *NYDT*, January 26, 1900.

[248] "Mayor Fagan's Defiance of Davis," *NYDT*, February 3, 1900.

[249] "Davis's Ball Without Fagan," *NYDT*, February 2, 1900.

[250] *NYDT*, February 4, 1900.

[251] "New Jersey News," *NYDT*, February 5, 1900.

[252] For the Great Hoboken Fire, see "Big Steamers Afire," *NYW*, June 30, 1900; "Hundreds Die in Fire: Three Great Liners Wrecked; Costly Wharves Destroyed," *NYDT*, July 1, 1900; "Over Two Hundred Perish in Burning Liners," "Ocean Steamships Caught in Berths of Fire," "Fire Gives No Warning," "Sixteen Escape by Miracle," "Daring Rescues Recorded," "Brave Hoboken Force, Though Small, Does Its Duty—Caring for the Injured," all reports in *NYT*, July 1, 1900; Reginald L. Foster, "The Great Hoboken Fire," *Munsey's Magazine*, Vol. 23, no. 6, September 1900; Gordon, "Great Harbor Fire."

[253] Gordon, "Great Harbor Fire," 4.

[254] *NYDT*, July 1, 1900.

[255] "Blame Tugboat Men," *NYS*, July 3, 1900; "Tugboat Men's Denials," *NYT*, July 4, 1900; "Complaints of Tug Captains," *NYDT*, July 4, 1900; Gordon, "Great Harbor Fire," 7–8.

[256] *NYS*, July 3, 1900.

[257] Although the Great Hoboken Fire of 1900 is not mentioned directly, for a broader context on fires during the era, see Rebecca Edwards, *New Spirits: Americans in the Gilded Age, 1865–1905* (New York: Oxford University Press, 2006), 1–6.

[258] *NYDT*, July 1, 1900; Gordon, "Great Harbor Fire," 10.

[259] "Mr. Cram on the Fire," *NYT*, July 3, 1900; "Loss of Life Needless, Cram Says," *NYDT*, July 3, 1900.

[260] Ibid.

[261] "Recovering Bodies of Dock Fire Victims—Attitude of Officials," *NYT*, July 4, 1900.

[262] "The Law is Seeking Cruel Tugboat Men," *NYW*, July 7, 1900.

[263] "For Better Docks," *NYT*, July 3, 1900.

[264] "Open Letter to the Mayor," *NYT*, July 3, 1900.

[265] "Noisy Fourth of July," *NYT*, July 5, 1900.

[266] North German Lloyd executive (name of executive who signed documented not easily determined) on behalf of Captain Moeller, Superintendent, to Fagan: New York, NY, July 6, 1900, *FA*. On the procession, see also "Eighty-Two Victims of Dock Fire Buried: Hoboken Draped in Black," *NYT*, July 6, 1900.

[267] "Four More Bodies Recovered," *NYW00*; "Dynamite Brings No Bodies: More Removed to Hoboken from the *Saale*—Half-Burned Debris a Menace to Health," *NYT*, July 9, 1900; Gordon, "Great Harbor Fire," 6–7, 11.

[268] Fagan returned to Hoboken from Asbury Park when he heard news of the fire, see "Fire Aftermath—Incidents of Unbelievable Brutality to Drowning Wretches," *JCN*, July 2, 1900. After ordering the dynamiting, he returned to his vacation, see Gordon, "The Great Harbor Fire," 11, 13. It is unclear which hotel the Fagan family stayed at during the summer of 1900.

In 1895, they stayed at the Brunswick, see "Park Personals," *Asbury Park Daily Press*, July 22, 1895; in 1898 and 1899, they stayed at the Monmouth, see "People Worth Knowing—They Come to This City from Far and Near," *Asbury Park Daily Press*, July 23, 1898; "Many Merry Dancers—Ball Rooms Crowded With Pretty Women," *Asbury Park Daily Press*, July 10, 1899. The Fagan family's first vacation home in Deal was located on Sydney Avenue below Norwood Avenue, see *Ancs.cf*: *U.S., City Directories, 1822–1995*, Asbury Park, New Jersey, City Directory, 1905, 139, 73/228; their second home in Deal was located at 307 Ocean Avenue, see photos in FA; see also *Ancs.cf*: *U.S., City Directories, 1822–1995*, Asbury Park, New Jersey, City Directory, 1920, 147, 63/198.

[269] Democratic National Committee, *Official Proceeding of the Democratic National Convention: Held in Kansas City, MO., July 4th, 5th and 6th*, (Chicago: McLellan Printing Co., 1900), 172.

[270] On Daly's death, see "Congressman Daly Stricken—New Jersey Legislator Dies Suddenly at Far Rockaway," *NYW*, July 31, 1900; "Congressman Daly Dead—Representative from the VIII New Jersey District Passes Away Suddenly," *NYDT*, August 1, 1900; "William D. Daly Dead—Succumbs to Uraemic Poisoning," *NYT*, August 1, 1900.

[271] "Mr. Bryan's Welcome in New Jersey Towns—The Crowds Overwhelming," *NYT*, October 26, 1900; "Bryan in New Jersey—Jersey City, Robert Davis Stronghold Exceeds All Other Places in Numbers and Enthusiasm," *NYDT*, October 26, 1900. On Bryan's customary attire, see Michael Kazin, *A Godly Hero*, 59.

[272] *NYDT*, October 26, 1900.

[273] Ibid.

[274] *NYT*, October 26, 1900; *NYDT*, October 26, 1900.

[275] Ibid.

[276] "Mr. Bryan in New Jersey: Second Day of His Trip Marked by Great Enthusiasm—Vast Crowds in Hoboken and Newark," *NYT*, October 27, 1900. For the Lyric Theater specifications, see Julius Cahn, *Julius Cahn's Official Theatrical Guide: Information of the Leading Theatres and Attractions in America*, Vol. 5 (New York: Empire Theatre Publishing, 1900), 57.

[277] "Bryan's New Jersey Trip: Second Day in 'Robber's Roost,'" *NYDT*, October 27, 1900.

[278] *NYDT*, October 27, 1900.

[279] Ibid.

[280] Ibid.

[281] On the presidential voting in New Jersey, see Foster, "Early Career of Mayor Frank Hague," 14–15.

[282] "New Jersey Political Notes," *NYDT*, October 29, 1900.

[283] For election background, see "In Hudson County: Seymour Sentiment Is Unanimous In this Banner Democratic District," *NYDT*, September 23, 1901; "A Hard Fight In Hudson—The Republicans Will Have To Battle Against A Fine Organization To Cut Down Democratic Pluralities," *NYDT*, October 7, 1901; "Fusion In Hoboken," *NYD*, October 11, 1901.

[284] On Verdon, see Rieser and Stinson, *Hudson County Today*, 156.

[285] "The Battle in New Jersey," *NYDT*, October 28, 1901; the interview was conducted on October 26th.

[286] *NYDT*, October 28, 1901.

[287] Ibid.

[288] "No Pay For Many Hoboken Officials—Mayor Fagan Will Not Sign Rolls Till Library Requisition Goes Through," *NYW*, August 31, 1901; "Holiday, But No Money—Anguish In Hoboken Because Mayor Fagan Held Up Payroll," *NYW*, September 2, 1901.

[289] *NYDT*, October 28, 1901.

[290] On Fagan's Great Danes, see Part 6 and related footnotes.

[291] *NYDT*, October 28, 1901.

[292] On the election, see "New Jersey—Forecasts of Leaders," *NYDT*, November 5, 1901; "Lankering In Hoboken—Late Returns Point To Election of Democratic Candidate For Mayor," *NYS*, November 6, 1901.

[293] On the new facility, see *State of New Jersey, Twenty-Fourth Annual Report of the Bureau of Statistics of Labor and Industries* (year ending October 31, 1901), 496; "Among The Foundries," *The Foundry* 20, no. 116 (April, 1902).

[294] Fagan Iron Works had been contracted to supply the iron for the building of the original Lackawanna Terminal at Hoboken, see "Big Terminal At Hoboken," *New Brunswick Times*, May 15, 1900. The firm would also be awarded a new contract to provide iron manhole covers, special castings, plugs, caps, and bends to Jersey City at $0.35 per lb., see *Municipal Engineering* 23, no. 2 (August, 1902).

Part 5: 1901–1909

[295] Maria Barbieri, as quoted in Jennifer Guglielmo, *Living the Revolution*, Chapter 5, Kindle loc. 2337–2444.

[296] Beverly Gage, *The Day Wall Street Exploded: A Story of America in Its First Age of Terror* (New York: Oxford University Press, 2009), 2–3.

[297] Jeffory A. Clymer, *America's Culture of Terrorism: Violence, Capitalism, and the Written Word* (Chapel Hill: University of North Carolina Press, 2003), 9. For newspapers exploiting "the rural mind," see Hofstadter, *Age of Reform*, 189.

[298] "No Naturalized Anarchists," *OBS*, August 20, 1892.

[299] Nell Irvin Painter, *The History of White People*, Chapter 17, Kindle loc. 4237–4245.

[300] On the 1898 incident as catalyst for Bresci, see Guglielmo, *Living the Revolution*, Chapter 5, Kindle loc. 2048–2051.

[301] "Humbert Lies In State—Jersey Anarchists Glad," *NYDT*, August 1, 1900.

[302] On Sophie Bresci, see "History of Assassin," *TET*, July 31, 1900; *NYDT*, August 1, 1900; "Anarchists Alarmed," *NYS*, August 1, 1900.

[303] *NYS*, August 1, 1900.

[304] *NYDT*, August 1, 1900.

[305] Ibid.

[306] "Hoboken Editor," *Passaic Herald News*, July 30, 1946.

[307] "Anarchist Law In Force," *NYT*, June 2, 1903.

[308] See "Union Men Fall Out Over Money Payments: Such is the Assertion of a Hoboken Employer," *NYT*, June 12, 1903.

[309] *NYS*, August 19, 1903.

[310] "Above Courts and The Union," *Century* 67, no. 1 (November 1903). On the incident, see also *NYS*, August 19, 1903; "Cleaned Out The Walking Delegate," *JJ*, August 18, 1903; "Ex-Mayor Fagan Fined: It Will Cost Him $47 For Striking A Walking Delegate," *NYW*, August 19, 1903; "Ex-Mayor Fagan—Must Pay $47 for Knocking Down Iron Workers' Walking Delegate," *NYT*, August 19, 1903.

[311] *NYS*, August 19, 1903.

[312] *JJ*, August 18, 1903.

[313] See figures in Tobin, "Mark Fagan," (6–7), noting that Jersey City had 2,099 African-American residents and a total population of 163,003 in 1890; 3,704 African-American residents and a total population of 206,433 in 1900; 5,960 African-American residents and a total population of 267,779 in 1910.

[314] "Negro Policeman is Arrested and 'Broken,'" *NYW*, June 2, 1903. On Reed's appointment, see "One of The Finest—Charles Reed a Colored Man Becomes A Special Policeman for The American Veneering Co.," *JCN*, May 28, 1903. For American Veneer's address, see W. Andrew Boyd, mgr., *Boyd's Hoboken and Jersey City Directory, 1903–04* (Jersey City: Boyd's Directory Company, 1903), 73.

[315] *NYW*, June 2, 1903.

[316] Ibid.

[317] "Fagan Again at Iroquois Club: First Week of New Organization a Very Busy One—Marks Probable Return of The Fagan Power," *JJ*, June 13, 1903. For the Iroquois Club, see also *JJ*, June 5, 1903; "Independents Have New Club House: Lease Taken For The Knights Of Columbus House On Bloomfield St.—Ex-Mayor Fagan Is One Of The Members," *JJ*, June 8, 1903; "'Larry' Fagan Will Run Again For Mayor," *NYS*, June 12, 1903; *JJ*, June 27,

1903; "Fagan Again At 'The Lamp Post:' Tells Downtown People Why the Iroquois Club Was Organized," *JJ*, July 2, 1903.

[318] *JJ*, June 13, 1903.

[319] On the Knights of Columbus in Hoboken, see the *Knights of Columbus' 55th Anniversary Dinner-Dance*, Hoboken Council No. 159 K of C, 1896–1951, program for Saturday, May 12, 1951, Union Club: Main Ballroom, Hoboken, N.J.

[320] *JJ*, June 8, 1903.

[321] "Turning Against Davis: Hudson County Democrats Organizing To Overthrow Him," *NYDT*, February 15, 1902.

[322] *JJ*, June 5, 1903.

[323] *JJ*, June 8, 1903.

[324] "Boon To The City In Rainy Spell," *NYW*, June 26, 1903. Showers were forecast on Monday, June 1903, see *NYS*, June 8, 1903.

[325] See "The Weather Report," *NYDT*, July 2, 1903.

[326] *JJ*, June 27, 1903. On The Lamp Post, James J. Farina, Hoboken municipal city clerk, and Jerry Lore, deputy city clerk, were very helpful in identifying it as a saloon and its general location in relation to city hall, interview by the author, Hoboken, NJ, July 9, 2010. The term "lamp-post drunks" appears in the student periodical of the Stevens Institute of Technology, Hoboken, NJ, see *Stevens Indicator*, May 1886. Further clues about The Lamp Post of 1903 may be drawn from a dramatization of one of its likely historical descendants. *The Lamppost Reunion* was a play set in a filthy Hoboken bar in which a Frank Sinatra–inspired character, "Fred Santora," returned to his hometown to see his old friends after a 25-year absence. One theatre critic described the production as "garbage—rank as the untended men's room that inspires many of its socko-est lines," see Alan Rich, "Theater," *New York Magazine*, November 3, 1975.

[327] *JJ*, June 27, 1903.

[328] Ibid.

[329] For the weather, see "July Begins With 90—Midsummer Lands All at Once," *NYS*, July 2, 1903.

[330] *JJ*, July 2, 1903.

[331] Ibid.

[332] The details of the seemingly quick fizzle of the Iroquois Club remain to be discovered; however, aside from the peculiar influence of Fagan and the unique urban setting provided by Hoboken, the Iroquois Club looked to have some of the dooming hallmarks typical of new political clubs of the day. The strong convictions of the factions which often formed such clubs were usually short-lived, perhaps too reactionary to be politically pragmatic or to remain viable long term. Further diluting many political clubs' original ideological cohesion was the fact that men, who were rising in

prominence but not yet belonging to a local organization with a well-out-fitted clubhouse, often hurried to join because of the amenities, making it usually not long before a majority of political clubs came to have a function which was largely social, see "Heard At The Clubs," *NYT*, June 21, 1903.

[333] "Ex-Mayor Fagan Off To Europe: Starts on His Maiden Voyage Across The Atlantic Ocean—Kept His Plans Quiet Until Last Moment," {newspaper clipping}, *FA*, very probably *OBS*, October 18, 1904. For suggested October departure date, see also *Ancs.cf*: UK Incoming Passenger Lists, 1878–1960; For Keresey, see *Ancs.cf*: 1900 United States Federal Census. For apparent rug sale receipts, see FA.

[334] Very probably *OBS*, October 18, 1904.

[335] Ibid.

[336] John Fagan {letter} to Lawrence Fagan: Dublin, IRE, March 14, 1905, FA.

[337] On the iron works fire, see "Lawrence Fagan Back From Europe Finds His Iron Works In Ashes," *OBS*, May 3, 1905; "Fagan's Iron Works Burned: Firemen and Employees Say The Loss Will Be Between $100,000 and $200,000," *JCN*, May 3, 1905; "Fagan Iron Works Burned: Owner, ex-Mayor of Hoboken, on Board Kaiser Which Will Dock To-Day," *NYT*, May 3, 1905; "Plant of the Fagan Iron Works Burned," *NYS*, May 3, 1905.

[338] *OBS*, May 3, 1905.

[339] See *Ancs.cf*: New York Passenger Lists, 1820–1957.

[340] *JCN*, May 5, 1905.

[341] *OBS*, May 3, 1905.

[342] On the club, see "Mrs. Washburn Tells History Of Hoboken Women's Club—Two Life Memberships to Be Given to 50-Year Members Thursday," *Hudson Dispatch*, May 4, 1954; Heaney, *Bicentennial Comes To Hoboken*, 82.

[343] Mary Fagan to Millie Stanton: Hoboken, NJ, March 6, 1900, FA.

[344]See "Strike Stops Foundry Work—Men Want The Closed Shop And 25 Per Cent. More Wages—Employers Say That to Give in Would End Their Chance of Doing Business in New York—Men in Allied Trades Suffer—Hunting for Non-Union Men," *NYS*, June 18, 1905; "Fagan's Iron Works Burned: Second Fire in Nine Weeks Completes Destruction of Big Plant," *NYT*, August 2, 1905; "Fagan Iron Works Burned Again," *NYS*, August 2, 1905; "Fagan Iron Works Threatened: Police Believe Incendiary Started Fire There—Other Attempts," *NYS*, February 1, 1906; "Dynamiter Tells On Union: One Of Moran's Jobs Was To Ruin Belmont Track—Another Was To Fire Fagan Iron Works—Hidden Store of Dynamite in Jersey—Walking Delegate's Rake-off on Inflated Expense Bills—Dates and Names," *NYS*, March 27, 1906.

[345] Louis Adamic, *Dynamite: The Story of Class Violence in America* (1934) 2008 Edition (Oakland: AK Press, 2008), 136–137. On the changing nature of the iron industry, see also Steven J. Ross, *Workers On The Edge: Work, Leisure,*

and Politics in Industrializing Cincinnati 1788–1890 (New York: Columbia University Press, 1985).

[346] *NYS*, March 27, 1906.

[347] "Four-Ton Larceny Case: Fagan Iron Works Heads Try To Recover Beams and One is Arrested," *NYT*, October 20, 1907. On the incident, see also "Ex-Mayor Fagan's Son Discharged By Court," *OBS* October 21, 1907.

[348] See "Passaic Steel Works Sale," *NYS*, May 29, 1909; "Sets Aside Sale of Steel Works," *NYDT* June 8, 1909; "Snap Steel Sale Set Aside," *NYT*, June 8, 1909; "Steel Works Sold," *NYS*, November 27, 1909.

Part 6: 1909–1921

[349] In 1908, the average lifespan for Caucasians was forty-nine years; thirty-five years for African-Americans, see Jim Rasenberger, *America 1908: The Invention Of The Model T. And The Making Of A Modern Nation* (New York: Scribner, 2007), 4.

[350] "Hoboken Politics: Lawrence Fagan Wants the Job of Mayor—War in Republican Camp," *NYS*, June 13, 1909.

[351] "Hoboken Has Hot Mayoralty Fight: Davis is Backing Stack and Warm Times are Assured," *TET*, August 18, 1909.

[352] "Hudson Democrats Restore Harmony," *TET*, September 11, 1909.

[353] The votes in the election tallied: Gonzales [4,908]; Fagan [4,520], see figures in *OBS*, November 3, 1909.

[354] "The Upset In Hoboken: Father of Twelve to Be The First Republican Mayor in 26 Years," *NYS*, November 4, 1909. On the 1909 election, see also "Gonzales Congratulated By Former Mayor Fagan," *OBS*, November 3, 1909; "Very Close In Hoboken: Chances That Republicans Elect Mayor on Electric Light Issue," *NYS*, November 3, 1909.

[355] James Kerney, *The Political Education of Woodrow Wilson* (New York and London: Century Company, 1926), 80–81.

[356] *OBS*, May 18, 1910.

[357] Connors, *Cycle of Power*, 24.

[358] Lincoln Steffens, *The Struggle for Self-Government: Being an Attempt to Trace American Political Corruption to its Sources in Six States of the United States with a Dedication to the Czar* (New York: McClure-Philips, 1906), 210. On Steffens, see Peter Hartshorn, *I Have Seen The Future: A Life Of Lincoln Steffens* (Berkeley: Counterpoint, 2011).

[359] Phillip Daab was about nine years younger than his brother Martin; see *Ancs.cf*: United States Federal Census, 1870. On Phillip Daab, see also "Phillip Daab Is Dead: Former Legislator, Owned Hoboken Baseball Club of 40 years ago—Zane Grey and Eddie Collins Players," *NYT*, August 10, 1936.

[360] "Seizing The Public Funds," *OBS*, June 11, 1910.

[361] "Lawrence Fagan Wins Fight Against Daab And Hoboken Inquirer: When the Case Comes Up in the Supreme Court, Smith and Abbet Throw Up Their Hands," *OBS*, June 10, 1910.

[362] Kerney, *Political Education of Woodrow Wilson*, vii–xvii.

[363] *OBS*, probably July 18, 1910, as quoted in James D. Startt, *Woodrow Wilson And The Press* (New York: Palgrave MacMillan, 2004), 62.

[364] *OBS*, July 18, 1910, as cited in Arthur Link, *Wilson: The Road to the White House* (1947), 1965 Edition (Princeton, NJ: Princeton University Press), 156.

[365] Tumulty, *Woodrow Wilson*, 19.

[366] On A.S. Alexander, see United States Mortgage and Trust Company, ed., pub., *Trust Companies of The United States*, 1907 Edition (New York, 1907), 167; *Stevens Indicator*, October 1912.

[367] A.S. Alexander to Wilson: Hoboken, NJ, July 22, 1910, *WWP*, 18–20.

[368] On H.E. Alexander, see "H.E. Alexander Dies in Philadelphia," *Editor and Publisher*, November 6, 1926.

[369] H.E. Alexander to Wilson: Trenton, NJ, July 23, 1910, *WWP*, 22–23.

[370] Ibid., July 27, 1910, *WWP*, 26–27.

[371] *OBS*, as quoted in *TET*, August 19, 1910, as quoted in Link, *Road to the White House*, 158.

[372] *OBS*, as quoted in *TET*, October 1, 1910, as quoted in Link, *Road*, 178.

[373] On Kerney and Ely, see Link, *Road*, 178; Kerney, *Political Education of Woodrow Wilson*, 80–81.

[374] Kerney, *Political Education of Woodrow Wilson*, 69–76; Link, *Road*, 188–196.

[375] Author holds a B.A. in rhetoric from Bates College.

[376] Link, *Road*, 135, 561.

[377] Kerney, *Political Education of Woodrow Wilson*, 74.

[378] Woodrow Wilson, as quoted in Link, *Road to the White House*, 194–195.

[379] "Campaign Is Indeed Over," *OBS*, October 26, 1910.

[380] On Lindabury, see William Edgar Sackett, ed., *New Jersey's First Citizens: Biographies and Portraits of the Notable Living Men and Women of New Jersey with Informing Glimpses into the State's History and Affairs*, 1917–1918 (Paterson: J.J. Scannell, 1917), 326–328.

[381] Lindabury to Wilson: Newark, NJ, October 27, 1910, *WWP*, 449–450.

[382] Ely to Wilson: Hoboken, NJ, November 3, 1910, *WWP*, 540.

[383] See *NYT*, January 10, 1911.

[384] Tumulty to Fagan: Washington, DC, February 11, 1914, *FA*.

[385] "Boycott by Paper Carriers Winds Up in Near Murder," *The Square Deal*, Vol. VII (February 1911—July 1911), 238. On the attack, see also "Mr. Kohnfelder Welcomed Back By Business Men," *OBS*, April 5, 1911.

[386] On Garrick and Sinatra, see Kitty Kelley, *His Way: The Unauthorized Biography of Frank Sinatra* New York: Bantam Books, 1986), 10–15, 30–31.

387 "In Service," {newspaper clippings}, *FA*.

388 "America Is At War—Seizure of German Ships Takes Place Without Difficulty," *OBS*, April 6, 1917.

389 "Hudson Observer Man Inspects Pier Camp Of Famous 'Double Deuces'—Only Newspaper Man Allowed On The Docks," *OBS*, April 21, 1917.

390 Ziegler-McPherson, *Immigrants in Hoboken*, 101–108.

391 King W. Snell, *With The Army at Hoboken* (New York: Wonderly, 1919), 50.

392 On Hague and his early political career, see Foster, "Early Career of Mayor Frank Hague;" McKean, *The Boss*, 2, 26–29; Leach, *Young Frank Hague*, 67–72.

393 "Hoboken Must Pay Up: The Furniture in the Office of Mayor Fagan Seized For Debt," *NYS*, June 16, 1898; "City Hall Attached—Sheriff Seizes Hoboken Municipal Building For Debt," *JCN*, June 16, 1898.

394 "Hague and Colleagues Win; Will Continue to Carry Out Progressive Methods Adopted," *OBS*, April 16, 1917.

395 "Editorial," *OBS*, May 5, 1917; "The True Inside Story of Commissioner Hague's Manly Fight," *OBS*, May 4, 1917; "Why Commissioner Hague Is Popular," *OBS*, May 3, 1917, as quoted in Raffety, "Political Ethics and Public Style," 54.

396 "Rough Treatment At Polls In Jersey City—Princeton Volunteers For Honest Ballot Association Are Assaulted by Crooks," *Daily Princetonian*, November 4, 1920.

397 On the MacKay investigation, see "Students At Polls Beaten By Ruffians: Princeton Men Tell of Attack by Jersey City Hoodlums at November Election—Held For Hours In Jail—Legislative Investigation Into New Jersey Municipalities Begins," *NYT*, March 11, 1921; "Name Mayor Hague In Election Inquiry: Princeton Students Testify That They Were Ejected From Jersey City Polls—Ballot Frauds Charged—Republican Votes Thrown Out While Democratic Candidates Were Not Excluded," *NYT*, March 19, 1921; "Says Hoboken Paid $100,000 For Land Valued at $36,400," *NYW*, April 21, 1921.

398 "Lawrence Fagan Dead: Two-Fisted Fighter in Politics, Lived to Wield Big Power in Hudson," {newspaper clipping}, *FA*, May 10, 1921.

399 "Last Will Of Late Lawrence Fagan," {newspaper clipping}, *FA*, May 1921; "Fagan's Entire Estate Left To Widow," {newspaper clipping}, *FA*, May 1921.

400 On Fagan's death, see "Former Mayor Fagan Passes Away At His Home This Morning: His Demise a Severe Shock to His Relatives and Numerous Friends—Complications Followed a Slight Cold That Speedily Sapped the Vitality of His Once Rugged Constitution," {newspaper clipping}, *FA*, May

9, 1921; "Ill Only A Few Days, Ex-Mayor Fagan Dies," *TET*, May 9, 1921; "Fagan's Son Gave Blood In Transfusion," {newspaper clipping}, *FA*, May 10, 1921; "Lawrence Fagan Dead: Two-Fisted Fighter," {newspaper clipping}, FA, May 1921; "Former Mayor Fagan of Hoboken is Dead: Called The 'Czar' of His Home City—He Was Dominant in Democratic Party," *NYW*, May 10, 1921.

[401] "Governor Edwards, Mayors Hague and Griffin Among Honorary Pall-bearers," *Hudson Dispatch*, May 12, 1921.

[402] *Hudson Dispatch*, September 21, 1923.

[403] "Looking Backward: Fagan Mansion One of Finest in Hoboken, Replaced by Modern Apartment Dwelling," newspaper article, circa 1950s, available at Hoboken Historical Museum online: www.hobokenmuseum.org. On the Great Dane at Hudson and Tenth Streets, see also *Hudson Dispatch*, September 21, 1923. Arthur L. Fagan Jr. recalled his father telling him the name of the family's Great Dane was "Malek;" he also recalled very possibly his father telling him of the family having another Great Dane named "Otto," interview by author, September 2011. For Great Dane description, see Joe Stahlkuppe, *Great Danes: A Complete Owner's Manual* (Hauppauge, NY: Barron's Educational, 2002), 13.

Afterword

[404] Ziegler-McPherson, *Immigrants in Hoboken*, 121, 125.

[405] Ibid., 121.

[406] Ibid., 125.

[407] *U.S. Census Bureau*, Source: 2020 Decennial Census.

[408] Figures from biggestuscities.com, "Jersey City Population History 1860–2023."

[409] *U.S. Census Bureau*, Source: 2020 Decennial Census.

[410] "Sales in New Jersey—Jersey City Plant in Foreclosure is Transferred," *NYT*, August 18, 1931; "Buys Jersey City Block—Continental Can Co. to Build Factory on 32 Vacant Lots," *NYT*, February 2, 1937.

[411] "Top New Jersey Newspapers Will End Print Editions, and One Will Close," *NYT*, October 30, 2024; "A Storied Newspaper Prepares to Print Its Own Obituary," *NYT*, February 1, 2025.

INDEX

A

Abbett, Leon, 60
Adamic, Louis, 127
African-Americans, 24, 36, 116
The Age of Reform (book), 33
Aldermanic Council, 15
Alexander, Archibald Stevens,
135–136, 139
Alexander, Henry Eckert, 136–
137
American Civil War, 10, 15, 19,
27–29, 122
American Hotel (Trenton), 41
American Progressivism (book),
22
American Tobacco Company,
139
American Veneer Company
(Jersey City), 116–117
anarchists, 109–114
Armageddon, 10,-11, 22, 95, 159
Arnold, Miss (W.C.T.U), 77–78
Asbury Park (NJ), 101
Atto, William J., 22

B

Banta, A.K., 84–85, 91
Barbieri, Maria, 109–110
baseball, 7, 131, 134, 150
Bates College, 138
Bayonne (NJ), 38–39
Bernardsville (NJ), 139
Besson, Elbridge V.S., 64
Besson, Alexander & Stevens
(law firm), 136
Bismarck, Otto Von, 23, 30
Blackmore's (iron foundry), 9,
34, 88, 125, 156
Bocock, John Paul, 61–62

bottom up themes, 11–14, 17, 22,
33–34, 54, 68, 109, 116, 159
Bremen (steamship), 93–94
Bresci, Gaetano, 111–112
Bresci, Sophie, 111–112
Brooklyn (NY), 70
Broome, Lewis, 38
Bruning, John, 91, 114, 125
Bryan, William Jennings, 109,
151
    1896 campaign, 86–88
    1900 campaign, 89–90, 102–
104
    appearing in Hoboken, 87,
103–104
    appearing in Jersey City, 89–
90, 102–103
Bush, Mrs. John O., 74–79

C

Camp Zachary Taylor (KY), 142
Cambell's Soup Factory, 100
Canada, 24, 43
Capelli, Anthony, 76–77, 91–92
Carlow (Ireland), 60
Carlyle, Thomas, 24
Central Park (NY), 31
Chicago (IL), 86, 88
Chicago Union School of Law,
86
Cigar Makers Union, 89
Colonial Life Insurance
Company of Jersey City, 64
Columbia Club (Hoboken), 70
Columbus Dispatch, 136
Coney Island, 73
Continental Can Company, 159
Continental Sunday, 70, 72
Convention of Pennsylvania
Iron Masters, 25, 127

Corsair (yacht)
Coyle, Michael, 37, 44–45, 51–52
Coyle's Liquors and Tavern, 44, 52, 119
Cram, J. Sergeant, 96–98
Crane, Stephen, 82, 94
craps (game), 116–117
Croker, Richard "Dick", 72, 122
Crushing, Martin, 26
Crusius, Nicholas, 65–66, 107, 149
Czolgosz, Leon, 110

D

Daab, Martin, 92, 105, 134
Daab, Philip, 134–135
Daly, William D., 88–89, 91, 101–102
Dana, Charles Anderson, 77–78
Darien, Andrew, 155–156
Davis, Robert
  early life and career, 60
  conflict with Fagan, 89, 91–92, 105–107, 118, 131–132, 135, 137, 158
  conflict with McLaughlin, 60–61
  Robert Davis Association and clubhouse, 92, 103, 118, 120, 132
Dawson Realty Company, 129
The Day Wall Street Exploded (book), 110
Deal (NJ), 101
Decker, Miss (W.C.T.U.), 77–78
Delaware, Lackawanna and Western Railroad, 104
Democratic National Convention
  of 1896, 86–87
  of 1900, 101

Democratic Party, 16, 44, 61, 86–87, 90–92, 101–102, 107, 118, 132, 137–138
Denmark (ME), 66
Detroit (MI), 66
Deutscher Klub (Hoboken German Club), 70
Douglas, George, 77–78
Douglass, Frederick, 24
Draft Riots (NYC), 27
Dublin (Ireland), 24, 28, 105, 123–124
Dynamite: The Story of Class Violence in America (book), 127

E

Ellis Island, 142–143
Ellis, William H., 50
Ely, Mathias, 57, 59, 133–134, 137–140
Elysian Fields, 7–9, 30, 135, 149
Employees' Protective Association, 128
England, 24, 28, 97, 125
  census, 27
Erie Railroad Strike (1878), 89
Erie, Steven P., 46
Esteve, Peter, 112
European Revolutions (1848), 30

F

Fagan Iron Works
  bankruptcy, 158–159
  Dawson Realty dispute, 128–130
  fire in May of 1905, 124–125
  business in Hoboken, 9, 43, 51, 64–65, 68–69, 91, 108
  business in Jersey City, 9, 15, 17, 69, 108–109, 112–115, 117, 124–125, 127–130, 158
  labor violence, 112–116, 127–128

Passaic Steel takeover attempt,
  130
Fagan, Anna, 25
Fagan, Arthur L., 90, 141–142, 145,
  159
Fagan, Arthur L. Jr., 155
Fagan, Bernard, 25
Fagan, Bridget (mother), 27
Fagan, Bridget (relative), 25
Fagan, Catherine, 42, 90, 125, 147
Fagan, Elizabeth, 26
Fagan, James, 28
Fagan, John (cousin), 123–124
Fagan, John (son), 42, 90, 125, 128–
  130, 148
Fagan, Lawrence
  assembly career, 36–41
  birth and early life, 8–9, 22–29
  conflict with Davis, 89, 91–92,
    105–107, 118, 131–132, 135, 137,
    158
  conflict with McLaughlin, 51–54,
    57, 60, 133, 158
  conflict with Hoboken City
   Council, 55, 76–77, 91–92, 106
  death, 148
  education, 26–27, 29
  financial services involvement,
    35, 43, 64, 70, 85, 136
  Guttenberg stake, 35, 49, 51, 53
  marriages to Hannah McHale, 42
  marriage to Mary Foley, 42–43
  mayoral campaigns and terms,
    of 1893, 47–64
    of 1895, 63–64, 72–76
    of 1897, 76–81
    of 1899, 82–85, 90–101, 103–107
    of 1909, 131–132

  police reform efforts, 55–59
  MacKay investigation of, 146–147
  See also Fagan Iron Works
  See also The Observer
Fagan, Madeline, 90
Fagan Mansion, 7, 13–14, 150
  See also Hudson and Tenth Streets
  (house)
Fagan, Mary (sibling), 27
Fagan, Mary (wife), 42–43, 90, 101,
    122–127, 148–149, 154
Fagan & Sons: Housesmiths and
    Bellhangers (Dublin), 28, 123
Fagan, Thomas, 27
Fagan, William, 27
Fanning, John, 56
Farman, Ned, 151–152
Fatima (hippopotamus) *aka*
    Murphy, 33
First Methodist Episcopal Church
    (Hoboken), 74
First National Bank of Hoboken, 85
First World War, 10, 142–143, 156
Foley, Michael, 42–43
Foner, Eric, 9
Foster, Reginald L., 94
France, 97

G

Gage, Beverly, 110, 112
Gallagher, James, 57
gambling, gambler, gamblers,
    gamers, gaming, 21, 57, 71,
    116, 133
    See also craps (game)
    See also Guttenberg horse rac-
    ing track
    See also policy slips
Garrick, Frank, 141

German, Germans, Germany
  immigrants, 7–8, 30–34, 50,
  59, 70–71, 123, 142–143, 157
Gilded Age, 18
Gilmore, Glenda, 21
Gonzalez, George, 132
The Good Roads Association,
  69–70
Gould, Jay, 57
Governor Edward Edwards, 148
Great Dane (dog), 107, 149–150
Great Famine (Ireland), 22–24
Great Hoboken Fire of 1900, 14,
  40, 93–100, 126
The Great Hoboken Fire (maga-
  zine article), 94
green goods, 56–57, 133
Griffin, Patrick, 132, 148
Guilfoyle, Dr. William H.
Guttenberg horse racing track,
  35, 49, 51, 53, 57, 65

H

Hackensack Water Company, 79
Hagenback, Carl, 31
Hague, Frank, 9–10, 143–146,
  148, 158
Hamburg-American Steamship
  Co., 31, 142
Hamilton, Alexander, 39–41, 90
Hamilton County Bill, 38–41, 90,
  156
Harty, Katie, 147–148
Hauck, Peter, 102
Helfer, Samuel H., 67
Heppenheimer, William C., 41
Hexamer, Alexander P., 70
Hoboken
  early history and Stevens
    family, 29–31
  German influence in, 8, 30–33,
    50, 70–71, 143, 156–157
  population trends in, 29, 36,
    63, 67–68, 70, 156–157

  seizure of waterfront in, 142–
    143, 157
Hoboken Baseball Club, 134
Hoboken Board of Police
  Commissioners, 92
Hoboken City Council, 27, 75,
  81, 85, 131
  conflict with Fagan, 55, 76–77,
    91–92, 106
Hoboken City Hall, 35, 45, 52–
  53, 63, 76–78, 107, 144, 153
Hoboken Evening News, 49–50,
  133
Hoboken Free Public Library,
  62–63
Hoboken Health Board, 67
Hoboken Historical Museum,
  154
Hoboken Land and
  Improvement Company, 158
Hoboken Police Department,
  44–45, 55–57, 59
Hoboken Public Instruction
  Commission, 83–84
Hoboken Public School No. 5, 83
Hoboken Saloon-Keepers
  Protective Association, 75
Hoboken Trust Company, 136
Hofstadter, Richard, 33
Holland Tunnel, 153
Holy Name Cemetery, 149
Honest Ballot Association, 145–
  146
The Horseshoe
  creation of Second Ward
    (1870), 15–16
  Dennis McLaughlin saloon in,
    61
  Frank Hague political
    education in, 143–144
  Fagan Iron Works in, 9, 15, 17,
    69, 108–109, 112–115, 117,
    124–125, 127–130, 158
  Holland Tunnel, 153

contemporary waterfront, 154
waste hazard in 1904, 14–15
typography of, 11–15
Hudson and Tenth Streets
(house), 7–8, 13–14, 17, 32, 66,
90, 118, 146–150
Hudson County
population growth, 29
Hamilton County legislation,
38–41
liberal alcohol culture, 72–78,
81
political corruption
allegations, 45–46, 48–49, 57–
62, 145–147
Hudson County Board of
Freeholders, 50, 60
Hudson Dispatch, 113, 133
Hudson River, 7, 9, 14, 22, 29,
39–40, 46, 73, 80, 95–96, 98,
149
Hudspeth, Robert S., 41

I

Immigrants in Hoboken: One-Way
Ticket, 145–1985 (book), 157
immigration, 29, 157
See also German, Germans,
Germany immigrants
See also Ireland, Irish immi-
grants
See also Italian, Italians, Italy
immigrants
immigrant quotas, 157
importing of exotic animals, 8,
31–34
Independent Citizens'
Association of Hoboken, 20
Independent politics, 20
See also The Iroquois Club, 117–
122
invisible sack of tools, 34

Italian, Italians, Italy immigrants, 10, 69, 76, 109–112,
141
Ireland, Irish immigrants, 9, 19,
22–26, 28, 48, 60–62, 123–124,
126
Irish-American Society of
Hoboken, 62
Irish-American political ring, 62
The Irish Conquest of Our Cities
(magazine article), 61–62
iron worker, iron workers, 21,
114
as very high-skilled labor, 25
as very low-skilled labor, 127–
128
The Iroquois Club, 117–122

J

Jackson Street Bridge, 64–65, 69
Jersey City
City Hall, 147
First District Court, 115
Heights, 70, 96, 102
Paulus Hook, 39
population trends, 29, 156–157
Second Criminal Court, 117
Second Ward (1870), 15–16, see
also The Horseshoe
Jersey City News, 51, 55
Jersey Journal, 7, 59, 113, 120, 129,
159
Jerseys (baseball team) aka
Skeeters, Ryanites), 131
Jewish Community (Hoboken),
68
Johns Hopkins University, 135
Julianna (steamboat), 30

K

Kaiser Wilhelm der Grosse
(steamship), 93, 122, 125
Kansas City (MO), 101

Kennedy, David, 21
Keresey, John, 122–123
Kerney, James, 138
Kiernan, Eugene, 83–84
King Umberto I, 111
Knights of Columbus, 118
Kohnfelder, Abraham L., 141
Kuper, Jacob E.W., 131

L

La Question Social, 112
The Lamp Post (saloon), 119–121, 153
Lankering, Adolph, 92, 105, 107, 134
The Lawrenceville School, 141
Lepore, Jill, 10
Letts, William, 37
Levin, Harry, 129
Lewiston (ME), 138
Lincoln, Abraham, 89
Lindabury, Richard, 139
Liverpool (England), 27–28
Living the Revolution: Italian Women's Resistance and Radicalism in New York City (book), 17
Local No. 43 (labor union), 114
Lord, Walter, 41
Lore, Jerry, 153
Lorillard's Tobacco Factory, 35
Lyric Theater (Hoboken), 103–105

M

Maggie, A Girl Of The Streets (book), 82
MacKay Legislative Committee, 146–147
Madison Square Garden, 31
manhood, manliness, manly themes, 22, 159

historians' discussion of, 10, 19–21
in Fagan/McLaughlin confrontation, 53
in Fagan's decision not to seek reelection, 106
in Fagan explaining his assault of Stiles, 115–116
in *Observer's* description of Frank Hague, 145
Mansfield & Fagan, 34–35, 43, 69
Manfield House (saloon), 43
Mansfield, Isaac, 34–35, 43
Marconi Wireless Telegraph, 125
Marion Station (Jersey City), 102
McCabe, James D., 26
McKinley, William, 102, 104, 110
McLaughlin, Dennis
conflict with Davis, 60–61
conflict with Fagan, 51–54, 57, 60, 133, 158
dubbing name Horseshoe, 15
Guttenberg stake, 48–49
political rise, 48–49
political fall, 53–54, 57, 59–61
McPhillipps, John, 50
Meyer's Hotel (Hoboken), 103
Milan (Italy), 111
Milwaukee (WI), 50
Monzo (Italy), 111
Morgan, J. Pierpont, 96
Morristown (NJ), 87–88, 151–152
Muckraking, 133
Municipal Iron Works, 129
Municipal Light, Heat, and Power Company, 91, 114
Munsey's (magazine), 94
Murphy (hippopotamus) *aka Fatima*, 32–33
Murphy, Police Chief (Jersey City), 117

N

Naboth's Vineyard, 104
Newhouse Media Group, 159
New Jersey Governor's Ball
   (Spring Lake), 43
New York City
   Dock Board, 97–98
   District Attorney's Office, 98
   Fire Department, 98
   Mayor's Office, 72, 99
   Police Department, 98, 72–73,
   128–129
New York Daily Tribune, 39, 71,
   75, 82, 84–85
New York Sun, 77–78, 95
New York Times, 99
New York World, 48, 51, 53, 57,
   61, 93, 116, 133, 158
New York Yacht Club (Hobo-
   ken), 8
Newark (NJ), 65, 68, 87, 135
Newark Bay, 65
Newark Riots (1967), 60
North Bergen Township (NJ),
   35, 38–39
North German Lloyd Steamship
   Co., 31–32, 93–94, 97, 99, 122,
   142
North Hudson Heat, Light, and
   Power Company, 85, 91
Northwestern University, 86
Nugent, James R., 135

O

The Observer, 9, 15
   charges against *Hoboken
   Inquirer*, 133–134
   circulation numbers, 134
   condemnation of anarchists,
   110–111
   coverage of Wilson
   gubernatorial campaign
   attacks on, 135–138

   praise of, 139–140
   Frank Sinatra employed by,
   141
   Fagan as editorial archon at,
   133–140
   founding and call for
   governance reform, 44–46
   reporting on Fagan Iron
   Works fire (1905), 124–125
   reporting on Fagan vacation
   (1904), 122–123
   reporting on First World War,
   142–143
   sale to Newhouse, 159
Odd Fellows Hall (Hoboken), 82
Old Excelsior Engine #2, 37
Omaha World Herald, 86
O'Neill, James, 141
O'Neill, James Jr., 141
Orange (NJ), 70
Orange Riots (NYC)
Osar, Karen, 154
Our Lady of Grace Church
   (Hoboken), 43

P

palisades (Hoboken/Jersey City
   Border), 11–14, 69–70
Parnell, Charles Stewart, 62
Parnell, John, 62
Passaic River, 65
Passaic Steel Company, 130
Paterson (NJ), 111–112, 130
PATH Train, 25
People's Safe Deposit and Trust
   Company, 64
Pestritto, Ronald J., 22
Philadelphia (PA), 25, 87
Philippine Islands, 102, 104
Phytophthora infestans, 23
Pingree, Hazen, 66–67
policy slips, 56–57
Portland (ME), 24

Post & McCord (architectural ironworks firm), 38
Princeton University, 9, 135, 141, 145
progressive, progressives, progressivism
    historians' discussion of, 10, 21–22
    in describing Mansfield & Fagan, 35
    in describing the *Observer*, 139
    in Wilson campaign, 135, 137
Il Proletario, 111
prostitution, 71
Pulitzer, Joseph, 57

Q

Quartet Club (Hoboken), 69

R

Rainbow's End: Irish Americans and the Dilemmas of Urban Machine Politics, 1840–1985 (book), 21
Raines Law, 72–73, 75–76
Reconstruction, 15
Record, George Lawrence, 138
The Red Badge of Courage (book), 94
Redistricting Act of 1870, 15
Reed, Charles, 116–117
reform, reformer, 22, 159
    Fagan described genuinely being one, 56, 61
    Fagan described sarcastically being one, 49, 62
    historians' discussion of, 10, 21–22
    Protestant reformers, 20, 30
    See also Scudder, John L. (Reverand)
    See also Women's Christian Temperance Union (W.C.T.U)

Reiche, Charles, 7–8
Reiche, Henry, 7–8
Reiche Family, 31, 65–66, 149
Rockefeller, John D., 63
Rohn, Peter, 154
Roosevelt, Theodore, 49–50, 72–73, 133
Russ, Edward, 83–84
Russo-Japanese War, 123

S

Saale (steamship), 93
Sackett, William Edgar, 48, 65
Salem (IL), 86
Salem State University, 152
saloons
    as hotels, 71, 75–76
    as musical theaters, 81
    Coyle's Liquors and Tavern, 44–45, 52, 119
    Capelli's, 76–77
    in Hoboken, 27, 71–77, 81
    Mansfield House, 43
    McLaughlin's in the Horseshoe, 61
    Raines Law controversy, 72–77
    The Lamp Post, 119–121, 153
Schlatter, Julius, 75
Scotland
Scudder, George, 34
Scudder, John L. (Reverend), 57–58, 74
Second National Bank of Hoboken, 62
Seide, Gustav E., 50–51, 133
Shannon, William V., 18
Sinatra, Frank, 10, 141, 152
Sinatra, Marty, 141
Singer Sewing Machine Company, 139
Smith, James Jr., 135
Snake Hill Almshouse, 35
Snell, Captain King W., 143

Southampton, England, 125
St. Paul's School (Concord, NH), 135
St. Peter's College Hall (Jersey City), 89
Stack, Maurice J., 131
Standard Oil Company, 63
Stanton, Edward, 50–51, 53, 57–61, 133
State Library Committee, 63
Steffens, Lincoln, 133
Steil, George H., 131
Stevens Institute of Technology, 30
Stevens, Edwin, 30
Stevens, John, 30
Stevens, Robert L., 30
Stiles, Daniel, 114–115
Strong, William, 72
Stuhr, William S., 82–84
Sunday Closing Laws
    in Hudson County, 43, 72–79, 81
    in New York City, 30, 72–73, 75–76
    See also Raines Law

T

Tammany Hall, 29, 72, 96, 99
Tangeman, John., 53
tenements
    in Hoboken, 79–81
    in New York City, 26
top down themes, 11–14, 17, 22, 33–34, 54, 68, 109, 116, 159
Trenton Evening Times, 80, 138
Trenton True American, 136
Trust Company of New Jersey, 64, 70, 85, 136
Tumulty, Joseph, 19, 135, 140, 144
Tumulty, Philip, 19, 51
Tweed, William Marcy, 29

U

Union of Architectural, Bridge, and Structural Iron Workers of America, 114
United States Army, 143
United States Census, 25

V

Verdon, William, 105, 107

W

Walbaum, Gottfried, 49
Wall, William H., 50
Weehawken (NJ), 38–39, 64, 79–80
Werts, George, 64
West Hoboken (NJ), 38, 79, 111–112
Whelan, Martin J., 131
Who Were The Progressives? (book), 21
Wilson, Helen, 147–148
Wilson, Woodrow, 9, 19, 135–140
Wilson: The Road To The Whitehouse (book), 17
Wittpenn, Otto, 136
Women's Christian Temperance Union, 74, 77
Women's Club of Hoboken, 126
Wyck, Robert Van Wyck, 99

Z

Ziegler-McPherson, Christina, 157